CONQUERING GOVERNMENT REGULATIONS

McNEILL STOKES

CONQUERING GOVERNMENT REGULATIONS

A Business Guide

McGRAW-HILL BOOK COMPANY

*New York   St. Louis   San Francisco   Auckland
Bogotá   Hamburg   Johannesburg   London   Madrid
Mexico   Montreal   New Delhi   Panama   Paris
São Paulo   Singapore   Sydney   Tokyo   Toronto*

Library of Congress Cataloging in Publication Data
Main entry under title:

Conquering government regulations.

   1. Trade regulation—United States. 2. Administrative procedure
—United States. I. Stokes, McNeill.
KF1600.C56   343.73′08   81-8182
                                   347.3038   AACR2
ISBN 0-07-061640-X

1 2 3 4 5 6 7 8 9 0   KPKP   8 9 8 7 6 5 4 3 2 1

The editors for this book were William R. Newton and Beatrice E.
Eckes, the designer was Elliot Epstein, and the production supervisor
was Paul A. Malchow. It was set in Century Schoolbook by University
Graphics, Inc.

Printed and bound by The Kingsport Press.

CONTENTS

PREFACE

The Founding Fathers viewed government as the enemy of freedom. They restricted the scope and power of government. Jefferson said, "That government is best which governs least." One of the grievances against the crown in the Declaration of Independence was, "He has erected a multitude of new offices and sent hither swarms of officers to harass our people and eat out their substance." Therefore, when the founders had won their freedom from Great Britain, they formed a government of limited powers. They drew constitutional lines that instituted checks and balances to prevent the President, Congress, or the courts from assuming all power. This separation of federal powers was further strengthened by the division of powers between the states and the federal government. The Constitution granted to the federal government only enumerated powers, and the Tenth Amendment spelled out explicitly that all powers not granted to the federal government or denied to the states are reserved to the states or to the people.

During the Civil War a military draft was instituted, and a temporary income tax was levied. The federal government emerged from the war with far greater prestige and power. In the unparalleled economic expansion which came after the war, individuals operating in a relatively free enterprise system cornered markets, fixed prices, and organized trusts and monopolies. Such names as Rockefeller, Vanderbilt, Carnegie, Morgan, Huntington, and Fisk became prominent as industrial, financial, and business giants: the Robber Barons. Their freedom from government regulation, state or federal, led to gross inequalities and inspired among the have-nots a change in attitude toward government. In the 1890s, in the interest of equality, party platforming demanded government interference and regulation such as the regulation of railroads and the breakup of trusts and monopolies.

From that time to the present the trend has continued to increase the power and expand the activity of government at all levels. Theodore Roosevelt and the New Nationalism used the power of government to bust trusts. The Democrats under Woodrow Wilson extended the trend by providing government support for agriculture and instituting the federal income tax. But it was Franklin D. Roosevelt's New Deal which outdid Wilson's New Freedom. To fight a crippling economic depression Roosevelt used his great political popularity to move boldly to expand the power of the federal government beyond anything before his day. Since the Roosevelt New Deal, these powers have continued to grow in response to World War II and especially to stabilize the economy and to support the civil rights movement.

The Fair Deal of Truman, the New Frontier of Kennedy, and the Great Society of Johnson continued a modern liberalism of the New Deal characterized by a burgeoning executive branch which aggressively sought to do all things for all people, eclipsing the states, the cities, and the private sector in favor of strong federal initiatives and massive federal spending. Congressman Elliott H. Levitas summed it up best and succinctly in a speech, "The New Deal Is Dead, May It Rest in Peace," when he pointed out, "We are at a historic turning point, a point where we must not forsake our basic beliefs, where we must not forfeit our fundamental ideas. Instead we must do what Franklin Delano Roosevelt did forty years ago. We must find innovative new ways of handling the problems of the current times."

Even though some of the history is well known, it is important and helpful to us today in understanding the crucible from which our country has been cast. In a very short period our economic system has been forged on an anvil of private and individual initiative that has produced roughly one-half of the world's wealth by our citizens, who comprise only about 5 percent of the world's population. These developments are reviewed to remind us that a complete reversal of attitude toward government has occurred in this country. It has come about in response to changing conditions and with the acquiescence of the citizens. The most obvious changes that have taken place are the miracles of technology which have freed us from backbreaking labor and made possible an undreamed-of standard of living. The United States has changed from a rural agricultural society of relatively independent family units into an urbanized, industrialized society of highly interdependent individuals in a new world community. Simplicity has given way to complexity. This basic transition has brought great changes in our attitudes toward the federal government and in our aspirations for freedom, equality, and security.

Jefferson's concept of freedom from government is in dramatic contrast to our present society, which may be overgoverned. To act affirmatively and to carry out the innumerable economic and social action programs, it has become necessary to create a bureaucracy, a fourth branch of government, consisting of civil servants not responsible to the electorate and in many cases responsible to no one. This is a new threat to freedom brought on by action which was designed originally to promote governmental equality. There are no checks and balances on the bureaucracy, which has thus become the dominant force in the federal government. Over 7000 regulations which have the force of law are promulgated by the bureaucracy each year, while only about 400 laws are passed by Congress. We have slipped under a Napoleonic Code which is published daily in the *Federal Register*.

In our highly interdependent society there cannot be complete freedom from government, but we must preserve freedom under government. Few could seriously contend in our modern technological society that the government should not provide reasonable protection against securities fraud or guard against price fixing and unreasonable restraints of trade. Nor could the government abandon machinery for the orderly process of collective bargaining or cease allocation of the frequencies of the electromagnetic spectrum. We must, however, shift the emphasis of the bureaucracy from penalizing and stifling citizens to aiding citizens.

It is obvious that our society has achieved a new stage of maturity. It is no longer young. It is middle-aged. We are in an age of transition, moving toward greater interdependence, a more industrialized and urbanized pattern of life. There is no need to bemoan our fate. There is no turning back the clock. The question is how our ancient virtues can be inculcated in people on a new stage, under different circumstances, in a new setting. We must understand the issues and continue to deal with government regulations in a businesslike fashion. It is the challenge before us to make the transition from freedom from government to freedom under government.

The bureaucracy and government regulations are inherent in every stage in the daily operation of business and professionals. All persons associated with business and the professions must arm themselves with awareness of the government regulations that affect their businesses, ways to respond to regulations, and also ways to plan for government regulation. This book is a jargon-free, plain-language discussion of government regulations and what businesses can do to use them for benefit and to conquer their negative aspects. The illustrative case histories demonstrate the results that can be achieved and cover numerous federal agencies. Obviously one of the first steps that must be taken by businesses is to develop planning for favorable or unfavorable agency actions and to anticipate future options. This planning should involve top management and deal with the economics and complexities of possible compliance. Businesses must understand the major social, political, economic, and technological driving forces which might lead to government regulation. And businesses must develop alternative courses of action so that they can be in a proactive position rather than a reactive position to the possible effects of government regulation.

Businesses must be able to determine the direct and indirect costs of government regulation. They must have a methodology that can measure the costs of regulation to an individual business and develop plans of action to minimize the cost impact on it. They must also know the steps that can be taken to stem the rising tide of paperwork required by government and to reduce the burden of a number of government forms which are tendered by government bureaucracy. There are practical ways in which businesses can complain about paperwork to eliminate or simplify its burdens. Government agencies initiate many outlaw forms which businesses need not legally file, and there are forms which do not entail practical penalties if there is a failure to comply with them.

Businesses must learn to utilize the Freedom of Information Act, the Privacy Act, and the Government in the Sunshine Act to turn the tables on agencies. These acts contain techniques in which businesses can gain information about competitors and participate more effectively in government proceedings on the basis of information in governmental files. It is imperative that businesses keep abreast of government regulations that affect their businesses and allocate their resources to minimize the impact on them. They must know how to lobby agencies in order to get the agencies to issue, modify, or not issue regulations that affect them. There are practical techniques for influencing rule making informally as well as formally, including writing your own industry regulations in order to avoid agency regulations. These practical tactics of rule making can be employed by individual companies or by associations. In addition, businesses may need to influence the public relations climate for dealing with government regulations.

Can you fight the government? Certainly. Citizens win against the government in the majority of instances. But, too often, businesses faced with an enforcement action by the government surrender cheaply rather than fight dearly. There are winning tactics and strategies for contesting government actions such as stonewalling, delaying actions, negotiating with agencies, using contests and litigation, and understanding the constitutional rights and privileges of enforcement action. Businesses have the right to lock out government inspectors in some instances and to insist on a search warrant. They can effectively contest agency enforcement actions by utilizing practical and legal substantive and procedural defenses to such actions.

Can you beat city hall? You bet you can. All too often, out of either fear or ignorance, businesses simply do not assert their rights or do not assert them in time. Local governments do cause injuries to businesses and should be held accountable. It is important for businesses to know what rights they have against their local governments and to assert them so that they avoid the limitations on suits against local governments. Local governments are highly suable, and they have money to pay judgments against them.

To be good corporate citizens, businesses should attempt to keep in mind that the ultimate political process in the United States requires getting involved in politics. There's an old saying, "Get involved in politics and get out of business." One of the best ways to get involved in politics is to start a corporate political action committee which gets the attention of your elected officials. There are many things that can be done in taming the agencies, such as various administrative and legislative reforms including sunset legislation, legislative-veto bills, decentralization, and breaking up agencies. The procedures by which the government accomplishes a desired goal are as important as the goal which the government seeks to accomplish, and business must be in a position to influence both. The issues are grave and far-reaching; they could involve not just headaches to businesses but major financial impacts.

McNeill Stokes

DEDICATION

This book is dedicated to my wife, Judy Ford Stokes, who is President and Owner of Judy Ford Stokes and Associates, Inc., one of the largest food management consulting firms in the country. She is one of the best practitioners of using government regulations for her clients' benefit and minimizing the negative effects of regulations.

ACKNOWLEDGMENTS

I would like to express my gratitude and acknowledge the invaluable contributions of many individuals who have aided in the writing of the chapters in this book. In particular, I would like to acknowledge the contribution of Gary A. Marple and Ellen I. Metcalf, Arthur D. Little, Inc., with the assistance of Jerri DeKriek in writing Chapter 1, "Business Planning for Government Regulations"; Michael E. Simon, Partner, Arthur Andersen & Co., in writing Chapter 2, "What Regulation Costs"; Carl A. Beck, former Chairman, and David M. Marsh, Executive Director, Business Advisory Council on Federal Reports, in writing Chapter 3, "Reducing Paperwork"; Jeffrey H. Joseph, Manager, Business-Government Affairs Division, Chamber of Commerce of the United States, in writing Chapter 5, "Lobbying the Agencies on Rule Making"; Robert Keith Gray, Chairman, Gray and Company, with the assistance of Ben Zingman and Joanna Hanes of Hill and Knowlton, Inc., in writing Chapter 6, "Public Relations and the Regulatory Process"; Al Langer, Publisher, *McGraw-Hill's Regulatory Impact Service*, in writing Chapter 7, "Living with Agency Action"; Justin Dart, Chairman of the Board, Dart Industries Inc., and Chairman of the Executive Committee of Dart & Kraft, Inc., with the assistance of James O. Lindberg, Corporate Group, Vice President, Public Affairs, and the University of Southern California Center for the Study of Private Enterprise, in writing Chapter 13, "Political Action Committees"; and Congressman Elliott H. Levitas, with the assistance of Ron Farley, Congressional Administrative Aide, in writing Chapter 14, "Taming the Agencies."

I would like to express my great appreciation for the assistance in legal research in my chapters by Elizabeth Belden, Attorney at Law, Atlanta, Georgia; and by Renee Huxley and Catherine Zachs while they were students at Emory University. The historical insight given to me by Dr. Judson C. Ward, Executive Vice President and Dean of Faculties at Emory University, greatly enhanced the Preface. I would also like to acknowledge the aid that

I received in reviewing these chapters by Ira J. Smotherman, Partner, Stokes & Shapiro, Henry Huettner, Attorney at Law, Fisher & Phillips, Marilyn J. Hill, Government Liaison Specialist for Donohue & Associates, Inc., and Richard Hiller, Vice President, Coca-Cola Co., and, particularly, my extreme gratitude to my secretary, Ellen J. Sutton, who managed the entire manuscript process. I appreciate the good friendship and keen insights of Patricia S. Nettleship, Chairman of the Board, North Pacific Construction Co., and Joe F. Canterbury, Jr., Attorney at Law, Dallas, Texas, with whom I often discuss approaches to dealing with government regulations.

I am extremely grateful for the understanding of my wife Judy, and my children, Ford and Ashley Stokes, which has been invaluable during the long periods of time I have necessarily spent in writing and compiling this book.

McNeill Stokes

ABOUT THE AUTHORS

McNeill Stokes is a partner in the law firm of Stokes & Shapiro of Atlanta, and
Washington. He holds degrees in chemical engineering and law from Vanderbilt University, and he maintains membership in both engineering and
legal professional associations. Mr. Stokes is one of the nation's leading
experts on dealing with government regulations and is the author of *Construction Law in Contractors' Language, International Construction Contracts,* and *Labor Law in Contractors' Language,* published by the
McGraw-Hill Book Company. He is a frequent speaker at conventions and
seminars and on many occasions has testified before congressional committees and White House conferences. He was one of the attorneys involved in
the Bakke reverse-discrimination case and the OSHA search-warrant case,
and he handled a serious constitutional challenge to OSHA in the U.S.
Supreme Court, during which the Solicitor General described his approach
to government as "a cannon on the loose."

About the Contributing Authors

Carl A. Beck is President of the Charles Beck Machine Corporation, a small manufacturer of industrial machinery in King of Prussia, Pennsylvania. He has
been active for several decades in representing the interests of small business
in Washington in various capacities, including serving 4 years as chairman
of the Business Advisory Council on Federal Reports.

Justin Dart is chairman and chief executive officer of Dart Industries Inc., a subsidiary of Dart & Kraft, Inc., and is also chairman of the Executive Committee of the Dart & Kraft Board of Directors. He has always been extremely
active in business and civic affairs and holds leadership positions on the Conference Board, the Business Roundtable, and the Board of Trustees of the
University of Southern California, and he served on the Board of Directors

xiv

of United Air Lines and its parent corporation, UAL Inc., for 38 years. Dart Industries Inc. under his leadership has implemented one of the most active political action committees in the United States and has been at the forefront in sharing his knowledge and success in political action committees with many other companies.

Robert Keith Gray is chairman and chief executive officer of Gray and Company, a national public relations and public affairs firm in Washington. Previously he was vice chairman of Hill and Knowlton, Inc., and head of its Washington office. He and his staff daily observe the regulatory process and regularly represent clients in the regulatory arena.

Jeffrey H. Joseph is manager of the Business-Government Affairs Division of the Chamber of Commerce of the United States. He is also an adjunct professor of business-government relations at the George Washington University. He has written and spoken extensively on the legislative process and the impact of regulation on business. He received his M.A. degree in international relations from the University of Pennsylvania, his J.D. degree from the University of Baltimore School of Law, a certificate from The Hague Academy of International Law, and his B.A. degree from the George Washington University.

Al Langer is publisher of *McGraw-Hill's Regulatory Impact Service*, a semimonthly newsletter which tracks and analyzes federal regulations. As a development manager within the McGraw-Hill Information Systems Company, Mr. Langer is responsible for creating information delivery systems for the construction industry and other discrete professional markets. He has more than 20 years' experience in publishing and public relations for both government and private industry.

Elliott H. Levitas is a member of Congress, serving in the House of Representatives from the Fourth Congressional District in Georgia. He serves on the Government Operations Committee and is concerned with determining the effectiveness and accountability of the broad spectrum of the federal bureaucracy and of government services to the people. As a congressman, he has established a major impact on the federal legislative process in his championing of the legislative veto, which would permit Congress to abolish rules and regulations perpetrated by nonelected bureaucrats in federal agencies. Before being elected to Congress he was a practicing lawyer, specializing in the regulatory area. He is a graduate of Emory Law School and was a Rhodes scholar.

Dr. Gary A. Marple is an experienced policy-level counselor to executives in both industry and government. His 17 years with the management counseling operations of Arthur D. Little, Inc., have concentrated on assisting executives who wish to identify and develop strategic options having both immediate practicality and longer-term competitive superiority. Clients represent many industries, including automobile companies, banks, beverage companies, consumer housewares firms, consumer electronics companies, publishing houses, and government agencies. Dr. Marple holds a B.S. degree from Drake University and an M.B.A. degree from Michigan State University and was a postdoctoral fellow at the Massachusetts Institute of Technology.

David M. Marsh has been executive director of the Business Advisory Council for the past 10 years. Previously, he was in the Washington office of a major corporation and a trade association. A native of Washington and an ex-Marine, he was graduated from Bowdoin College and the George Washington University Law School.

Ellen I. Metcalf is a senior management consultant with 17 years of experience with Arthur D. Little, Inc., consulting to industry and government concerning consumer behavior, strategic marketing planning, new-product introductions, and long-range strategic planning. Her experience in counseling clients whose businesses were severely threatened by external events led to a series of position papers on managing uncertainty, the process of identifying potential external change and developing corporate responses to the threats and opportunities which change poses. She has a B.A. degree from Tufts University and an M.A. degree in management from Simmons College.

Michael E. Simon is a partner in Arthur Andersen & Co. and is in charge of the firm's management advisory services practice in Cleveland. He was one of the partners responsible for conducting the cost-of-regulation study performed by Arthur Andersen & Co. for the Business Roundtable. Mr. Simon is a graduate of Indiana University and is a certified public accountant in several states.

1 BUSINESS PLANNING FOR GOVERNMENT REGULATIONS

GARY A. MARPLE

ELLEN I. METCALF
Arthur D. Little, Inc.

The marketplace in which industry must function has been increasing in complexity. Pressures for regulating the comportment of corporations come from a variety of constituencies: the consuming public, special-interest groups, competitors, endangered industries, and a multitude of specialized regulatory agencies.

Changing attitudes of these constituencies tend to be reflected in changing policies and actions. The policies and actions, in turn, have a substantial impact on corporate operations and planning. The changes are frequent, but they are not sudden: warning signals generally precede changes in policies and actions with sufficient time so that corporations are able to plan for change.

However, the market signals are numerous, frequently conflicting, and variable. Planning for *all* the signals would divert valuable resources (personnel, capital, and management attention) away from the pursuit of corporate objectives. To date, many methods have been devised to cope with the uncertainties resulting: forecasting, delphi techniques, simulation, and sensitivity testing are four techniques for reducing uncertainty in forward planning. However, to be effective, all these techniques require an understanding of not only the most likely future course of events but the likely *alternatives:* alternative futures. The development of planning around alternative futures is often called contingency planning. Contingency planning for regulatory action is the subject of this chapter.

Alternative futures as a planning tool are based on two key assumptions:

- Planning based on a single forecast of most likely events is vulnerable to changes which make the plan unworkable or which make the corporate goals on which the plan is based unattractive. No forecast is sufficiently accurate to be invulnerable.

- The nature of the changing processes under way in the world is such that important impacts on any given industry or corporation can arise from what appear to be remote social, economic, political, and technological trends. Assessing these trends will considerably reduce the chance of being caught off guard by any given change.

By developing contingency plans around alternative futures, corporations can maintain control over their planning process rather than simply reacting to changes as they occur in their environment.[1] Companies which rely on a single long-range plan in which they have invested much time, energy, and thought often seek to reduce change imposed by government regulations[2] by three approaches: (1) trying to influence agencies; (2) contesting policies; and (3) complying with regulations without altering company directions. Often such approaches result in a diversion of corporate resources which serves to lose forward corporate momentum and sometimes results in a loss of confidence by the public. Corporations that have developed contingency plans, on the other hand, need not divert their resources in such a manner: their advance planning has prepared them for the change, and they have a plan which considers the appropriate strategy for addressing the regulatory agency, the marketplace, and required changes in corporate objectives. Government regulation, which is frequently viewed as a negative force for industry, can in fact be advantageous to corporations and industry. In 1970, William E. Fruhan, Jr., urged air carriers to take advantage of opportunities available to them because of government regulations.[3] And many followers of the automobile industry have concluded that General Motors, in a costly and venturesome move to downsize rapidly, was able to take advantage of regulations: it actually gained market share in the process.[4]

The next section addresses the major driving forces which serve as the impetus for governmental regulation. The following section gives a step-by-step guide to developing alternative futures; the last section describes the contingency-planning process.

MAJOR DRIVING FORCES BEHIND GOVERNMENTAL REGULATION

There are four major forces which influence governmental policies and action: social, political, economic, and technological forces. Understanding these forces and their potential impact on regulatory agencies is a first step to coherent planning. This is not a simple task. These forces can operate independently, in harmonious combination, or in conflict with each other. The greater the range of forces that might affect the regulatory climate, the greater the uncertainty of the future course of events.

Social

The vast majority of governmental regulations have been influenced by social forces. The well-known switch in attitude, for example, from caveat

[1]Rochelle O'Connor, *Planning under Uncertainty: Multiple Scenarios and Contingency Planning,* Report 741. The Conference Board, Inc., New York, 1978.

[2]M. E.Porter, "Strategy under Conditions of Adversity," working paper, Harvard Business School, Boston, 1977.

[3]William E. Fruhan, Jr., "The Fight for Competitive Advantage under Regulation," working paper, Harvard Business School, Boston, 1970.

[4]"G. M.'s Juggernaut," *Business Week,* Mar. 26, 1979, pp. 62–77.

emptor (let the buyer beware) to caveat vendor (let the seller beware) has been the root of much legislation: truth in lending and truth in advertising, to give two examples. Public attitudes toward acceptable business practices and the role of the governing agencies to protect the public interest have changed dramatically over the years.

In addition, however, people have learned that organizing into groups that lobby for certain actions has a multiplier effect: the effect of the whole (the organization) is greater than the sum of its parts (the individuals comprising the organization). Thus can minority viewpoints have a majority impact on governmental action. Ralph Nader's Citizens for Concerned Action, the John Birch Society, the Sierra Club, and the Moral Majority are examples of organized groups which have had an impact greater than that of the individuals themselves. Organized labor is another example of individuals effecting change through concerted action.

Social change has fueled changes in working conditions (minimum wage laws, workmen's compensation, job safety regulations, and so on); in product safety (autos, flame retardancy, cigarettes, saccharin, and drugs); in efficacy (laetrile, Geritol, and other products); in information dissemination (true interest rates, proof of advertising claims, etc.); and in individual rights (of criminals, the mentally disturbed, the handicapped, and the elderly).

Social change often has second- and third-order impacts. For example, the push of organized labor for fewer working hours (through paid holidays, vacations, and shorter working weeks) not only has netted workers more leisure time (at a cost to employers) but also has given them incentives to purchase goods and services for their leisure-time use, thus increasing personal consumption expenditures on leisure-time products and services.

Political

Politicians suggest or introduce legislation and also must vote on legislation introduced by their colleagues. Legislation is proposed for a variety of reasons: personal conviction of a legislator, public pressure on the legislator from his or her constituency, pressure from commercial interests, and legislative committee pressure. Likewise a politician may vote for a piece of legislation because the politician supports it or because by voting for it the politician collects a favor from or repays a favor to other legislators.

Legislative changes are thus a result of other driving forces, such as social and economic change, and are *responsive* to the general environment in all its conflicting measures. The Supreme Court, in its broad interpretation of the law, is a political driving force that does not so much respond to the environment as reflect the judicial bent of its justices. The Warren Court and the Burger Court differ sharply in their interpretations, for example: the differences are most likely greater than changes in social opinion can explain.

Legislation, like social change, can lead to conflicting demands on businesses. For example, auto manufacturers must be responsive to corporate average fuel economy (CAFE) standards, which escalate each year, *and* to safety standards, such as barrier crash tests, which also escalate over time. Fuel economy has been achieved mainly through downsizing and lightening cars. Crash barrier standards are often achieved through heavier reinforcements. The two sets of standards may be on a collision course in which achieving one objective precludes achievement of the other.

School districts have likewise seen court-ordered integration of districts coupled with strictures against using busing as a means of achieving integration.

Economic

The mainstream of United States citizens has enjoyed a standard of living which, except for short dips during infrequent recessions, has risen since the 1930s. Gains in worker productivity, coupled with technological innovation, have allowed high levels of disposable income. Recently, high levels of inflation have eaten into disposable income. Relative economic security for the mainstream of United States citizens, due to unemployment compensation, social security, and disability payments, has coincided with increased demands for employment fringe benefits (including company-supported education, medical benefits, increased vacations, and so on), for freedom of information (without which accountability is merely a slogan), and various reform movements which are generally lumped together under the name of consumerism.

Thus, the parentage of many movements toward change is difficult to trace. Which came first, social driving forces or economic ones? Which has the greater impact? It has been contended, for example, that the black movement in the United States was fueled once economic conditions improved. The women's movement began with wealthy, better-educated women; even today, the women in this movement are more representative of advantaged women than they are of the undereducated, the poor, or minority women.

At present, two general trends are in apparent conflict. On the one hand there is a decided tendency to have government (often state or local government but also the federal government) play an increasing role in affairs, serving as a watchdog to business in particular. On the other hand, rising taxation (direct or indirect) to pay the tab for governmental involvement has led to a movement to monitor the government through tax ceilings such as California's Proposition 13.

Technological

Technology has played an important role in the standard of living in the United States. It has been employed to boost productivity through better and more efficient machinery. Medical technology has produced longer life expectancies for the population. And we have grown accustomed to the technological conveniences which give us more free time and more options on how to spend it: the range and oven which can be programmed to cook a meal "automatically," paper-thin calculators which can perform a multitude of complex calculations, electronic games, and so on. Technology is now being employed in attempts to meet regulations.[5] The automobile industry has used such sophisticated technology as computer-aided design to help pare down the size and weight of cars without compromising structural integrity; electronics in the autos themselves has helped increase fuel efficiency. Ford's proco engine, with its computer-controlled gasoline-injected system, is an example.

Technology itself, in its applications, has spawned a demand for governmental regulations. The ability to collect, store, and disseminate massive amounts of information through computerization has led to great fears of "big brotherism" as described in George Orwell's *1984*. And the ability of medical support systems to sustain some sort of life in a person incapable of living without that support, coupled with the new technology of organ transplants, has raised a series of legal issues as to the right to die and the legal definition of death.

Thus technology, too, has direct and indirect impacts on legislative agencies and is also used to help implement agency policies.

As can be seen, these four driving forces act and react in complex ways that create change. Companies which plan for change and thus are prepared for it can often capitalize on change and still manage their own destinies.

DEVELOPING ALTERNATIVE FUTURES

There are five major steps in developing alternative futures. The first step is to identify the specific driving forces relevant to the company. This is accomplished through a massive sifting and sorting process of data collection and analysis. The second step is to identify the agencies which are most likely to have an impact on the company and to describe them in terms of their "personality"—the way in which they view the industries they regulate, their normal approach, their enforcement tools, and how and when enforcement procedures are used. The third step utilizes the same process to identify and describe present and potential competitors. These three steps result in a fourth step which requires that the information be consolidated and arranged in a cogent, meaningful way into a "base case" condition which appears to be most consistent with recent trends. In the final step, alternatives which are plausible but currently appear less likely are developed. In the subsections below, each step is described in greater detail.

Identifying Specific Relevant Driving Forces

To identify the specific forces which lead to regulation that will have a substantial impact on a business, it is important to have a broad, up-to-date data base covering the social, political, technological, and economic trends

---

[5]William J. Abernathy and B. S. Chakravarthy, "Government Intervention and Innovation in Industry: A Policy Framework," working paper, Harvard Business School, Boston, 1978.

and changes most relevant to the business being examined. The data base need not always be built anew: it can be adapted or updated from existing data bases. However, any data-base collection procedure must be flexible so that new alternative futures can be added on a continuing basis.

The categories of information collected usually include:

- Demographic
- Social-cultural
- Economic
- Legal-regulatory
- Technological
- Industry or business
- International

The data need to be analyzed to detect interrelationships among forces and trends in these forces. In working with data bases, interrelationships, and trends, a number of concepts have been developed concerning how to use data bases in the alternative-futures framework. A variety of relatively simple conceptual models that help to integrate the data bases and interpret the relationships and trends have also been developed. Each of these analytical techniques is discussed further below.

One key concept for interpreting data involves searching for what can be termed "driving forces": the fundamental, social-cultural, political, economic, and technological forces that, through their interactions, establish much of our business and social environment or, in this case, regulatory environment. As noted earlier, while driving forces are usually trends in themselves, they also produce other trends, in the process often either supporting or conflicting with other driving forces. A driving force is generally described as a movement of such strength that no single industry participant, social group, or even nation can by its own actions significantly change its direction or end goal.

Examples of specific driving forces each of which could be grouped under one of the four general driving forces (social, economic, technological, and political) include the following (although not all necessarily apply to the regulatory environment facing a given business).

Demographic Patterns

Among these patterns are changes in population growth, age distribution, household formation, employment patterns, levels of education, housing patterns, and mobility. For example, the aging of America has led to a push for the rights of senior citizens.

Economic Conditions

These include changes in disposable income, discretionary income, unemployment, underemployment, gross national product, inflation, balance of payments, consumer expenditures, and interest rates. For example, a devaluation of the dollar may lead to a loosening of trade barriers, which encourages foreigners to import our goods and helps our balance of payments. A high standard of living may change our national needs from basic survival to laws concerning the quality of life.

Resources

There are changes in the cost and availability of raw materials (petroleum, lumber, coal, and natural gas, for example), capital, and labor. Scarce petroleum resources and increasing reliance on foreign oil have led to regulated fuel economy through CAFE standards, increased demand for fuel economy standards, and increased demand for governmental control over oil company profits.

Social Values

Recent years have seen changes in the role of the family, school, religion, and government in the shaping of our country; attitudes toward work, leisure time, and personal obligations; parochialism, nationalism, and internationalism; attitudes toward private enterprise; attitudes toward materialism; feelings of independence, dependence, isolation, and apathy; attitudes toward egalitarianism, autocracy, and plutocracy; and so on. Recently, in what has been described as the "psychology of entitlement," it has become commonplace for individuals to hold corporations responsible for their products even when individuals have not adhered to the warnings or instructions accompanying the products. In many cases the courts have concurred.

Illustrative Example

In 1942, the Oliver Machinery Company sold a new bench saw to the U.S. Navy for use at Pearl Harbor. The machine was equipped at that time with the latest available safety equipment, including blade guards that differed only slightly from those now used by saw manufacturers. In October 1971, a worker in an El Paso, Texas, plant, which had bought the saw as surplus from the Navy, lost part of his hand on this machine. The worker later testified that he was aware that the machine was dangerous and that the blade guard had been removed. The accident, according to the court testimony, took place when the worker attempted to cut a large piece of wood. The worker allegedly lifted the saw blade as he pushed the wood down on the table, thereby pushing his hand through the saw blade and amputating his fingers. The machinery company argued that the accident could not have happened had the blade guard been installed, as it was on the original equipment when sold to the Navy 29 years earlier. Nevertheless, the jury found the Oliver Machinery Company at fault and awarded the worker $50,000.[6]

[6] *The Product-Safety Function: Organization and Operations,* The Conference Board, Inc., New York, 1979, p. 10.

Government Regulation

There are changes in the role agencies play, the areas under their purview, their means of enforcing their policies, and so on. For example, antitrust legislation has been around for a long time, but in 1950 mergers came under antitrust control.[7] Senator Edward M. Kennedy has suggested that mere bigness might be sufficient to draw antitrust attention, a view not necessarily upheld by the Supreme Court, which in decisions such as in *General Dynamics*[8] refused to base its conclusions merely on market share or concentration figures.

Technology

There are changes in the role of technology in industry; in those who bear the cost of technological changes' side effects; in the impact of technology on industry size, concentration, economies of scale, employment, and indirect links to other industries; and so on. For example, high-technology industries with high barriers to entry because of significant economies of scale are often the targets of antitrust activities.

Business Conditions

Among changes in business conditions are those in foreign competition, industry concentration, multinationalism, and industry maturity. For example, industries in a growth stage do not need to compete with each other for sales because the market is growing (e.g., mopeds in the early 1970s). However, as the market tapers off and they begin competing with each other, they may be scrutinized by the government for their business practices.

Specific driving forces can be identified in a number of ways: by examining trends and looking for commonality in their character or their causes, by reading new material in different fields, from interviews, from experience, and from specific analyses. Sometimes they can be discovered by asking questions as to why particular trends or driving forces such as egalitarianism gained sudden strength at a particular point in history rather than earlier or later. In other cases, they can be noted by searching for counterforces, which almost always will be present in response to the forces or trends that have already been identified.

Selecting those driving forces that impact an industry or a company is the second step. It requires a thorough understanding of how a business works and why it works and has worked as described. The workings of the industry should be traced as far back as possible to assure that synergistic and economic ties with other industries, government activities, etc., are covered. An analysis of driving forces which would lead to the regulation of selected industries might include these examples:

[7]Betty Bock, "Consistency and Change in Antitrust in the United States," *Toward a National Antitrust Policy,* The Conference Board, Inc., New York, 1976, pp. 39–43.

[8]*United States v. General Dynamics Corp.,* 415 U.S. 486 (1974).

Illustrative Examples

Demographic patterns Increased population density and corresponding automobile use led to smog and other pollutant problems and to a demand for emission controls. A high birthrate led to substantial numbers of children and to a push for the regulation of television programs and advertisements, the labeling of the contents of children's products (e.g., additives), and the removal of substances such as sugar from baby foods.

Resources The Arab oil embargo led to a recognition of American dependence on foreign oil and on the intentions of the Organization of Petroleum Exporting Countries (OPEC) and to the need to conserve energy and thus to demands to regulate fuel consumption. Dwindling supplies of certain types of fish and game led to quotas and bans.

Government regulation Increased attention is being paid to safety, fuel efficiency, and emission controls in the auto industry. The ability of General Motors to capture market share in the face of regulation may lead to intensified antitrust efforts. The Toxic Substances Control Act has set up a system to evaluate, monitor, and control the use of chemicals throughout industry. The Occupational Safety and Health Administration (OSHA) has established, among other things, acceptable levels of asbestos.

Social values Consumers, unhappy with a loss of independence when Congress mandated the locking of transmissions until seat belts were fastened, forced government retrenchment from this position. At the same time consumers exhibited increasing concern over the safety of products and services, causing the creation of safety statutes and regulatory agencies.[9]

Economic conditions As cars became more expensive to own and operate, consumers became more deeply concerned about the value of what they received, and there were more numerous complaints in two major areas of dissatisfaction, service and the purchase of used cars. The complaints led to increased governmental regulation in these two areas. The pressures of the mismatch of social security payers and payees are believed to be part of the drive to abandon compulsory retirement despite the other economic implications of continuing employment of the elderly (e.g., increased unemployment of younger workers).[10] And inflation and recession are implicated in moves to reduce the exemption of labor unions to antitrust laws.[11]

Technology The high cost of technological solutions to emissions, safety, and fuel efficiency requirements have further weakened marginal auto manufacturers in the United States. In Europe, without the same restrictions, the high cost of retooling and economies of scale in a slowing growth have done much the same thing. In the electronics industry, first photocopy machines and then video tape machines have led to a renewed interest in copyright laws.

Business conditions As the automobile industry becomes more and more multinational, European and Asian car manufacturers, in particular, are forming various agreements for joint marketing and components manufacture. In the United States, General Motors was successfully sued for misrepresentation when it was discovered that the company had been using engines interchangeably. Weakened United States auto manufacturers have turned attention toward General Motors and antitrust laws. Jap-

[9]*The Product-Safety Function: Organization and Operations,* The Conference Board, Inc., New York, 1979, p. 10.

[10]J. Roger O'Meara, "Will Mandatory Retirement Be Outlawed?" *The Conference Board Record,* May 1976, pp. 6–7.

[11]Murray L. Weidenbaum, "A Shot of Antitrust for Labor Unions," *Business Week,* Mar. 26, 1979.

anese companies have been investigated for charges of dumping products at prices below cost in weakened United States industries (e.g., television sets, automobiles).

Explanatory Models

As noted previously, driving forces are complex and interact both harmoniously and in conflict. The difficulty of the task of explaining the process has led to the development of a variety of explanatory models. These models can be manipulated by changing their variables and thus can be used to develop alternative futures. For example, the birthrate, which has recently been deviating from its historical trend, can be increased, say, to 2.5 or lowered, say, to 1.5. Such a change will, over time, change other demographic variables such as age distribution, household formation, population growth or decline, and the labor force and will also change other driving forces such as economic conditions.

Explanatory models have been developed in the following areas:

- Relationships between affluence levels, socioeconomic maturity levels, hierarchy of human needs, and patterns of growth in sales of different types of products and services

- Alternative modes of government intervention in the private sector the circumstances of which are likely to make a particular mode dominant, patterns of transition from one mode to another, and implications for business relationships with government

- Ways in which deeply embedded cultural needs influence the acceptability of change, new forms of government and regulatory procedures, adoption of new technologies and similar matters, and conditions likely to lead to countermovements

- Diffusion of technology: quantitative estimates of the level and rate of diffusion, its impact on the economics of industries, and its potential for creating new industries which take over part or all of older industry business

Identifying and Describing Agencies

Regulatory agencies were created as a kind of fourth branch of government and were designed primarily to remain more firmly insulated than regular agencies from political pressure, Congress, the President, and voter groups. They are staffed by specialists who have acquired their expertise by concentrating their careers within one agency and program. The head of the agency may change with political fortunes, while the basic personality of the agency and the direction in which it flows may either remain unchanged or reflect the personality of the head.

The agencies of particular concern to an industry must be identified. While at first blush this seems obvious (food companies must be responsive to the Food and Drug Administration, or FDA, for example), the identification process is more complex. The Consumer Product Safety Commission (CPSC), for example, touches all consumer products companies; and agencies have come into existence to monitor air pollution, water pollution, employee safety (National Institute for Occupational Safety and Health, or

NIOSH), the hazards of chemicals being used, and so on. The list can be very extensive indeed.

Once an agency has been identified, it should be "tracked": a description of its mode of operation, its charter (including the regulatory actions it may take), its personnel, its power with other legislative bodies, and the targets it chooses should all be traced from the past to the present. Trends can thus be noted.

Identifying and Describing Competitors

Past, present, and future competitors in an industry must likewise be identified. Here, too, a company should not just accept the obvious but think in terms of substitute products or services. For example, home video may in fact "compete" with movie theaters, and regulation of this fledgling industry may well substantially impact the movie theater business and the entertainment industry in general.

Close attention must be given to competition within a given industry. Competitors' actions or reactions to a driving force could have a widespread effect on the direction of an entire industry. Willingness or hesitancy of commitment to a course of action often determines the number of futures open to a particular company and affects the resources available to it for utilization.

Each corporation has its own mode of operation: the techniques it uses to facilitate change, meet challenges, deal with agencies, etc. This mode is an indication of the corporation's decision-making style. Even with the increasing uncertainties that a corporation faces, its responses will reflect that style.

Thus, as with the agencies, a corporation should track the responses of its competition, so that it can predict competitors' reactions to regulatory maneuvers.

Developing the Base Case

Using the above materials, a "base case" future is developed. The base-case future normally is presented in terms of a set of most likely trends, which are related to the specific relevant driving forces, likely agency behavior, and likely competitor response.

The very large quantity of material that must be considered in the course of an alternative-futures study places a premium on formats and modes of presentation that make it easier to grasp the totality of the material provided. The following type of format may be useful for the base case:

- Division of the material into categories, using either those described earlier or a modified version to match the structure of a particular industry

- Presentation of each trend in a one-sentence statement, followed by a one-paragraph rationale for each of the trends, giving the basis for its existence, appropriate cross-references, and, in some cases, its relationship to the driving forces of which it is an expression

- A brief summary of the key features of each category covered

Illustrative Example

To use the automotive industry as an example, a future base case might be as follows:

Demographic patterns The most active car-buying group (23- to 34-year-olds) will account for 22 percent of the potential car market and hold social values (see below) which will focus on more comprehensive warranties and a car return policy.

Resources Continued reliance on foreign oil, plus stability of OPEC alliances, leads to continued pressure for escalating CAFE standards.

Government regulation CAFE standards will continue to increase; federal car inspection standards will be in force by 1985 and will increase pressure for a so-called maintenance-free car; emission control standards have stabilized, but diesel is not exempt from the standards. New flammability standards which call certain automobile materials and gasoline tank placements into question have been set. Antitrust activity has abated owing to the threat of "foreign" cars becoming dominant (of the top five manufacturers, three are foreign, although each has manufacturing or assembly facilities in the United States).

Social values Consumers are complaining about the shoddy workmanship of United States–made cars and are pushing for more comprehensive warranties *and* for the right to return the merchandise for their money back (i.e., a full refund) if not satisfied. They are suspicious of auto manufacturers and oil companies, suspecting them of withholding technology which would reduce our dependency on foreign oil. Because of these factors they are buying more foreign cars (1 out of 4 cars is now foreign), further weakening United States car manufacturers.

Economic conditions As the bite of fuel costs and increased auto costs continue to impact on families, autos have become more specialized: there are the urban car, which is heavily used and is traded in frequently; and the family car, which is used less frequently and is expected to last 20 years. The former car is apt to be foreign; the latter, of United States manufacture. As a result, regulations are being considered to mandate a 20-year car.

Technology A new fuel which will virtually do away with the need for emission control has been developed. However, it will require the virtual retooling of all automobiles, and two of the United States manufacturers will be unable to do so without government support.

Business conditions Owing to the size of foreign car shares, it has become economical for some foreign manufacturers to assemble cars and even to manufacture some components in the United States. This trend calls for a redefinition of "foreign" versus "domestic" cars. Of the top three manufacturers, only one is a United States corporation. Antitrust activity has abated until the matter can be resolved.

In addition to the trend statements and category summaries, it is important to develop a descriptive statement of the entire base case that presents the essence of what seem to be the key determinants, sources of conflict, instruments for resolution, and so on. Finally, it often is useful to abstract certain key issues whose resolution can have a major impact on the future and to prepare material on any new explanatory models that may have evolved in the course of the base-case study.

Selection of Alternative Futures

Prior work, including the industry-oriented component of the data base, will have provided a background for identifying the specific driving forces to which regulation of a particular industry is most sensitive. A relatively small number of key variables can be selected to characterize a range of futures that will cover the most important situations for a particular industry or company. An initial set of combinations of states or values of these variables is selected as *alternative futures*. While the number of futures for study can be expanded indefinitely, at this stage more than three to five alternatives will tend to be unmanageable and may prove to be more than really are needed.

There are two steps in the selection process: determination of the key variables and selection of combinations of these variables to define the future end states.

Selection of Key Variables

Key variables are selected from observations of the interactions between broad environmental trends and their specific driving forces and the primary determinants for the regulation of the industry. The variables themselves, however, almost always will be the exogenous factors, since the primary objective of the alternative-futures process is to help an organization determine how to manage its internal and controllable activities and to influence external events to the extent practicable so that it can adapt to and exploit factors and events that are outside its full control. A fairly limited number of key variables dominates the operation of most industries and organizations. As a general rule, one can start with as many as five or six candidate variables, but these normally will be reduced to two or three during the process of future end state selection.

End State Selection

End state selection simply amounts to selecting suitable combinations of "values" for specific key variables. To do this, there may have to be a degree of integration back through the variable selection and definition process. There are two major objectives to be met in end state selection:

- First, it is very desirable to select variables which are not highly correlated. If two variables *are* highly correlated, little or no purpose is to be served by selecting both, since one of the two can represent both.

- Once the final variables have been specified, it is desirable that the end points selected provide an envelope, or coverage, that "surrounds" the base case. With the base case as a point of departure, the most desirable situation is one in which both "greater than" and "less than" end state combinations involving each key variable are chosen. This process obviously is closely related to sensitivity testing and is part of the effort to ensure that a broad range of possible futures is incorporated. The goal is to get reasonable representative futures that cover a range of possibilities important to a company. With an infinity of possible futures, no four or five will give a high degree of coverage, but these can form a base to which additions can easily be made. This addition process can be encouraged by the monitoring system, which will be one of the end products and which can help to indicate when events begin to represent a departure from *all* the representational futures that have been examined.

If in the computer industry antitrust were considered one of the key factors of the regulatory environment, alternative futures might be (1) the breakup of International Business Machines Corp. into two or more companies and (2) the merger of smaller manufacturers because of vastly reduced antitrust. The treatment must be internally consistent; thus, the scenario which has the expanded number of United States manufacturers must recalculate shares of market, and the consolidated scenario must do likewise.

CONTINGENCY PLANNING

The base-case and alternative-futures development provides the basis for contingency planning, which will be undertaken in three steps: (1) assessing the impact of each scenario on the industry as a whole and the company in particular, (2) developing a specific plan of action for each scenario, and (3) developing monitoring techniques to assess where events are heading and how well the planning process is working.

Assessing the Impact of Each Scenario

Each future will have a markedly different impact on the corporation. Some futures may strengthen its market position; others may weaken it. The same is true of the competition. As specific details as possible should be developed for the industry and the company based on each scenario: size of market, market shares, changes in cost of operations, price elasticities, market segments, changes in foreign or domestic opportunities and threats, changes in distribution structure, and so on.

Developing a Specific Plan of Action for Each Scenario

Once the anticipated impacts have been delineated, a company can determine the appropriate actions to take in order to

- Encourage or discourage the future from occurring
- Take advantage of or blunt the negative impact of the situation if it does occur

The plan should be specific, including timing of actions, personnel to use, extent of resources to be committed, targets of actions, posture or position of the company, and changes in distribution, pricing, and promotion. For example, actions might include congressional lobbying, a public speaking campaign, legal maneuvers, and even corporate reorganization. Postures can range from conciliatory to rigid. The issue may warrant a vast commitment of resources and capital or need only a minimal infusion.

It is also important to discover the actions, personnel, and resources which each scenario has in common, for these parts of the plan can be begun immediately without jeopardizing the company. This may be accomplished by utilizing matrices.

Illustrative Example

A consumer products company involved in litigation determined that its losing the case would have a substantial impact on its business: it would be apt to lose share, all its distribution policies would have to be revamped, and even its ability to maintain its extensive distribution would be seriously impaired. Moreover, its costs would most likely escalate, and at the same time it might have to lower prices to maintain market position. Seeing the impact on sales, profits, and even corporate organization, the company renewed its commitment to infuse large amounts of resources to avoid losing the case and developed highly specific corporate contingency plans in the event that it did lose. The company was even able to distinguish actions which could be taken in the present to blunt the impact of losing that would not have a negative impact on present operations.

Monitoring and Evaluation

Once planning has taken place, the company must monitor external events so it can be aware of which path the future is taking (including some new twists not previously anticipated) and can adjust corporate planning accordingly. Monitoring requires an understanding of what signals precede an event (or have done so in the past) or a change in agency positioning and the normal timing from signal to action. Responsibility for monitoring must be assigned within the company; once signals have been received, the company must have a set of procedures for implementing the actions suggested in the contingency plan (or, if the change was unanticipated, for quickly developing the impact and appropriate contingency plan).

Monitoring must also include evaluation of the contingency plan adopted. How effective are the actions taken? Is the posture appropriate? Are there other actions which ought to be tried?

As can be seen, the process is iterative: today's solution may be tomorrow's catastrophe. However, proper use of this technique allows a firm to maintain maximum control over its future rather than being at the mercy of its environment.

2 WHAT REGULATION COSTS

MICHAEL E. SIMON
Partner
Arthur Andersen & Co.

Most government regulation originates from genuine concern for the achievement of desirable economic and social goals. The proliferation of regulatory agencies and programs in the United States during the 1960s and 1970s was a response to the public's perception that without government intervention the market system would fail to provide safe and healthful workplaces, equal employment opportunity, clean air and clean water, safe products, and an equitable distribution of scarce materials such as fuel oil at "fair" prices.

For much of the 1960s and 1970s there was little recognition of the fact that each regulatory goal, no matter how desirable, had its cost. When cost was raised as an issue, the usual response was that whatever the regulation cost, the benefits were worth it. The regulatory process achieved such momentum that benefits were simply assumed to exist and costs were addressed casually if at all. Given that environment, it should not be surprising that some regulations resulted in the imposition of large cost burdens on the private sector and on the nation's economy. Business, government, and other interested groups have seriously questioned whether the costs of meeting regulatory objectives are excessive. They have also stated their belief that less costly alternative methods could be employed to achieve desired goals.

A number of estimates have been made of the costs of government regulations. Some estimates have included all levels of government, all businesses in the United States, and both economic and social costs. Others have focused on individual areas of regulation, selected types of costs, and specific industries. For example:

- Murray L. Weidenbaum and Robert De Fina of the Center for the Study of American Business at Washington University in St. Louis estimated the total cost of federal regulation in 1977 to be $79.1 billion. Roughly $9.5 billion of that sum was attributed to environmental regulations. Their estimate was based in part on estimates provided by several industry- and agency-specific studies conducted by others. Subsequently, on the basis of continued growth in the budgets of the regulatory agencies, Professor Weidenbaum estimated that the cost of federal regulation in 1979 exceeded $100 billion.[1]

- The Office of Management and Budget (OMB) estimated total costs of regulation in 1975 to be in the range of $113 to $135 billion. The economic evaluation of OMB's study by the General Accounting Office (GAO) concluded that this estimate was significantly overstated but did not establish an alternative estimate.[2]

- Edward F. Denison, then with the Brookings Institution, estimated that the incremental costs to protect the environment and the safety and health of workers in 1975 was $10.5 billion, of which $9.5 billion was attributed to environmental regulations. He also estimated that in 1975 those factors had resulted in a 0.5 percent annual reduction in growth of output of net national product per unit of input.[3]

- The Council on Environmental Quality (CEQ) study estimated the incremental cost for all businesses to comply with pollution abatement control requirements in 1977 to be $12.8 billion.[4]

- Arthur Andersen & Co. in a study for the Business Roundtable enlisted the participation of forty-eight companies and found that those companies had incurred direct incremental costs of $2.6 billion in complying with the regulations of six federal agencies in 1977.[5]

Each of these studies had a different scope and featured a different methodology. What they all had in common was the conclusion that the costs of regulation were very high indeed.

WHY MEASURE COSTS?

As the 1970s drew to a close, the public gradually came to the painful realization that the nation's resources were finite, not infinite. The implications of that simple fact have been hard for Americans to accept: we cannot necessarily afford the cost of every desirable goal; priorities must be established.

The studies of the costs of regulation cited earlier were useful in raising the public's awareness that these costs were high. That, coupled with the realization that the nation could ill afford to incur unnecessary costs, has led to a significant improvement in the regulatory process. First by order of the President[6] and later by congressional legislation,[7] federal regulators are being required to perform a more rigorous analysis of the expected effects of each major regulation. The analysis includes a clear description of the objectives of the regulation, that is, the benefits to be achieved from it, consideration of alternative ways of achieving the objectives and the economic impacts of each alternative, and an explanation of why the selected alternative has been

---

[1]Arthur Andersen & Co., *Cost of Government Regulation: Study for the Business Roundtable*, Executive Summary, March 1979, p. 20.

[2]Ibid.

[3]Ibid.

[4]Ibid.

[5]Ibid.

[6]Executive Order 12044 of the President of the United States.

[7]The 1980 Regulatory Flexibility Act, as well as several bills requiring regulatory analysis that are before Congress.

chosen. Equally significant are the provisions for public participation much earlier in the process, before the regulators are committed to a particular course of action.

The requirements for regulatory analysis and the provisions for a public dialogue early in the process provide an effective mechanism for those who want to assure that objective cost information is considered seriously in formulating regulatory policy. From a public policy standpoint there are at least three reasons for focusing attention on the cost impacts of a particular regulation:

1. Are the benefits cited for a particular regulation worth the costs to the nation of that regulation?
2. Is the compliance action required by the regulatory program the least costly way of achieving the benefits sought?
3. Can the nation afford the added costs that are being imposed by the regulation?

Answering the three questions obviously requires information about benefits and costs. Some of that information will be in monetary terms. Benefits and costs should be expressed in monetary terms when measurements can be made objectively. Some benefits and some costs cannot be quantified easily. When they cannot be measured objectively, it is sufficient to describe them without assigning monetary values.

James C. Miller III, the noted economist, has described admirably the value of an analysis that quantifies benefits and costs that can be measured objectively and identifies, but does not attempt to quantify, benefits that cannot:

One of the most important advantages of benefit-cost analysis is that it can free regulators to focus more on the subjective areas of benefits and costs, where quantification in money terms is more difficult. Let us imagine the regulators having a simple ledger (for a given regulatory initiative). On the left side are listed first those benefits that can be quantified in money terms and second those that cannot. On the right side are listed first those costs that can be quantified, and then those costs that cannot. By netting out the quantified benefits and costs, the regulator is then able to focus on those pluses and minuses which are not easily capable of quantification. An analogy might illustrate the point. Imagine there are two very large piles of sand, and one is asked which is the larger. If the piles of sand are comparable in size, the decision is very difficult. However, if a "bucket brigade" were organized and [equal] bucketfuls were taken from each pile in sequence, it would become progressively easier to tell which had been the larger. That is, as their absolute sizes diminish (as the quantified benefits and costs are netted out), their relative sizes become more apparent.[8]

Business books and records provide a unique source of information on the costs of complying with regulations. Benefits are usually measured on a communitywide or broader basis and are relatively more difficult to measure objectively than costs. The sources of information for measuring benefits are

---

[8]Prepared statement of James C. Miller III before the Subcommittee on Consumer Protection and Finance and the Subcommittee on Oversight and Investigations, U.S. House of Representatives, Oct. 24, 1979.

diverse and are not necessarily subject to the same disciplines as the books and records of companies. By contrast, a substantial portion of the costs of compliance with regulations is determinable from company books and records.

With a federal policy that requires serious analysis, with public participation, of economic impacts and alternatives to regulation, business has the opportunity, if not the obligation, to provide credible cost information that will contribute to the development of regulatory policies in the national interest. Businesses need to determine the direct and indirect costs of government regulation of various facets of the businesses, especially when government regulations actually or potentially affect one of the strategic driving forces of the businesses such as raw-material or energy supply, labor force makeup, production techniques or facilities distribution systems, and advertising or marketing procedures. They need to measure their costs of regulation so that they can plan ways to minimize adverse cost impacts.

The remainder of this chapter describes how companies can calculate both historical and projected costs of compliance with regulations and report the costs in an effective manner.

WHAT ARE THE COSTS OF REGULATION?

The costs of regulation fall into three general categories:

1. *Regulatory agency costs.* The costs incurred by the regulatory agencies are borne by taxpayers and can be determined by examining the budgets of the agencies.

2. *Direct costs of compliance.* Actions taken by individuals, businesses, and governmental units to comply with regulatory requirements result in costs incurred by the regulated individuals or entities that are directly attributable to the compliance action. The amount of the costs is identifiable through accounting means, particularly in the case of businesses and governmental units. The direct costs are borne ultimately by individuals: consumers, investors, and taxpayers.

3. *Indirect costs of compliance.* There are also many less visible indirect effects of regulation which cause substantial costs to those who are regulated and to the economy as a whole. Indirect effects can be difficult to identify and even more difficult to quantify in monetary terms even though the costs are very real. Indirect costs of compliance include those in which compliance with the regulation results in productivity losses, investment disincentives, lost opportunities, delays, misallocation of resources, shortages of supply, loss of competitive edge to foreign producers, and added inflation.

The foregoing categorization distinguishes between the costs of the regulators and the costs to the regulated. Moreover, it provides a clear demarcation between direct compliance costs which can be determined by accounting means from business books and records and indirect compliance costs which are much more difficult to identify, quantify, and support with adequate documentation. Thus, regulatory compliance costs can be collected, analyzed, and reported by using a structure that distinguishes between those which are verifiable and should be credible to almost all segments of the public and those which will prove more difficult to pin down in a manner acceptable to all parties.

Principles for Determining the Direct Costs of Compliance

The Arthur Andersen & Co. study of regulation for the Business Roundtable cited earlier in this chapter was unique because it applied uniform, verifiable cost accounting principles for measuring the costs of *individual* regulatory programs and rigorous standards for documenting results. The Business Roundtable initiated the study among its members to determine whether or not a methodology could be developed and applied to measure costs of regulation consistently for a number of agencies and a range of industries and whether the results of the study would be credible and useful to the regulators as well as the regulated and to those responsible for overseeing the regulators.

The Business Roundtable study was successful on all counts. Its methodology and objectivity have been acclaimed by regulators, those responsible for overseeing the regulators, and those who are regulated. As the chairman of the Joint Economic Committee of Congress stated:

The Business Roundtable's "Cost of Government Regulation" study has contributed to a heightened interest in cost-effectiveness by defusing an important concern of those who oppose our attempts to control excessive regulatory costs—the concern that regulatory costs cannot be measured accurately enough to make informed choices among alternatives or to be included in a regulatory budget.[9]

The administrator of the Environmental Protection Agency (EPA) and chairman of the U.S. Regulatory Council commented in a similar vein:

The Business Roundtable's "Cost of Government Regulation Study" is a commendable attempt to quantify some of the costs. The study's strength rests on the use of a consistent methodology, based on the concept of incremental costs, which is applied across six regulatory programs and forty-eight companies. The result is a rigorous and professional analysis.[10]

Moreover, several agencies of the United States government have used information gathered in the study in their policymaking processes.

The principles for measuring the direct costs of compliance were an important reason for the credibility of the Business Roundtable study. Twelve cost principles, adapted with little substantive revision from this study,[11] are presented below to provide a sound basis for ongoing efforts to determine the direct costs of compliance.

1. The Costs to Be Measured Are the Costs of Those Actions Taken to Comply with a Regulation That Would Not Have Been Taken in the Absence of That Regulation

Measuring the cost of regulatory compliance actions requires screening out actions that would have been taken even if the regulation were not in place.

[9]Senator Lloyd Bentsen in a letter to the editor of *Regulation,* November–December 1979, p. 59.

[10]Douglas Costle in a letter to the editor of *Regulation,* November–December 1979, p. 3.

[11]Arthur Andersen & Co., *Cost of Government Regulation: Study for the Business Roundtable,* The Report, March 1979, chap. 4.

After that screening, what remains are the "incremental actions," actions taken only because they were required by regulation.

This cost principle, usually known as the "incremental-cost principle," is based on the idea that if costs are to be an integral part of the decision of whether or not to issue a new regulation or to rescind or modify an old one, the only costs pertinent to the decision making are those that would be incurred or were incurred only because of the proposed or existing regulation.

The business community has incurred substantial costs on behalf of the safety and health of its employees, the protection of the environment, and other factors associated with socially responsible corporate practices. Additional costs have been incurred to respond to demands of the marketplace and to labor pressures. In addition, the federal government has established regulations formalizing many of the practices already in place and adding thousands of new regulatory requirements that impose yet another layer of costs.

The direct costs of compliance are a portion of the last layer, the costs of actions taken to comply with a regulation that would not have been taken in the absence of that regulation. The direct costs are based upon informed judgment as to which actions would have been taken in the absence of regulation and information drawn from the companies' accounting and engineering records.

Illustrative Examples

A company incurred $500,000 in scholarships to minority institutions and special training programs for minority and women employees. The actions were taken as part of the company's affirmative-action program under the federal government's equal employment opportunity program. The company decided that it would have taken the same actions as a matter of corporate social responsibility even if it had not been required to have an affirmative-action program. Since the action would have been taken anyway, it did not result in a direct cost of compliance.

A second company also incurred $500,000 in scholarships to minority institutions and special training programs for minority and women employees as part of its affirmative-action program. Its management decided that while the company had long had a strict policy of nondiscrimination in hiring and promotions, it would not have undertaken the special scholarship and training programs in the absence of the regulatory requirement. In this instance, the entire cost of the program, $500,000, was a direct cost of regulation.

The incremental-cost determination requires each company to apply its best judgment to decide which actions would have been taken in the absence of regulation. The introduction of judgment into the calculation of direct cost of compliance has been questioned. However, different companies do indeed make different judgments as to which actions to take in the absence of regulation. By requiring companies to make that judgment, the methodology measures costs to comply with regulations that would have been applied to other purposes in the absence of regulation.

In the case of the Business Roundtable study, the focus on incremental costs turned out to be an important reason both for the study's usefulness and for its credibility.

One key point must be remembered by those comparing the benefits of a regulation with its costs: since the costs of compliance actions include only actions that would not be taken in the absence of regulation, it follows that a comparison with benefits should include only benefits that would not occur in the absence of regulation. That is, *incremental* benefits should be compared with *incremental* costs.

2. Costs Are to Be Segregated by Year

Some cost determination efforts will focus on the historical costs of regulations; others will emphasize the estimated future costs of existing or proposed regulations. In either case, consolidation of results with other companies and comparisons with other studies will be facilitated if the data collected are segregated and reported by using each company's fiscal year or some other agreed-upon 12-month period.

3. Costs Are to Be Identified and Collected for Specific Compliance Requirements

Whether a cost determination effort concentrates on historical costs or on estimated future costs, the identification of costs of compliance actions to meet individual compliance requirements will add measurably to the usefulness of the results. The following definitions clarify the terms:

- "Compliance requirements" result directly from a law or from a regulation or administrative ruling by a government agency.

- "Compliance actions" are activities undertaken by a company to meet a regulatory (compliance) requirement.

4. Recognition of Costs Follows the Accrual Basis of Accounting

Costs of complying with federal regulations are to be determined on the accrual basis of accounting, the basis used by most companies in their regular books of account and financial statements. Capital costs should be measured on the basis of expenditures or accruals for capital items rather than through depreciation. Calculating the costs in that manner measures the diversion of funds during the period from other possible uses to complying with regulations. Two other reasons for measuring expenditures rather than attempting to measure depreciation are pragmatic:

- In studies that focus on historical costs of compliance, it would be necessary to identify, for each asset in use in the year studied, the portion related solely or partially to the regulation or regulations under study. It would then be necessary to determine the cost, in the year acquired, of the portion of the asset attributable solely to the regulation or regulations. Finally, it would be necessary to compute depreciation for the year, taking care to assure that the asset had not been fully depreciated prior to that time.

- The many different but acceptable methods of computing depreciation used by different companies in the same industry would make the results difficult to compare.

5. Costs Are to Be Identified and Collected in Four Classifications

To enrich the analysis, direct costs of compliance should be collected in four classifications:

- *Capital costs.* The incremental capital costs of regulation consist of expenditures for those portions of property, plant, or equipment that are required to bring the company into compliance with a regulation. To ensure consistency among companies, one type of cost that some companies capitalize for financial statement purposes should be excluded from capital costs: allocations to capital projects of home office and year-end and administrative expenses. Conversely, applicable planning and design costs and special tooling and equipment costs should be included with capital costs even if they are not normally capitalized for financial statement purposes.

- *Operating and administrative costs.* Operating and administrative costs consist of costs incurred as a result of (1) operating facilities or equipment installed to comply with regulations, (2) performing activities necessary to comply with regulations that affect the manner in which manufacturing or other operating functions are carried out, (3) completing required paperwork, (4) meeting with government personnel on regulatory matters, and (5) performing other administrative activities required in the course of meeting compliance requirements. This classification includes the cost of operating all facilities or equipment installed to comply with regulations regardless of whether the capital cost was incurred in the year being studied.

- *Research and development costs.* This classification consists of costs for determining and developing product or process modifications needed to meet regulatory requirements.

- *Product costs.* Direct product costs consist of material, labor, overhead, and other costs incurred to make a product conform to a regulatory requirement. This classification consists of costs that can be measured on a unit-of-production basis. The unit cost is then multiplied by the number of units produced to determine incremental product costs.

Subclassifications within each of the four classifications can be established to provide a finer analysis of the types of costs incurred. For example, "preparation of reports" and "employee training" could be established as subclassifications within the operating and administrative cost classification, and "product testing" within the research and development classification. Similarly, source codes could be added to distinguish between labor costs and nonlabor costs.

6. The Preferable Sources of Cost Data Are Accounting and Financial Records

The preferable sources of cost data, companies' accounting and financial records, include general and subsidiary ledgers; payroll records; records of capital expenditures, authorizations, and reports; property records; and operating statements and source documents such as invoices and time cards. Data available in accounting and financial records at times will be supplemented by data drawn from production and engineering records in order to obtain the type of detail required by the methodology.

In accordance with sound accounting principles and practice, cost allocations and estimates should be made when available sources do not provide necessary cost details. Such circumstances will occur in determining historical costs as well as in estimating future costs. For allocations and estimates to be acceptable, they should be conceptually sound, be performed by or in conjunction with an individual qualified to make the estimates, and be documented.

Illustrative Examples

If an estimate is required to determine the cost of a water filtration plant built as part of a new facility for the purpose of meeting the EPA's water effluent guidelines, an architect or engineer familiar with that project would be qualified to assist in making the estimate. If an estimate is required to determine the portion of an individual's time spent completing equal employment opportunity (EEO) reports, the individual or his or her supervisor would be qualified to assist in making the estimate. In both examples, the estimate should be documented in sufficient detail to explain how it was developed.

7. Costs Are Measured at the Point in the Business Cycle at Which Compliance with a Regulation is Required

To prevent either double counting or omitting the cost of complying with a regulation, it is necessary to identify the point during the business cycle (between purchase of raw material and sale to the ultimate consumer) at which the regulation is imposed. The cost should be measured only at that point. Each company will include only the costs of regulations with which it is required to comply.

Illustrative Examples

EPA regulations require new automobiles to meet specific emission standards prior to sale. The manufacturer adds equipment to each car to comply with the EPA's requirement. A company that leases cars purchases a fleet of cars from the manufacturer. It is the manufacturer, rather than the purchaser of the automobiles who paid a higher price because of the added equipment, who should report the cost to comply.

A company was required to reduce interior noise levels in one of its plants. To comply, it purchased new, quieter production machines. The company purchasing the machines would recognize all or a portion of the machine cost as a cost of compliance. The manufacturer of the machine, who was not precluded by regulations from producing and selling the old line, would not recognize the increased product cost to muffle noise as a cost of compliance.

8. Cost Reductions Are Deducted from the Direct Costs of Compliance

In some situations, complying with a regulation may result in direct and quantifiable cost reductions, such as the net income derived from sales of a by-product resulting from a process or an operation required to comply with a regulation. When such cost reductions occur and can be identified and quantified, they will be deducted from the cost of regulation.

Illustrative Example

A chemical plant installs a water treatment facility to reduce the amount of effluents being discharged into a river. As a result of installing the facility the company recovers chemicals which previously were discharged. The chemicals can either be recycled in the company's process or be sold to outsiders. Both the net income from selling the chemicals and any savings arising from recycling the chemicals should be treated as cost reductions.

The cost reductions referred to here do not include benefits as the term is normally used. For example, cost reductions do *not* include revenues from new or existing products created as the result of regulation, investment tax credits, or the use of funds arising from accelerated depreciation deductions.

Illustrative Example

A manufacturer of pollution control equipment has increased demand for its product as a result of government regulations. Also, the company develops new products to satisfy the need of its customers to comply with regulatory requirements which affect them. The revenues from these products will not be treated as cost reductions.

9. Costs Not Directly Attributable to Compliance Actions Are Excluded

Costs that are not directly attributable to complying with a regulatory requirement will not be included as a direct cost of compliance. For a cost to meet the directly attributable test, it should satisfy the following criteria:

- The cost incurred must be for an element essential to the accomplishment of the compliance action.
- A reasonable, verifiable basis must exist for attributing the cost to the regulatory compliance action and for measuring the cost.

The effect of applying this test is to include only those costs which represent resources which could be redirected to other productive uses if the compliance action were no longer performed. Conversely, costs which are relatively remote from the compliance action and which would be incurred even if the compliance action were not taken are to be excluded.

Illustrative Example

Indirect expenses will be included only to the extent that they are necessary to the accomplishment of a compliance action and can be attributed to the applicable direct costs. The application of this principle will generally be made in one of two situations:

- When all or a substantial portion of a department's or a cost center's time or direct cost is included in a compliance action, it is reasonable to include all or a pro rata portion of operating costs of the department or the cost center other than home office expense.
- When only a minor portion of direct costs of a department or a cost center is included, only operating costs which can be related specifically to the direct costs will be included. An example is labor fringe benefits.

10. Payments to the Federal Government Are Excluded from Direct Costs of Compliance

Payments for income and excise taxes, foreign trade tariffs, and import duties will not be included. Payments for payroll taxes will be included to the extent that they are included in fringe benefits associated with the labor cost of compliance actions. Fines and penalties or assessments resulting from noncompliance with regulations are not to be included since they are costs of *non*compliance rather than compliance.

Illustrative Examples

An importer of casks of French wine is required to pay federal excise taxes as part of the cost of the bottling operation. The payment of taxes would not be included as a cost of regulation.

The EPA determined that a company was not in compliance with a regulation and levied a fine of $10,000. The fine was a direct cost of noncompliance and should be excluded from the direct cost of compliance.

11. Intracompany Profits or Losses Are Excluded from Direct Costs of Compliance

In measuring the costs of regulation to a company as a whole, intracompany profit or loss margins will be excluded even if the resulting cost varies from the price at which the goods or services could be purchased from a third party.

Illustrative Example

To comply with Occupational Safety and Health Administration (OSHA) regulations concerning the level of dust and fumes in an abrasive-blasting room, a company had one of its operating divisions design and install an exhaust ventilation system for the division affected by the regulation. The cost charged to the user division included a normal profit margin. This intracompany profit should be excluded from the cost of the system for purposes of this study.

12. The Costs or Benefits of Indirect Effects Are Not Included with the Direct Costs of Compliance

The costs or benefits of the indirect effects of regulations should not be included with the direct costs of compliance. Indirect effects include:

- Changes in productivity
- Cost of forgoing alternative uses of resources (opportunity costs)
- Inability to bring new products to market or to enter new lines of business or markets
- Impact on the consumer of not having products or services available because of regulatory delays or restrictions
- Shortages of supply
- Loss of competitive edge to foreign producers

- Increased costs adding to inflation

- Increased or decreased sales and profits

The costs of indirect effects are properly classifiable as indirect costs of compliance, the third category of compliance costs. Although not properly classifiable with direct costs, indirect costs are very important, sometimes even more significant than direct costs. Accordingly, to the extent practicable, indirect effects should be identified and described. If feasible, the costs of each effect should be estimated, by using as many of the other eleven cost principles as are applicable, and classified under indirect costs of compliance.

Illustrative Examples

To comply with OSHA safety standards, a company installed additional safety devices which alter the procedures necessary to operate certain machinery. As a result, machine operators require additional time to produce products. The added costs are identifiable and should be collected as an indirect cost of compliance.

To satisfy noise levels required by OSHA standards, a textile company replaced a piece of existing equipment. The new equipment operates 40 percent more efficiently than the equipment it replaced. The annual reduced cost resulting from increased productivity of the new equipment is quantifiable. The company should collect the amount as a reduction to the cost of compliance.

A company's planned capital expansion program must be substantially reduced because most capital funds have been allocated to specific programs to comply with new regulatory requirements. The impact of this decision on the company's current or future operations can be estimated by using the company's financial model. The cost should be classified as an indirect cost of compliance.

The premises are the same as in the preceding example, except that the company has no reasonable way of estimating the effect which the diversion of capital had on its operations. In this instance, the incident should be included in anecdotal form in a discussion of indirect effects without attempting to state the effect in monetary terms.

A pesticide company is prohibited from selling a product owing to an EPA requirement. The lost sales or profits are an indirect effect. However, the cost of disposing of the product held in inventory (including the inventory cost) is a direct cost of compliance.

How Can You Measure the Direct Costs of Compliance?

Because the methodology for measuring the direct costs of compliance developed by Arthur Andersen & Co. for the Business Roundtable study has met the test of credibility, it provides the basis for the methodology described in this chapter. Measuring the direct costs of compliance with regulations in a manner designed to provide accurate results requires five principal tasks. These five tasks are applicable regardless of whether the measurement focuses on historical costs already incurred or on future costs to be incurred.

Task I: Define the Scope of the Project

The Business Roundtable study collected the direct incremental costs incurred by forty-eight companies in complying with the regulations of six federal agencies in 1977. Costs were collected for each regulation or regulatory program of the six agencies. Other studies performed by individual companies have included the costs imposed by all federal regulatory agencies. Studies performed for a specific industry have addressed the costs of complying with specific regulations of the federal agency whose regulations most deeply affect that industry.[12] Each of the studies has collected historical costs of compliance. The methodology can also be applied to estimate future costs of existing or proposed regulations.

The effort required to collect cost information will vary directly with the number of regulatory agencies and regulations included in a study. Similarly, the number of years to be included will have a direct impact on the effort required. A decision to collect regulatory cost information on an ongoing basis rather than in a special one-time project may stretch out the data collection effort required, but it will probably necessitate some changes in corporate procedures and systems.

The first step in defining the scope of a project is to decide how the results are to be used. The Business Roundtable study's chief purpose, for example, was to demonstrate that a uniform methodology could be applied to yield valid results. That study and earlier studies by others have made people aware of the fact that regulatory costs are very high.

Those studies were instrumental in establishing a climate for further studies that concentrate on the historical or projected impact of a particular regulation or regulations on a particular industry or industries. A key advantage of focusing on the costs of a few problem regulations is that it takes considerably less effort for a company to collect the information. In terms of impact on the regulatory process, projects in which many companies in an industry or in a geographic region join to study the costs of a specific regulation can be expected to receive major attention in the federal government's regulatory analysis process.

Studies which encompass many regulations, whether performed individually or by groups of companies, can also be useful in the regulatory analysis process if the principal focus is on individual regulations or regulatory programs. That specificity is important because the government's regulatory analysis process focuses on individual regulations or programs. The broader studies may also prove useful in informing stockholders, employees, and others in the community of the costs of compliance with a broader range of regulations.

---

[12]An example is Arthur Andersen & Co.'s study for the Pharmaceutical Manufacturers Association of the costs incurred in 1978 by nine pharmaceutical manufacturers in complying with certain regulations of the Food and Drug Administration.

Task II: Identify Compliance Requirements

The second task is to identify compliance requirements for each regulation included in the study. It sets the stage for identifying specific actions taken in response to the regulation or regulations.

Task III: Plan and Organize the Data Collection Effort

The third task is to plan and organize the data collection effort.

Step 1. Regardless of whether the project encompasses many regulations or few, whether it will be performed in conjunction with other companies or alone, or whether the company is large or small, one person should be designated to be in charge of the project. Depending on the size of the company, additional people may be needed for the effort.

Step 2. The second step is to identify the operating units affected by the regulation or regulations under study, if the company has more than one location, and the affected procedures, processes, and products.

Step 3. The third step is to develop a work plan for conducting the study, estimate the resources required, and establish due dates. Key factors that will affect the estimates of resources required for the project are:

- The number of operating units or divisions to be included in the study
- The number of separate and dissimilar physical locations or operating units
- The number of separate but very similar physical locations or operating units
- The nature, location, and level of detail of the company's financial and accounting records
- The existence of departments specializing in implementing and monitoring the company's compliance with the regulations under study
- The degree of difficulty in collecting the data, depending on the types of records used as sources of data
- The availability of an internal audit staff to review results in order to determine that the methodology has been followed and that the results are properly documented and reasonable

Step 4. The project leader should use the work plan as a basis for arranging for periodic progress reporting to the chief executive officer or the officer's designee. The support of top management is essential to the success of the project.

Step 5. The final step in planning and organizing the effort is to train those who will participate in collecting data in the methodology to be used and the standards of documentation.

The planning and organization task is the key to successful completion of the project. By planning and organizing the data collection effort and by training members of the project team, the project leader will know what is needed to complete the project.

Task IV: Collect the Data

This task entails the actual collection of data on the cost of regulation.

Step 1. Identify the actions taken in the period under study to comply with the requirements of the regulation or regulations under study. In Task II compliance requirements of the regulation or regulations under study were identified. Task III identified the procedures, processes, and products affected by the regulation or regulations under study. By cross-checking each compliance requirement against the procedures, processes, and products of each operating unit with the manager of the unit, the project team will be able to identify the actions taken to comply with the requirements of the regulation. In performing this step, the team will need to refer to the cost principles described above to make sure that the actions identified fall within the scope of the project.

Step 2. For each compliance action identified in Step 1, determine the extent to which the company would have taken the action *in the absence of regulation*. In determining the extent to which an action would have been performed in the absence of regulation, consider the present-day environment to be one in which the federal regulation does not exist and never did exist, but in which all other factors, such as social pressures, interest groups, and marketplace considerations, are present.

Step 3. If the compliance action is one that the company would have taken even if the regulation did not exist, there is no need to determine the cost of the action, since there will be no *incremental* cost. If, however, the compliance action or portions of the action would *not* have been taken except for the regulation, further work is needed by the project team to determine the incremental cost of regulation resulting from the compliance action taken:

- Calculate the incremental cost of the specific compliance action in accordance with the cost principles described above.

- In some instances the cost of the compliance action can be taken directly from accounting sources. To arrive at the incremental cost of compliance, deduct the cost of the action that would have been taken in the absence of regulation. If no action would have been taken in the absence of regulation, the amount to be deducted will equal the cost of the compliance action.

- In many instances, the cost of the compliance action will be somewhat more difficult to obtain, for instance, when the costs of the action are not segregated or easily identifiable in accounting records because the action is part of a larger action, say, a capital project. In such cases, the logic of the calculation is similar to that cited above except that the project team first must separate the cost of the compliance action itself.

Illustrative Example

Consider a company that had built a new facility to expand operations. To comply with certain EPA water effluent guidelines, the company installed a sophisticated water filtration system as part of the new facility. However, the cost of constructing the system was not separately identified and accumulated in the company's property records. In such a situation, the project team would use engineering cost estimates, invoices, and other records to separate the cost of the compliance action taken: construction of the sophisticated water filtration system.

The project team would then determine that in the absence of regulation the company still would have installed a water filtration system. However, it would have been a much simpler system, one that would have eliminated enough effluents to bring total discharge down to an acceptable level for that particular facility, taking into consideration factors such as the extent to which the water was used for industrial, drinking, and recreational purposes. The project team would then obtain estimates of the cost of constructing the less sophisticated filtration system from the company's engineers. That cost would be deducted from the cost of the system that was built, the difference being the incremental cost of the compliance action.

Project team personnel would document (1) how they defined the compliance portion of a large project, the purpose of which may have been broader than just compliance with a regulation; (2) the source of the cost data; and (3) calculations required to determine total and incremental costs.

Step 4. The project team then summarizes the data collected by compliance requirements and by each of the four cost classifications. The form of the summary will depend greatly on the scope of the study. The Business Roundtable study, for example, was so large and so many data elements were collected that an automated system was developed for analyzing, validating, and summarizing the data collected. Manual summarization is practical when a study focuses on only a few specific regulations.

Task V: Review and Verify the Data

All the tasks described to this point—defining the scope of the project, identifying compliance requirements, planning and organizing the data collection effort and training participants, and collecting the data—are designed to assure a well-conceived study that uses a valid and consistent approach. These tasks alone, however, do not assure that results of the study will withstand public scrutiny. Task V, the review and verification of the data, is designed to assure that data are reported accurately.

To provide credible results, the methodology specifies four levels of review within each company of the data collected. The reviews are to be performed by (1) management of each operating unit in which costs are collected, (2) the project team, (3) internal auditors, and (4) key executives including the chief executive officer (CEO). In smaller companies or in companies without internal auditors, one or more of the levels of review will not be present.

Step 1. Management of the operating units or divisions will review the data collected in their respective units or divisions to ensure that all major items have been considered and that they concur with the underlying assumptions and reasoning which went into determining costs, particularly assumptions regarding actions that would have been taken in the absence of regulation. Management at this level will also review the incremental costs for reasonableness relative to the operations of a unit or division as a whole.

Step 2. The core project team will review the data collected to ensure that:

- The data collection methodology has been followed properly.
- The data submitted are supported by adequate documentation.
- All operating units within the company have followed consistent assumptions and allocation methods.
- Intracompany transfers have been properly treated.
- Cost data have been neither double-counted nor omitted.
- The results are reasonable in relation to the study objectives and the compliance actions performed by each operating unit.

Step 3. Each company's internal auditors will also review the data. Their review will take place throughout the course of data collection. Internal auditors will verify compliance with the data collection methodology and then will check the reasonableness of cost computations and assumptions and the adequacy of documentation. They will check to see that there is a sufficiently well documented audit trail for tracing the incremental cost associated with a given compliance requirement. The internal auditors' overall objective is to ensure that the results are correct and supportable.

Step 4. Key executives including the CEO and the financial officer will review summaries of all preceding results. The summaries, prepared by the project team leader, should contain a description of significant policy issues that arose throughout the study and a description of how these issues were resolved, a summary of the results of the study within the company, and other information requested by individual company executives. The CEO and other key company executives will review closely the decisions made by the project team regarding the actions that would have been taken by the company in the absence of regulation.

In the Business Roundtable study, Arthur Andersen & Co. played a major role throughout the study and provided an additional independent review of each company's results. In addition to developing the methodology, Arthur Andersen & Co.:

- Trained companies' project leaders and participated in companies' training meetings
- Provided support through field reviews, a central hot line to answer questions, and computer software for validation and analysis of companies' results

- Reviewed results to ensure that each company had properly interpreted and applied the methodology and that its results were both supported by adequate documentation and reasonable in relation to those of other companies in the same industry

Measuring the Indirect Costs of Compliance

Few studies have focused on the cost of indirect effects, the indirect costs of compliance. Studies of those costs will be important to improve our understanding of a significant part of the regulatory burden.

The cost principle presented earlier in this chapter addresses indirect costs and provides what could be a start toward the collection of those costs. Similarly, the methodology presented for identifying the direct costs of compliance is also applicable for identifying indirect effects and estimating their costs when it is feasible to do so.

How Can the Results of the Study Be Used Effectively?

One noted business leader stated:

[We share the] view that the goals of many federal regulatory programs are desirable. We also believe the private sector must supply credible leadership in its arguments against unnecessary or untimely regulations—no easy task given the monumental complexity of analyzing the direct and indirect costs of such government intervention.[13]

Regulatory policymakers recognize that specific and objective information about the costs of regulation is still sparse, and they encourage the development of pertinent valid information as a vital contribution to regulatory policymaking.[14] The regulatory analysis process virtually demands such information.

It is equally clear that presentation of the facts can influence regulatory policy in the national interest. This point is probably the primary reason for a company or a group of companies to undertake a cost-of-regulation study.

There are additional uses for such studies. Today analyzing, reacting to, and complying with regulations represent a major activity for any company, no matter how large or how small. Many companies that participated in studies such as the Business Roundtable's found that by closely examining the ways in which they were coping with regulations they were able to identify opportunities for improvement which led to significant monetary savings.

In addition to the tangible benefits, companies reported that by participating in the studies individuals became much more familiar not only with regulations but with a company's operations, procedures, and processes. Plant managers gained insights that would help them cope more effectively

---

[13]Alva O. Way, who at the time was senior vice president, finance, General Electric Company, and president of the Financial Accounting Foundation, in a letter to the editor of *Regulation,* November–December 1979, p. 4.

[14]Douglas Costle, in the letter cited in footnote 10, stated: "We are constantly exploring the potential for regulatory reforms and we appreciate the constructive input that studies such as the Business Roundtable study provide to regulatory decisions." Many others have expressed similar beliefs.

with visits by OSHA inspectors. Operating personnel came to understand the financial consequences of regulatory constraints on their operations. Many companies also found that the insights gained through the studies enhanced their ability to communicate clearly to stockholders, employees, and citizens in their communities on the constraints and costs of regulations.

COSTS OF COMPLIANCE CAN BE IDENTIFIED AND COLLECTED ON AN ONGOING BASIS BY MODIFYING A COMPANY'S DATA COLLECTION SYSTEMS AND PROCEDURES

For companies interested in doing so, provisions can be made in their data collection systems and procedures for the collection of at least a portion of compliance costs as part of the normal data collection process. For operating and administrative costs that are not collected as projects, tracking compliance costs on an ongoing basis can be a complex undertaking which requires continuing, recurring efforts by those responsible for classifying and entering data. For example, identifying and collecting on a routine basis the costs necessary to develop the reports required by regulation can involve considerable timekeeping by individuals. For costs such as these, special analyses and projections may be more practical than ongoing data collection. For three of the four cost classifications (capital costs, research and development costs, and product costs), however, comparatively small changes in a company's planning and reporting systems and procedures will enable the company to identify and collect compliance costs on an ongoing basis with very little data collection effort.

Most companies have formalized planning procedures for authorizing the acquisition of capital assets, undertaking research and development projects, and making significant changes in products. Before any activities take place, the responsible official must describe what is to be undertaken, how much it will cost, and why it's necessary. Frequently complying with a regulation is either explicitly or implicitly part of the justification. Modifying the process to identify the portion of the action that represents compliance with a specific regulation which would not be taken in the absence of the regulation and determining the cost attributable to the compliance action should not be an unduly burdensome change in a company's planning and authorization system. The two changes to the planning system would:

- Require the justification and approval process to identify in specific monetary terms the planned cost of the compliance action

- Employ a coding scheme to use in collecting the planned activities and their planned costs

Companies also track actual costs of capital acquisitions, research and development projects, and product costs against planned and authorized costs. That process will also serve as the means of adjusting planned compliance costs for those projects to the actual costs incurred.

As one federal official stated, "While the government has always been mindful of the problems regulation is intended to solve, it has now become a great deal more sensitive to the problems that regulation creates."[15] One of those problems is the cost of compliance. Although the federal regulatory process requires analysis of economic impacts before a regulation is issued, credible data to support the analysis have been sketchy. However, a proven and credible methodology is now available to measure compliance costs. Business, which bears the initial costs of compliance, is in the best position to measure those costs.

Companies that do measure costs of regulation contribute data that are important in establishing federal regulatory policies in the national interest and achieve internal efficiencies by focusing on their own compliance activities.

---

[15]Lucy Falcone, Department of Commerce, in a letter to the editor of *Regulation,* November–December 1979.

3 REDUCING PAPERWORK

DAVID M. MARSH
Executive Director

CARL A. BECK
Former Chairman
Business Advisory Council on Federal Reports

What is our [expletive deleted] government doing to us? Is there any hope for relief? Where can I get help? How should I go about it? These are the gripes of business executives heard each year by the Business Advisory Council on Federal Reports (BACFR). The fact is that help is available and that there are many ways to combat the burdensome and useless paperwork requirements of government. Businesses on their own initiative, working with industry representatives or with BACFR, can take practical steps to cut unnecessary costs and paperwork burdens to the bone.

This chapter will explore the who, what, where, how, and when to attack "form pollution." There will be case histories of success or near success in the most recent problem areas: energy, foreign trade, environment, pensions and welfare, and other regulatory and economic reporting and record-keeping topics. First the cost and magnitude of the paperwork problem will be examined.

MAGNITUDE OF THE PAPERWORK PROBLEM

As demands for government services increase, new government programs are created and existing services are expanded. With the growth of government programs come increasing requests to the public for information. The government's demands for information cost the public dearly. Indeed, the paperwork burden may be a critical factor in whether or not a business survives. Money and management time spent by a business in filling out government forms are not available to be put back into the business.

In its final report to the President and the Congress, the Commission on Federal Paperwork estimated that private industry alone spends between $25 and $32 billion each year in keeping records and filling out forms. This is no small sum. The total paperwork bill imposed by the federal government on all sectors of the public is thought to be $100 billion. This cost produces little or no profit. The time and money spent in satisfying government's insatiable appetite for information fuel inflation and contribute little to the increased productivity essential to a healthy economy. There are also other hidden but very real costs to the public. The time and energy spent in filling out forms are irreplaceable. The public is demoralized, frustrated, and exasperated by the flood of paperwork which confronts it.

In his letter transmitting the October 3, 1977, *Final Summary Report of the Commission on Federal Paperwork* to the President and the Congress, Congressman Frank Horton, chairman of the commission, stated:

The theme we heard repeatedly throughout the country is that the vast majority of Americans want to obey the law. Most Americans want to cooperate and participate in furthering Federal programs and national goals. However, these people can be frustrated by a Government which, in their view, does not trust them.

Many people feel, and the Commission agrees, that a multi-billion dollar wall of paperwork has been erected between the Government and the people. Countless reporting and recordkeeping requirements and other heavy-handed investigation and monitoring schemes have been instituted based on what we view as a faulty premise that people will not obey laws and rules unless they are checked, monitored and rechecked.

This situation and this assumption must be reversed if we are to restore efficiency within the Government and confidence in Government by the people and if we are to realize the potential for cooperative attainment of our goals as a Nation. Many of the major conclusions and recommendations of the Commission on Federal Paperwork are aimed at this goal.

While business bears a substantial burden, similar views are heard from the health care industry, educational institutions, state and local government officials, and individual citizens. These assessments of the mood of business executives and other members of the public make remedial action imperative.

Obviously government, like business, needs accurate and meaningful information to plan properly, issue reasonable regulations, and otherwise carry out its functions. Paperwork proposals don't come out of thin air. The paperwork is normally based on somebody's idea, law, or regulation issued as law. Once Congress or the state, county, or local body has spoken, a department, agency, or authority goes to work preparing regulations, directives, forms, and record-keeping requirements. Agencies tend to interpret their legislative authority as broadly as possible, enabling diverse, far-reaching courses of action. It is hoped that, throughout the process of legislation, regulation, and form development, affected firms and members of the public are given adequate notice and opportunity for reasoned comments and that they take advantage of this opportunity.

The experience of those in industry, however, is that too often there is insufficient notice, too short a period or no period for comment, and, worse still, failure by government officials to evaluate and act on the comments that are received. Steps now exist to alleviate this situation. When reasonable people sit down and consider a governmental paperwork proposal, results are usually favorable to all concerned and in the public interest. However, individual businesses must take the offensive and complain in a meaningful way about specific forms and paperwork burdens.

Furthermore, businesses must be aware of which requests for information must be complied with and which are illegal. Businesses can easily reduce their own paperwork burden by not responding to forms which are not legitimate. The United States government may be one of the world's worst bootleggers. Federal agencies must submit record-keeping and reporting proposals to the Office of Management and Budget (OMB) for review and clearance. If a form does not bear an OMB clearance number or does not explain why a number is not needed, it is an unlawful or "bootleg" form and need not be filled out.

EXISTING PAPERWORK CONTROLS

In 1942 Congress enacted the Federal Reports Act. There was a paperwork glut then, and things haven't changed much. The Federal Reports Act controlled government paperwork policies for years. Basically, the act set up a central paperwork control system in the OMB. Later, the General Accounting Office (GAO) was given the responsibility for review of the forms of independent regulatory agencies.

However, Congress recognized that federal paperwork policies still fell short, and in December 1980 the Paperwork Reduction Act was signed into law. This act, Public Law 96-511, represents a serious attempt by Congress to control the runaway government paperwork problem. It can be broken down into three major sections: (1) consolidation of control over federal paperwork requirements, (2) subjection of paperwork requests to scrutinization, and (3) establishment of a Federal Information Locator System (FILS) as a central clearinghouse of information. Through these provisions it is expected that the act will minimize the paperwork burden for the public, minimize the costs to the government, coordinate federal information policies, avoid duplicate requests, and at the same time maximize the usefulness of the information that is collected.

The act consolidates within the OMB Office of Information and Regulatory Affairs control over federal government paperwork. The director of the OMB is responsible for developing and establishing uniform information management policies, reviewing proposed legislation and regulations relating to information collection, promoting agency sharing of information, and evaluating agency information activities. The development of uniform and efficient procedures is fundamental to the successful implementation of the act and subsequent solution of the paperwork problem.

The director of the OMB is also responsible for some important paperwork control functions. OMB clearance powers extend to all agencies, including for the first time the Internal Revenue Service (IRS) and certain bank supervisory agencies. The OMB reviews and approves information requests proposed by agencies. Each agency must submit to the OMB a copy of any proposed rule which contains a requirement for the collection of information on or before publication in the *Federal Register*. The OMB has 60 days to comment on the proposed rule. This comment includes a determination that the request is necessary to achieve the agency's objectives. Even if the request is necessary, however, it must be ascertained that the information is not available from another source within the government and that there is no less burdensome way to obtain the information. Prompt communication between the business community and the OMB is necessary at this point; otherwise a challenge to the proposed rule may be lost. There is no judicial review of the OMB's decision to approve or not to act on a reporting or record-keeping requirement.

Once an information request has been approved, it is assigned an OMB control number, indicating that the OMB director has determined that the information is necessary, that it is not duplicative, and that it will be collected efficiently. If an information request does not contain an OMB clearance number or does not specify that the form is exempt, it is an unlawful form and need not be filled out. Furthermore, any request for information made to the public must contain a statement informing the recipient why the information is being requested, how it is to be used, and whether a response is voluntary, necessary to obtain a benefit, or mandatory. These paperwork control requirements are a recognition by Congress that paperwork burdens need to be lessened. One way to accomplish that goal is to inform businesses and affected individuals as to which forms *must* be filled out and which can be ignored. In addition, the act directs the director of the OMB to reduce existing paperwork burdens by 15 percent by October 1, 1982, and by an additional 10 percent for the following fiscal year.

The act also creates FILS to identify information being collected by the government, reveal duplication, and assist the OMB in its clearance process. This provision is intended to reduce the cost of paperwork procedures that is borne by the government itself. FILS will contain no data submitted by the public. The controls established by the Paperwork Reduction Act should reduce the expenses incurred by both business and government in complying with paperwork procedures and increase efficiency in the management of federal information procedures.

The act requires that FILS be established by April 1, 1982. A few federal agencies were already using a more limited search system, the Information Requirements Control Automated System (IRCAS), which the Department of Defense had initiated in 1977.

FILS embodies an information referral service which businesses can tap to identify the information requirements of the federal government. The ability of FILS to ferret out duplication should be one of its most useful features, particularly when combined with the sunset provision of the Paperwork Reduction Act that limits approval of each reporting or record-keeping requirement to a maximum of 3 years.

In addition, OMB Bulletin 80-11, dated June 19, 1980, directs each agency to prepare an annual information collection budget (ICB). The ICB must contain an estimate of the total hours currently imposed upon the public to comply with requests for information and forecast total burden-hours for the coming year. After meetings with the OMB each agency will receive a final overall burden-hour paperwork ceiling for the fiscal year.

WHERE AND HOW TO GET HELP

In these days of massive paperwork demands by government, members of the public and business executives are constantly asking: "What can I do, and where can I get help?" Despite the oppressive number and complexity of forms and surveys heaped on the public, there are several ways to get help.

On the industry side there are also efforts to control the paperwork problem. The Business Advisory Council on Federal Reports was formed in 1942 at the request of the director of the Bureau of the Budget. BACFR works with hundreds of businesses and trade associations to keep paperwork under control. Many organizations look to BACFR as the major medium to ensure consideration of business views on proposed federal forms. For instance, industrial relations managers in a variety of industries formed a review panel for comments on proposed Occupational Safety and Health Administration (OSHA) reporting and record-keeping requirements. The industrial relations personnel are often backed up and represented by specialists in their industry organizations or associations.

Businesses which are unaware of control procedures are uniformly relieved to hear that both government and industry are "watching the store" and taking action. To this end, businesses and organizations are given notice of regulations regarding reporting and record-keeping requirements. While there are instances when not enough business comments reach government, there seems to be an increased awareness of and reaction to the reports piled on industry. Businesses and trade associations, for the most part, have expressed themselves forcefully. The Paperwork Reduction Act provides the opportunity for public participation in the formulation of record-keeping and reporting requirements. Active public participation is the essential ingredient in any recipe for paperwork control.

BACFR is an obvious avenue of approach for beleaguered businesses. Its address and telephone number are:

Business Advisory Council on Federal Reports
1001 Connecticut Avenue, N.W., Suite 925
Washington, D.C. 20036
(202) 331-1915

It is exceedingly rare that a business executive is not a member of a local, state, or national trade association. This trade association may provide assistance with reporting and record-keeping requirements.

It is now the policy of the OMB and federal agencies to require that each form sent out have the name, address, and telephone number of a responsible government official who should be of help. Call the official, and if a satisfactory answer is not received, call or write BACFR and any local or national organizations or associations that might become involved. Naturally some forms may require consultation with an accountant or an attorney.

For problems with federal department and agency forms, the OMB may be reached at:

Office of Information and Regulatory Affairs
Office of Management and Budget
726 Jackson Place, N.W., Room 3208
Washington, D.C. 20503
(202) 395-6880

Whether it's a federal, state, or local form that causes difficulty, don't forget appropriate elected officials. Part of their duty is to help their constituents. A number of officials and organizations are available to help. While it may not be necessary in each instance, if a problem persists, get in touch with all those identified previously, perhaps by a letter to one person or organization with a copy to all the others.

Remember to be specific. When writing anyone other than the issuing department or agency, enclose a copy of the form, transmittal letter, and instructions. Describe in detail the individual complaint or problem. In writing those identified above, businesses will want to address these points:

- Is the form authorized by law, and does it cite the statute and/or regulation which is claimed to be the authority for its issuance?

- Is there a statement as to whether submission of the form or questionnaire is mandatory or voluntary? The OMB requires a clear statement of whether the form is mandatory, required to receive benefits, or voluntary.

- Is there a better way for government to collect the information it seeks? For example, should the form go only to a sample of business respondents? Would a shorter, simpler, less detailed form be adequate, especially for small firms? Or can the frequency be reduced?

- In the case of unnecessarily burdensome forms, estimate how many hours it will take or has taken the company to complete them, and include the cost of collecting the data and/or record keeping.

- When information requested is the same as that provided on similar forms, identify the forms, the issuing department or agency, and the information which can be identified as duplicative.

- Do the form and the accompanying documents provide adequate assurance of protection of information that you believe to be confidential?

- Are the data requested readily available from regular accounting or other business records? If not, that fact should be highlighted in correspondence with the agency and, if necessary, with others previously mentioned.

- Federal forms must have an OMB clearance number, usually found in the top right-hand corner. If they do *not,* they are probably unauthorized and illegal.

If enough business executives make the points emphasized above on enough occasions, the war on paperwork can be waged much more effectively. When an agency holds a hearing on a paperwork proposal, take time to testify or comment for yourself or your trade association. Those working in the field of paperwork control cannot fight the battle alone. If businesses pitch in together, results favorable to all will follow. When businesses lie down on the job, paperwork will suffocate them in very short order.

STEPS BUSINESSES CAN TAKE TO CURB FEDERAL PAPERWORK

There is no substitute for face-to-face discussion of a burdensome reporting requirement by the proponents of the form, the clearance official from the OMB, and the businesses which will have to respond to the requirement. The face-to-face approach with the responsible government agency and the OMB is the best approach. It is the experience of BACFR and individual businesses that if a formal request for consultation is made to the OMB and the agency originating the form, substantial progress can be achieved to mitigate the burdensome effect of an existing or a proposed form. Because of the technical nature of many proposals, business representatives present must be fully competent regarding the subject to be discussed. The agency involved and the OMB will appreciate the constructive criticism.

Illustrative Example

The Employee Retirement Income Security Act (ERISA) became law on September 2, 1974. ERISA was not the first pension law requiring reporting. Its predecessor, the Welfare and Pension Plans Disclosure Act, had several reporting requirements. The first ERISA form filed with the OMB for Federal Reports Act review was EBS-1, the plan description form. It was evident from the outset that this form was far too lengthy and complex. Further, it called for narrative responses which would have been impossible to assess. These factors led the OMB to grant a BACFR request for a panel meeting on the proposed form. The net result of the meeting and industry comments was a vastly curtailed form: six check-the-answer pages in lieu of twenty narrative pages. The new ERISA Form 5500, *Annual Return/Report of Employee Benefit Plan,* was a more troublesome and burdensome form. Even though the short Form 5500C was developed for plans with fewer than 100 participants, it was burdensome for small businesses. For some time, even though Form 5500 was published for comment in the *Federal Register* and industry views were submitted to the OMB, little substantive progress seemed to be made. BACFR and its members, expert in ERISA, decided to urge a joint conference with the Department of Labor and IRS personnel responsible for the form. The government officials welcomed the session and agreed to delete from Form 5500 two entire columns of meaningless figures on acquisitions and dispositions, for an estimated 10 percent reduction in the work of responding to the form.

Despite considerable success with these two ERISA forms, they remain burdensome because of detailed provisions in ERISA itself. Also because of the reporting requirements of ERISA, the Pension Benefit Guaranty Corporation (PBGC) has a number of reporting requirements. Remedial amendments which have been introduced in Congress may provide additional relief.

In certain instances complete success in remedying onerous requirements is prevented by changes in the law. One such instance was an amendment to the Trans-Alaska Pipeline Act that shifted report review authority covering regulatory agencies from the OMB to the GAO. Moreover, the GAO was denied the power to turn down any proposed form. The effect of this change, amending the Federal Reports Act, is evident in the discussion which follows.

The Federal Trade Commission (FTC) line-of-business (LB) initiative has gone through revisions, hearings, and legal challenges. The FTC Line of Business Program is certainly one of the most contentious and controversial reporting programs ever proposed. It survived, after some modification, in large part owing to an irrelevant amendment to the Federal Reports Act. Although some efforts of businesses to eliminate burdensome forms may not be successful, businesses must continue to take the initiative against an offending agency. Running into a paperwork brick wall may not be fun, but it is necessary and can eventually knock down the wall or at least put a crack in it. The methods employed can persuade the OMB to disapprove a proposed form.

Illustrative Example

The FTC *Line of Business* (Form LB) proposal grew out of the transfer of the collection of less detailed but related information in the *Quarterly Financial Report* from the Securities and Exchange Commission (SEC) to the FTC. At a January 1971 BACFR meeting, an industry panel criticized the LB proposal on the grounds of inadequate assurance of confidentiality protection, the difference between the proposed standard industrial classification (SIC) system for collecting data and the way in which most diversified companies kept their books, the possibility of subpoenaing individual company reports, the questionable usefulness of the data, and other reasons. The proposal would have required the largest manufacturers to file reports on profits, costs, research and development, and promotional expenses by product lines specified by the FTC. The FTC estimate that filing this proposed form would cost each company $800 was incredible. Small businesses considered laughable the FTC contention that the LB program would benefit smaller firms. Following the change in the Federal Reports Act, the FTC filed its third revision of its LB proposal with the GAO in March 1974. By consolidation it reduced its prior line-of-business categories from 455 to 228. After numerous comments by industry and others, the GAO gave the FTC limited authority to conduct an initial round of reports. The GAO noted that approval of subsequent annual reports would be contingent upon a significant reduction in or elimination of problems in the initial data request, including the unreliability of data.

Things might have turned out differently had not Congress in November 1973 amended the Federal Reports Act. The amendment, based in large part on the contention that the OMB might not give the FTC complete approval to collect LB data, stripped review authority over independent regulatory agencies from the OMB and lodged it in the GAO. That might have been all well and good had it not been for the fact that the GAO, unlike the OMB, was denied the right to reject ill-conceived reporting proposals. Furthermore, the amendment was unassailable as it was attached as a rider to the popular Alaska pipeline bill. In subsequent years the LB program was debated in Congress, principally in connection with FTC appropriations, and was the subject of limited comments at a hearing before the FTC. An LB report form for 1974 incorporated some recommended revisions, which were carried forward in the 1975, 1976, and 1977 versions. In addition, many of the companies subject to filing the FTC LB reports went to court in what turned out to be an unsuccessful attempt to block the program.

Occasionally businesses are frustrated by an arbitrary failure by agency personnel to grant a request or accommodate reasonable viewpoints. If this situation persists, businesses should also persist. Write or call different people in the agency. Get in touch with the agency head, but keep at it; if you give up, paperwork demands can ride roughshod over you. Some good can be salvaged through persistence, illustrated by success on Environmental Protection Agency (EPA) clean-water reports.

Illustrative Example

In 1976 unapproved bootleg forms generated under Section 308 of the Clean Water Act began proliferating from the EPA, which requested detailed process, technical, and financial data. Individual businesses and BACFR brought the requests to the attention of the OMB, which actively disputed the EPA claim that these forms were exempt from OMB clearance under the Federal Reports Act. The EPA reluctantly abandoned its position and agreed to submit the forms for "generic clearance" from the OMB. This submission, in 1978, covered plans for a 3-year period and consisted of eight primary areas of data: equipment, facilities, engineering and technological processes, energy requirements, wastewater treatment, impacts, costs, and "other factors the EPA Administrator deems appropriate."

BACFR and numerous companies and associations questioned the legality of this request, considering it a device for EPA administrative convenience rather than an instrument in conformance with the spirit and rules of the Federal Reports Act and procedures of OMB Circular A-40, and objected to the depth and breadth of the proposed lines of reporting technical, economic, and financial data as being both unduly burdensome and too far-reaching for the purposes of the act. The OMB agreed to a hearing, and industry was unanimous in its testimony that the request for generic clearance:

- Raised a question as to the legal authority of the OMB to issue such generic clearance, much less to clear a generalized request unaccompanied by even a suggestion as to the specific questions to be asked

- Did not make use of substantial data and information regarding water pollution already collected and available, including information relative to water discharge permits under the National Pollution Discharge Elimination System

- Demanded excessive and sensitive details on cost data down to the individual plant level and, in the case of many smaller businesses, data which was either unavailable or obtainable only at great cost

- Embodied unduly extensive and impractical filing requirements for process changes

- Provided inadequate protection for the preservation of confidentiality of sensitive company information

- Did not address the problems of inability to comply, particularly on the part of the small-business community

A breakthrough finally occurred when EPA changed its position to allow BACFR and other affected industry representatives to make detailed comments as soon as each form was developed.

Occasionally the government must develop forms on an emergency basis. In such a situation the most desirable course is to assemble promptly a small yet representative panel. The meeting of the panel may produce beneficial results through an open and candid discussion between government officials advocating use of the form and businesses in affected industries. Prompt action is the only way when the government is determined to develop forms on an emergency basis.

Illustrative Example

During the summer of 1979, as a result of concern about the supply of heating-grade oils for the coming winter, the Department of Energy asked the Bureau of the Census to conduct a monthly survey. The survey would measure the use and stocks of fuel oil in the manufacturing sector as well as the stocks and sales of oil in the fuel wholesale and retail sectors. As is often the case, time was of the essence. Only 3 days were given for BACFR to assemble business representatives from the ten most seriously affected industries. Through the cooperation of companies and trade associations, a representative panel met with officials of the Bureau of the Census and the Department of Energy. Discussion of such issues as whether to collect inventory data on an ownership or a possession basis led to improvements in the forms, and as soon as copies of the final forms were obtained, they were given wide distribution by BACFR to companies and associations not represented at the meeting. Further, response on a quarterly basis was substituted for monthly filings.

All too often businesses sit on their hands and take no action or insufficient action on paperwork proposals that could prove costly and annoying. Typical business responses which may be successful include complaints that a form is poorly designed, the questions are irrelevant or require subjective judgments, the study is premature or invites misinterpretation, the questions miss the point, and the estimates of reporting burdens are grossly low.

Illustrative Example

The EPA submitted a proposed survey in 1979 to the OMB for review. The survey form, which covered a wide range of questions for thirteen industry groupings identified by EPA as "major generators of hazardous waste," ran to nine pages. It covered the respondents' SIC codes, the nature of the plant sites, and such unrelated questions as the plants' production, average cost of capital and capital expenditures, and detailed information regarding hazardous wastes. Industry responded in force. Business comments hammered at the following issues:

- There is a *duplication* of some of the information requested by other EPA, congressional, and court-ordered inquiries.

- The survey form is *poorly designed*. A significant number of questions either *are irrelevant to the objectives* or *require subjective judgments* that most respondents are not prepared to make.

- The study is *premature*. A study of this magnitude should be based only on final, promulgated regulations. This form references regulations that the EPA either has not yet proposed or has proposed but not yet promulgated.

- The survey *invites misinterpretation* by respondents. Although the questions frequently refer to a broad category of "hazardous waste," the answers depend upon knowledge of *specific* hazardous wastes. No guidelines or lists of hazardous wastes are provided with the survey form or otherwise.

- The *financial questions miss the point* as to what constitutes a cost deterrent to the development of new hazardous-waste management capacity. There is little or no historical information on hazardous-waste management because there has been no way or reason to track such costs in previous years.

- The *estimates of reporting burdens for respondents are decidedly low.* The key assumptions underlying the 4-hour estimate are clearly unwarranted.

Industry viewed the proposal as overly detailed and premature. The OMB agreed and voiced concern about the form. The result was that no form was sent out. The EPA withdrew the form in a face-saving move to head off outright OMB rejection.

The foregoing has touched on a few of the hundreds of forms that businesses must handle each year. It is important to peck away day by day. Equally important is understanding the interrelationship of today's form to similar information requested in the past. The job of advocating collection of only essential, useful, and obtainable data is an ongoing process which involves all types and sizes of businesses.

Because it provides stricter controls over more categories of paperwork, the Paperwork Reduction Act offers an unprecedented opportunity for relief to business. With diligent work, industry can reduce its reporting and record-keeping costs. Attainment of this reduction will require broad and whole-hearted participation by all segments of the business community working with organizations such as the Business Advisory Council on Federal Reports.

4 OBTAINING INFORMATION FROM AGENCIES

McNEILL STOKES
Stokes & Shapiro
Attorneys at Law

The files of government agencies are vast reservoirs of information. The contents of these reservoirs are diverse. The information may concern an individual, a business, or agency procedures and decisions. It may be generated by activities from within an agency or by entities that submit information to the agency. Whether the information is agency-generated or submitter-generated, business-oriented or agency-oriented, public or private, it is equally a part of the reservoirs to which businesses may obtain access.

Government files contain a great deal of information which concerns businesses either directly or indirectly. The files contain information about governmental procedures, regulations, rulings, and orders which may have a direct effect on a particular business or on its competitors; they contain information about the procedures, activities, and management of a business, information about the personnel, employment practices, and salaries of a company, and vast quantities of financial information about a business. Each year businesses are required to file detailed reports of almost every aspect of their affairs with various agencies of the government. These records are maintained by the government somewhere in its files.

Whether a business or an individual can tap these reservoirs is governed by three federal statutes. The Freedom of Information Act (FOIA), the Privacy Act, and the Government in the Sunshine Act structure the availability of government information. Together they proclaim the public's right of access to government records and files, yet they acknowledge the necessity to afford some protection to certain types of information. The FOIA is the most important of the congressional responses to the developing need for greater openness in government.

There are a variety of ways in which a business can use the FOIA. In fact, 80 percent of all FOIA requests are made by corporations or their lawyers. As the business community and private individuals are requested to supply the government with more paperwork, more information is available to anyone who wishes to request the material under the FOIA.

Since the purpose underlying the FOIA is to allow public access generally to the reservoir of agency information, it is desirable to look into the composition of this reservoir and the ways in which the application of the FOIA has affected various types of information which may be of interest to a business. The agency reservoir includes submitter-generated business information, agency-generated information concerning businesses, government research of interest to businesses, agency-promulgated guides and manuals which may affect businesses, and agency-generated information concerning potential or actually filed charges against a particular business. Within each of the categories the agency will have both protected and unprotected information. There remain many questions concerning which information is protected and, if the information is protected, when it should be requested nonetheless. Because of this uncertainty, there is no reason why a business should not go ahead and make a request. Even if some of the requested information is not disclosed, the portions of the requested information which are not protected must be disclosed.[1] If the unprotected parts are not disclosed, the requester may take full advantage of the remedial sanctions which are provided in the act.

FREEDOM OF INFORMATION ACT

The Freedom of Information Act, unanimously passed by Congress, was based upon the simple yet basic belief that the American public had the "right to know" the activities of its government. Such a right was founded in the constitutional guarantees of freedom of speech and of the press of the First Amendment. Prior to the passage of the FOIA the burden was on the private citizen to prove a right to examine government records. The records were, for the most part, maintained in secrecy; the contents and even the existence of many records were fiercely protected. An individual would have had to prove a real need to obtain records from the agency watchdogs. With business information this need would have been almost impossible to prove.

The FOIA represents a real shift to a policy of government openness. The act substitutes a "right to access" standard for the previous burden on the individual of proving a need to know. The act is based on the notion that just as the government belongs to the people, the information of the government should likewise belong to the people. It intends to increase public access to government records by prescribing liberal disclosure requirements and providing guidelines for the agencies in making the decision to release or to withhold documents. The FOIA also represents a substantial shift in policy by providing, for the first time, that judicial remedies will be available to those wrongfully denied access. It specifically gives district courts the power to enjoin agency withholding and to order the production of documents wrongfully withheld.[2]

The FOIA accomplishes a meaningful change in the public's access to gov-

---

[1] *Grumman Aircraft Eng'r Corp. v. Renegotiation Bd.*, 425 F.2d 578 (D.C. Cir. 1970).

[2] 5 U.S.C. § 552(a)(4)(B).

ernment information through the shift in the burden of proof, the provisions explicitly making almost all records available to any person, the creation of workable standards to be followed, and the availability of judicial remedies for wrongful withholding. At the same time it attempts to strike a balance between the need for disclosure and the need for protection. On the one hand, it acknowledges the public's right to know by opening agency records to greater public access; on the other hand, it recognizes that certain types of information must be protected. The act seeks to preserve the confidentiality which is undeniably essential to certain areas of governmental or business operations by providing nine exemptions from mandatory agency disclosure. These exemptions are important to a business not only because they limit what information may be obtained by that business but also because they provide the standards for what information can be obtained by a competitor. An exemption can be a real barrier to a business seeking information, while at the same time it can provide needed protection to a business seeking to prevent release of its own records. Actually, all the provisions of the FOIA can have that same effect: they can work to the advantage of a business when used to obtain information yet definitely disadvantage a business when used by a competitor. Use of the FOIA can help to make or break a business.

The FOIA provides that each agency shall make available to "any person" all records unless the information falls into one of the nine enumerated exemptions. The definition of "person" of the Administrative Procedure Act (APA) includes an individual, a corporation, and other types of associations.[3] The act requires the disclosure of government records to any person because the singular concern is with what must be made public. The FOIA never provides for disclosure to some and withholding from others. It remains the rule that any person is to be allowed access regardless of the reason for the request. The goal is liberal disclosure to any member of the public.

The act's mandate applies to "each agency." The FOIA broadly defines "agency" as including executive and military departments, government or government-controlled corporations, all other establishments in the executive branch, and other independent regulatory agencies.[4] It does not apply to the legislative and judicial branches, the President and the President's immediate staff, and advisory committees which are subject to the Federal Advisory Committee Act.

The act provides for two basic types of access to agency information. The first is in the form of publication. The second is in the form of availability for inspection and copying. Each agency is required to publish in the *Federal Register:*

(A) descriptions of its central and field organization and the established places at which the employees (and in the case of a uniformed service, the members) from whom, and the methods whereby, the public may obtain information, make submittals or requests, or obtain decisions;

[3] 5 U.S.C. § 551(2).
[4] 5 U.S.C. § 552(e).

(B) statements of the general course and method by which its functions are channeled and determined, including the nature and requirements of all formal and informal procedures available;

(C) rules of procedure, descriptions of forms available or the places at which forms may be obtained, and instructions as to the scope and contents of all papers, reports or examinations;

(D) substantive rules of general applicability adopted as authorized by law and statements of general policy or interpretations of general applicability formulated and adopted by the agency; and

(E) each amendment, revision or repeal of the foregoing.[5]

Furthermore, each agency is required to make the following information "available for public inspection and copying":

(A) final opinions, including dissenting opinions, as well as orders, made in the adjudication of cases;

(B) those statements of policy and interpretations which have been adopted by the agency and are not published in the Federal Register; and

(C) administrative staff manuals and instructions to staff that affect a member of the public.[6]

Each agency is also required to maintain and publish indexes of information required to be disclosed.

In addition to the records made available as described above, each agency must make available any records which are solicited by a request which "(A) reasonably describes such records and (B) is made in accordance with published rules stating the time, place, fees and procedures to be followed."[7]

What constitutes a "record" is not clearly defined by the FOIA. Not all the courts that have examined the question have agreed on what constitutes a record, but some generalities can be stated. Almost all courts have extended the concept of a record beyond written documents. They have included things such as movie films, tape recordings, x-rays, and other things which can be copied. They have of necessity excluded items such as physical evidence which can't be copied. A dispute exists as to whether personal notes made by an agency employee constitute agency records. In contrast to the requirements of other statutes, the FOIA does not require an agency to obtain or make any records which it wouldn't have kept otherwise. Only existing records which are already maintained by the agency must be made available upon request.

FOIA Exemptions

The FOIA was designed to nurture disclosure but at the same time to provide protection for certain types of information. Protection was afforded by exemption. The nine exemptions listed in the act do not dictate mandatory

---

[5] 5 U.S.C. § 552(a)(1)(A)-(E).
[6] 5 U.S.C. § 552(a)(2)(A)-(C).
[7] 5 U.S.C. § 552(a)(3).

withholding but merely protect the information from having a status of mandatory disclosure. The exemptions are:

1. Properly classified national defense or foreign policy information.

2. Internal personnel rules and practices of an agency.

3. Information protected from disclosure by another statute. The other statute must either prohibit disclosure or confer discretion to withhold or release the information. If the other statute confers discretion, it must either establish criteria which guide the exercise of discretion or refer to specific types of information.

4. Trade secrets and other commercial or financial information which have been obtained from a person and are confidential or privileged.

5. Internal communications which consist of deliberative or legal opinion and are privileged in civil litigation.

6. Information contained in personnel, medical, and similar files which, if disclosed, would constitute an unwarranted invasion of personal privacy.

7. Investigatory files compiled for law enforcement purposes but only if disclosure would result in one or more of six enumerated harms.

8. Certain bank records.

9. Data on oil wells.

The APA provides a cause of action for a person "adversely affected or aggrieved" by agency action.[8] It also requires agency action to be "in accordance with law."[9] Since the exemptions to the FOIA merely prevent mandatory disclosure rather than dictate withholding, the FOIA does not limit agency discretion. By itself, it only protects a business's interest in confidentiality to the extent that the particular agency collecting the information maintains the confidentiality.

BUSINESS-GENERATED INFORMATION

Each year businesses submit great quantities of forms and reports to various agencies of the federal government. The forms detail many aspects of a business's affairs. Agency files contain trade secrets, research data, product safety evaluations, forecasts of future development plans, information on customers and sources of supply, estimates of market shares, descriptions of labor and other production costs, reports of affirmative-action programs, information on key company personnel, annual reports of company-sponsored employee benefit plans, and balance sheets and other financial data on the company, including tax returns. This list is far from exhaustive, but it is an indication of the rich deposits of information in the government's reservoirs. There is no question that most businesses would be deeply interested in examining the information on a competitor contained in government files.

Some of this business information may be made available to a requester,

[8] 5 U.S.C. § 702.
[9] 5 U.S.C. § 706(2)(A).

and some will be withheld under one of the exemptions. Although the FOIA sets forth some standards for the withholding of records, the exemptions are not mandatory. The agency must itself endorse the interest in nondisclosure, or it may just proceed to release records which technically might be withheld under the act. Different agencies will respond differently to a request for business information. Although some generalizations can be made about agency attitudes toward the release of business information, they should not be taken as definitive. The best policy to follow when records are desired is to go ahead and make a request. Even if an agency has previously withheld particular documents, they might later be released. Some documents, over time, will lose their confidential nature and thus will lose their exempt status.

The exemption which is most clearly applicable to business information is Exemption 4, which exempts from mandatory disclosure "trade secrets and commercial or financial information received from a person which is privileged or confidential."[10] This exemption was enacted to afford some protection to information submitted by a business to the government.

Trade secrets have been more zealously protected than any other category of business information. By using the term "trade secrets" the FOIA imports the common-law principles on trade secret status into the act. There are multiple definitions of a trade secret but the category has been afforded the strongest protection of any exemption. Its definition has generally been extended from tangible items such as formulas to nontechnological data such as compilations of marketing information and sales statistics. If the material desired is afforded trade secret status, it enjoys a presumption of confidentiality. However, some information will be considered a trade secret by some jurisdictions but in others will be considered merely commercial information and be subject to the standard for disclosure applied to such information. It is much easier to obtain the release of business information which does not fit into the definition of a trade secret.

If information can be classified as commercial or financial rather than as a trade secret, it will not be afforded a presumption of confidentiality. Business information which is not a trade secret must meet three separate requirements to be withheld from a requester. If it fails to meet just one of these requirements, it must be released. The information must be:

- Commercial or financial
- Submitted by a person
- Privileged or confidential

Commercial or Financial

First, information must be commercial or financial to be afforded b(4) protection. If the information which is desired is neither commercial nor financial, it must fall under another exemption to be withheld. Courts have delin-

[10]5 U.S.C.§ 552b(4).

eated the broad categories of commercial and financial to some extent. Items which the courts have found to be protectible commercial information in FOIA case law include:

- Business sales statistics

- Intricacies of production or testing of products

- Applied technology of industrial plants

- Profit-oriented research work

- Technical ideas and projections in contract bids

- Contingency plans for business operations

- Identities of key employees by job, skill level, race, and sex

- Names of oil-field suppliers and contractors

- Prices paid for contracted goods

- Loan application information and updating data on operation[11]

Items which the courts have found to be protectible financial information include:

- Loan application figures

- Cost accounting methods of contractors

- Profit and loss data

- Specific interest rates charged by banks to select customers

- Overhead and operating costs

- Levels of profits

- Pricing data

- Customs forms including money brought into the United States

- Amounts and sources of personal income

- Amounts of payments received by individuals

- Other credit-related information[12]

These listings are of general assistance in defining the type of information involved and in categorically locating how a court has treated the information in the past. However, the exemptions are not mandatory, and any particular treatment of a specific request cannot be accurately and absolutely predicted. Other factors do come into play in determining the ultimate result of an FOIA request. It is still best to request any information desired despite previous treatment by the courts.

Some business information will be denied protection because it has no real commercial value. The exemption for commercial information will be

[11]*O'Reilly* 14.07 at 14.23-14.24.
[12]*O'Reilly* 14.07 at 14.24.1-14.25.

rather narrowly construed by courts. For example, although it can be argued that a noncommercial scientist's research design does have remunerative value to the scientist, this has been held not to be commercial value. The words "commercial" and "financial" will be given their ordinary meanings.

Illustrative Case

The International Brotherhood of Teamsters (IBT) had filed an application with the National Mediation Board (NMB) for an investigation of its designation as the collective bargaining agent of some employees of American Airlines. American Airlines responded with a request for the information which had been filed with the NMB by the IBT in support of its application. The NMB denied the request, alleging that the information was exempt from disclosure. Defendants relied partially on Exemption 4, which provides for nondisclosure of "trade secrets and commercial or financial information" as justification for its denial of the request. All the parties agreed that the information requested by American Airlines was not a trade secret. However, defendants alleged that since "labor unions, as unincorporated associations engaged in providing services to employees, are plainly in the channels of commerce," the information sought by American Airlines was related to commerce and thus was exempt from disclosure. The court stated that this argument would place any communication from a labor union to a government agency within the coverage of Exemption 4 and held that that clearly was not the intent of Congress in enacting the exemption. The court noted that the information might give an employer an advantage in initiating an antiunion campaign and might also be valuable to a competing union. However, that alone was not enough to constitute "commercial" information. The court held that the protection of the exemption "is not necessarily co-extensive with the existence of competition in any form." The information must have a more direct relationship with commerce than the information sought by American Airlines to come within the exemption. The court directed that the information requested by American Airlines be disclosed.[13]

Submitted by a Person

Not only must business information be commercial or financial to receive exempt status, it must also be submitted by a person or a corporation outside the government. Business information prepared by the government, even if it pertains to commercial or financial aspects of a business, will not qualify for b(4) protection. This is true even if the information is prepared from information which has been submitted by a business.

Illustrative Case

The Renegotiation Board has the responsibility of eliminating excess profits earned by national defense contractors on contracts with the government. A company holding a contract with the government must submit forms setting out receipts, accruals, costs, and profits relating to performance of the contract. The Board then determines whether it thinks excessive profits may have been earned and tries to reach an agreement with the contractor to eliminate those excess profits. If an agreement can't be reached, the Board may enter its own order determining the amount of excess profits. If the contractor doesn't agree with the amount, a de novo proceeding, that is, an entirely new proceeding, may be held in the Court of Claims to redetermine the amount of excess profits.

---

[13]*American Airlines, Inc. v. Nat'l Mediation Bd.*, 453 F. Supp. 430 (S.D.N.Y. 1978).

Some students at Georgetown University Law Center sought disclosure from the Renegotiation Board of documents relating to the renegotiation of the national defense contracts of several corporations. The Board denied the students' request, and the students brought suit under the FOIA. The Board contended that Exemption 4 applied to the unilateral orders and the renegotiation agreements which the students sought. The court held that Exemption 4 applied only to information received from outside the government. The reports sought by the students were prepared by the Board and so weren't eligible for b(4) protection.

The unilateral orders are determinations of excess profits reached by the Board through the application of its own analysis to the information submitted by contractors. Like the unilateral orders, the renegotiation agreements, although based on information submitted by the contractors, are actually the Board's own conclusions. This information does not fit under the exemption for "trade secrets and commercial or financial information obtained from a person" and so must be disclosed.[14]

In addition, the exemption does not apply to documents prepared by persons under contract with the government. The information is not considered as coming from "outside the government." The exemption was held not to apply to an appraisal report prepared by an outside appraiser under contract to the General Services Administration (GSA).[15] Information which appears to come from outside the government may not be afforded the protection of Exemption 4 if it is compiled by someone actually working for the government.

Privileged or Confidential

The third requirement which business information must meet to be afforded protection under b(4) is that it be privileged or confidential. A promise of confidentiality made by the government at the time when information was obtained may be a factor in determining whether the information will be subject to disclosure. However, when the public has a right to information, an agency's promise of confidentiality cannot defeat the public's right of access to the information. The greatest controversy concerning business information revolves around the question of what is confidential. The leading court decision defining confidentiality sets forth two alternative tests. It states that commercial or financial information is confidential if disclosure is likely to:

- impair the government's ability to obtain necessary information in the future; or

- cause substantial harm to the competitive position of the person from whom the information is obtained.[16]

The first test is not relied on very often since it applies to information which the agency must obtain by voluntary cooperation and for which the agency must give an assurance of confidentiality. Business information is not

---

[14] *Fisher v. Renegotiation Bd.*, 355 F. Supp. 1171 (D.D.C. 1973).

[15] *Benson v. GSA*, 289 F. Supp. 590 (W.D. Wash. 1968), *aff'd*, 415 F.2d 878 (9th Cir. 1969).

[16] *Nat'l Parks & Conservation Ass'n v. Morton*, 498 F.2d 765 (D.C. Cir. 1974).

generally obtained through the voluntary cooperation of a business. The second test, then, is the one which poses the most numerous problems for an agency in deciding upon a request.

The test for determining whether information is confidential is objective. The mere fact that a business claims that the disputed information is not the type which the business would reveal to the public does not end the agency's inquiry. The agency must determine, on objective information, that this information is the type which the business would not voluntarily disclose. If the information has already been disclosed to the public, a claim of confidentiality will not stand up. For example, Hughes Aircraft Co. participated in an industrywide salary survey which involved an exchange of salary information with other companies. When Hughes Aircraft attempted to prevent the release of the same kind of information to a requester, the court held that that information had lost whatever confidential status it might once have enjoyed because of its release to the other companies. The availability of business information from another source also reflects on whether its release by the government would cause competitive harm to the company.[16a]

Illustrative Case

The Continental Stock Transfer and Trust Company requested that information which it had submitted to the Securities and Exchange Commission (SEC) in connection with its application for registration as a transfer agent be afforded confidential treatment. The SEC denied the request, and the company petitioned for review of the order. The court found one fact to be persuasive in its denial of the petition: that almost all the information was already available to the public. Some 95 percent of the issuer lists which the petitioners were trying to protect could be found in the *Financial Stock Guide Service Directory of Active Stocks,* and most of the remaining listings could be obtained from the *CCH Stock Transfer Guide Directory* or from *Moody's OTC Industrial Manual.* The court held that in view of such easy availability disclosure of the information by the SEC could not cause substantial harm to the competitive position of the company.[17]

In an FOIA action in which a submitter alleges that disclosure will cause competitive harm, a court will not withhold disclosure upon a bare allegation. Proof is required not only that the submitter faces competition but also that substantial competitive harm would result from disclosure. Some requesters attack a submitter's claim for exemption by using an antitrust type of attack to the competitive-harm test. This attack is an attempt to show that the submitter has a monopoly. Having no competition in the market, the submitter could not be injured by a release of commercial information. Thus, before a business can prove harm to its competitive position, it must first be able to prove that it operates against competition.[18]

[16a] *Hughes Aircraft Co. v. Schlesinger,* 384 F. Supp. 292 (C.D. Cal. 1974).

[17] *Continental Stock Transfer & Trust Co. v. SEC,* 566 F.2d 373 (2d Cir. 1977).

[18] *Nat'l Parks & Conservation Ass'n v. Morton,* 498 F.2d 765 (D.C. Cir. 1974).

Most businesses will not find it difficult to prove that they have competitors, but they must also prove that disclosure of the requested information will cause substantial harm to their competitive position.

A great number of the cases dealing with FOIA requests for business information concern government contractors. Government contractors and prospective government contractors are required to submit many forms and reports. These range from the forms filed in connection with a bid to those filed in connection with the equal-opportunity efforts of an employer. Many of these forms contain information which could be of great interest to a competitor.

Illustrative Cases

Sperry Univac sought information submitted by Burroughs Corporation in connection with an unsuccessful bid on a contract with the Navy's Automatic Data Processing Equipment Selection Office. Burroughs contended that disclosure of the information requested would allow Sperry Univac to estimate more accurately Burroughs's bids on future procurements so that Sperry Univac would have an advantage in preparing its own bid. The defendants agreed that release of information relating to the components of the bid would substantially harm Burroughs's competitive position. However, they proposed to release a recap table that summarized Burroughs's price proposals by installation location and was broken down into various methods of acquisition. The table was actually the bottom-line figure of a complex bid. Burroughs contended that this information also was exempt from disclosure. The court remanded for a hearing on the harm that could result from disclosure.[19]

The Council on Economic Priorities had requested EEO-1 forms and affirmative-action plans (AAP) submitted by Sears, Roebuck to the GSA and to the Office of Federal Contract Compliance Programs. Sears brought an action to prevent disclosure, alleging, among other things, that the information fell within exemption for trade secrets and confidential commercial data. Sears submitted six affidavits from five experts in support of its allegation that disclosure would harm its competitive position. The affidavits asserted that a competitor could deduce from the EEO-1 and the AAP employment totals estimates of labor costs, sales volume, and plans for expansion. The court held that the affidavits did not show, beyond general assertions, that release of the data would cause substantial harm to Sears's competitive position. Furthermore, it held that, without a comparison of the accuracy of estimates which could be made from the requested data with estimates which could be made from data already available to Sears's competitors, it could not make a finding that release would cause "substantial competitive injury." The court concluded that the "EEO-1 and affirmative action reports could not be of great usefulness to a competitor. Release of the data would provide only rough approximations of sales volumes, growth patterns or labor costs. Equally accurate approximations are already possible without the use of this data."[20]

There are other examples of cases in which the courts have concluded that disclosure of requested information would not cause substantial harm to the competitive position of the subject of that information. In many instances

---

[19] *Burroughs Corp. v. Schlesinger,* 403 F. Supp. 633 (E.D. Va. 1975).

[20] *Sears, Roebuck & Co. v. GSA,* 402 F. Supp. 378 (D.D.C. 1975).

the court will order disclosure of the information because the burden of proof has not been met.

Illustrative Case

In a suit under the FOIA, a nonprofit organization was seeking to inspect and copy records concerning the concession operations of the National Park Service. The court of appeals found that disclosure would cause substantial competitive injury to five of the seven defendants from surrounding businesses. Disclosure of the financial information would facilitate selective pricing, market concentration, expansion plans, and takeover bids by competing businesses. In addition, disclosure of the salary information could facilitate personnel raiding. However, the court held that the evidence wasn't sufficient to sustain a finding of injury to the other two businesses involved.[21]

The fact that the burden of proof rests on the party opposing disclosure makes it easier to obtain business information because the agency is the adverse party. The burden of proving that the business will suffer substantial competitive harm from disclosure rests with the government. The government may not be adequately equipped to carry that burden, and the information will then be disclosed.

Illustrative Case

A requester sued the government for audit reports and related financial data concerning the allowability of costs incurred by a government contractor. Although the government alleged that disclosure would reveal labor costs, production cost trends, and projected profit rates, the court said that the government allegations were "conclusory and generalized" and didn't meet the burden of proof necessary to establish that disclosure would harm the competitive position of the submitter.[22]

The problem is that unless the agency endorses the interest of the submitter in not having the information disclosed, it will disclose the information upon request. There is no clear, overriding notification requirement when records are requested pursuant to the FOIA. While some agencies explicitly provide that the submitter be notified of any requests for information submitted by that person, the notification requirement is not clearly set out as applicable to all agencies. In the area of b(4) information, implied-notice requirements and actual notification are becoming more of the rule than the exception.

The result is the reverse FOIA suit. The reverse suit occurs when the submitter of information finds out that a request for that information has been made and then attempts to intervene to protect the information from disclosure. Because the exemptions are not mandatory, it is to the advantage of the submitter to make an argument for withholding to the government. Reverse FOIA cases were often being brought, and from these cases the categories of protectible and disclosable commercial information were being defined.

---

[21] *Nat'l Parks & Conservation Ass'n v. Kleppe,* 547 F.2d 673 (D.C. Cir. 1976).

[22] *Military Audit Project v. Kettles,* No. 75-666 (D.D.C. 1976).

However, in the first reverse FOIA case to reach the Supreme Court, the Court struck a blow to such cases. In *Chrysler Corp. v. Brown*,[23] the Supreme Court declared that the FOIA did not provide a private right of action to the submitter of information. At the same time it went on to say that businesses could challenge the disclosure of information under the APA. Under the APA the standard of review to be applied to an agency's action is whether the action constitutes an abuse of discretion. Since the exemptions are clearly not mandatory, it will be hard for a business to have an agency decision to disclose information overturned. Many of the reverse issues were left unresolved by the Court's declaration that the FOIA did not grant a private right of action. It remains to be seen how the agencies and the courts will deal with the Court's holding.

RESEARCH INFORMATION

The government is a vast reservoir of research data which it has collected from companies that perform research for the government or have disclosed research information to the government. Using the FOIA to obtain research data can be a valuable resource for a company. For example, a company that wishes to submit a successful government grant proposal might obtain, under the FOIA, the number of successful grant proposals that the government has previously approved in order to get an idea of the format of a successful proposal. A company might want to compete for a second phase of research in which the first phase has been done by another company, and technical information on that phase would be necessary to prepare for the second phase.

Some research done by a company may be exempt from disclosure as a trade secret. However, there remains a great quantity of research data that for one reason or another will not fall under that exemption. For example, a noncommercial scientist's research design does not fall within the trade secret exemption. Since it is not commercial, it is not really a trade secret. Although it has been argued that a scientist has a very clear interest in non-disclosure, in that ideas are the scientist's stock-in-trade, the exemption hasn't been extended that far.

Illustrative Case

The Washington Research Project brought an action to compel disclosure under the FOIA of information pertaining to several research projects that had been funded by the National Institute of Mental Health. The projects all concerned the comparative effects of psychotropic drugs on the behavior of children with learning disabilities. The information in dispute contained three different types of documents:

1. **The grant application.** This included, among other things, identification of the research applicant and the applicant's affiliation with research organizations, qualifications, and experience. In addition, the application included budget estimates and research protocol or design.

2. **The site visit report.** This was a report on the observations of outside consultants

[23] 441 U.S. 281 (1979).

engaged by the Department of Health, Education, and Welfare (HEW) to review the application.

3. **The summary statement.** This was a summary of the observations and deliberations of the consultants.

The National Institute of Mental Health regularly discloses lists of all research grants which are awarded, but it does not disclose the research design, proposed methods, and specific aims of a project, nor does it release the names or proposals of any applicants whose applications are rejected. The court of appeals held that a noncommercial scientist's research design was not a trade secret and therefore had to be disclosed. However, the court did find that site visit reports and summary statements were exempt from disclosure as intraagency memoranda.[24]

Research of a noncommercial nature may be available to a requester if it does not fall within one of the other exemptions to disclosure. This is so even if these data would have commercial value in other hands; they must have commercial value to the person who has submitted the information to the government. Technically, the research data of a scientist have real commercial value in terms of career advancement and accompanying financial rewards. The value must be other than their value to the scientist in the employment market. The exemption so far has not been extended past the business market into the employment market.

Just as it appears that a trade secret must have commercial value, so it also appears that it must be "obtained from a person" to be exempt from disclosure. Thus, government-conducted research and testing are available to a requester. The government regularly runs a battery of tests on all kinds of products. These tests range from product safety evaluations to testing done in preparation of a government contract to buy a particular product. Much of the data obtained from the government's testing activities will fall outside any of the exemptions and so will be subject to disclosure.

Illustrative Case

Consumers Union brought an action under the FOIA to compel the Veterans Administration to release records of the VA's testing program for hearing aids. The VA's program is a means of evaluating hearing aids for purchase and distribution to veterans. Invitations to bid are sent to hearing-aid manufacturers, who must provide the VA with samples. The VA then tests the hearing aids and converts the raw scores from the tests into a single "quality point score" for each model submitted. Consumers Union requested the raw scores, scoring schemes, and quality point scores for 1968. The VA contended that these records were exempt from disclosure under the FOIA. The court found that the benefits of releasing raw scores obtained from testing outweighed any harm. The raw scores didn't fit under the exemption for commercial and/or financial information or trade secrets because they weren't obtained from outside the government. However, the court did find that the danger of the public being misled by release of the quality point scores outweighed any benefits of disclosure. The court ordered the release only of the raw scores.[25]

---

[24] *Washington Research Project, Inc. v. HEW*, 504 F.2d 238 (D.C. Cir. 1974).

[25] *Consumers Union v. VA*, 301 F. Supp. 796 (S.D.N.Y. 1969).

Data received from government testing may be withheld under one of the other exemptions. For example, testing results may be withheld when disclosure is specifically exempted by statute.

Illustrative Case

The Consumer Product Safety Commission (CPSC) had obtained television-related accident data from various television manufacturers. The data were consolidated, and the CPSC then prepared to release the information to the public after receiving a number of requests pursuant to the FOIA. Several manufacturers brought actions to enjoin release of the information. They argued that the information disclosure requirements of the Consumer Product Safety Act (CPSA) prevented disclosure in this case. The disclosure requirements were intended to provide safeguards for the release of information by the CPSC whether the release was done on the CPSC's own initiative or pursuant to requests made under the FOIA. Accordingly, the Supreme Court enjoined release of the information.[26]

At one time this exemption was subject to a very broad construction, and records were withheld whenever a statute denying disclosure could be considered applicable.

Illustrative Case

The Center for the Study of Responsive Law was conducting a study of airline safety and sought disclosure from the Federal Aviation Administration (FAA) of systems worthiness analysis program reports (SWAPS). The SWAPS contained the FAA's analysis of the operation, maintenance, and performance of commercial airlines. The Supreme Court denied disclosure, relying on the b(3) exemption for "matters specifically exempted from disclosure by statute." The statute involved was a section of the Federal Aviation Act of 1958 which permitted the administrator of the FAA to withhold information if, in the administrator's judgment, public disclosure would adversely affect the interests of the objecting party and if the information was not required to be disclosed in the public interest. The Court held that the b(3) exemption precluded disclosure by the FAA when read in conjunction with that provision of the Federal Aviation Act.[27]

The decision to allow a broad construction of the b(3) exemption led to a 1976 amendment to b(3) which overturned the Supreme Court decision. The exemption is now limited to matters that are "Specifically exempted from disclosure by statute, *provided that such statute* (A) requires that the matter be withheld from the public in such a manner as to leave no discretion on the issue or (B) establishes particular criteria for withholding or refers to particular types of matters to be withheld."[28]

The amendment to b(3) greatly limits the applicability of the exemption. It will no longer be available to preclude the disclosure of records unless they are actually and specifically exempted by statute. Much information which

[26]*CPSC v. GTE Sylvania, Inc.*, 447 U.S. 102 (1980).

[27]*Adm'r, FAA v. Robertson*, 422 U.S. 255 (1975).

[28]5 U.S.C. § 552(b)(3).

might previously have been withheld under the Supreme Court's interpretation of the b(3) exemption will no longer be afforded protection.

GOVERNMENT-GENERATED INFORMATION

In addition to the results of testing and research projects, governmental activities generate a great many records which could be of interest to a business. Some records generated by the government actually come from outside sources, as in the case of research projects initiated and funded by the government but conducted by a private entity. When information is prepared by a private entity for use by the government, it may be subject to disclosure, depending on the source of the information and the nature of the data.

Illustrative Case

Benson was a member of a partnership which had purchased property from the GSA. The partnership later sold the property and then became involved in a dispute with the Internal Revenue Service (IRS) over characterization of the profit. Benson sought the records of the transaction from the GSA to prove the correct characterization of the profit. When the GSA refused the request, he filed suit. The government alleged that the appraiser's reports were exempt because they contained information which was commercial and confidential. However, the court held that the exemption did not apply to the appraisal reports. The exemption was intended to protect information that a private individual wanted to keep confidential for his or her own purposes but revealed to the government under a promise by the government that the information would be kept confidential. Clearly this did not apply to appraisal reports because they were not kept confidential by the appraiser on the appraiser's own behalf and so were not confidential within the meaning of the statute.[29]

This is really a gray area under the FOIA because the information is submitted by a business yet is not information pertaining to that business; therefore, the reasons for the exemptions do not apply. At the same time the information does come from outside the government, and technically the exemptions might apply.

By contrast, there is also information in the agency files which is solely a product of agency activities. Since only information "obtained from a person" may come within the scope of protection for trade secrets and financial or commercial information, unless this information falls under another exemption, it must be released. These files contain much information about items of interest to a business which must be disclosed.

Much of the data compiled by the government about businesses will be ineligible for any protection. Not only may a business be interested in data that the government has compiled about a competing business, it may also be interested in information that the government has compiled about its own business.

[29] *GSA v. Benson,* 415 F.2d 878 (9th Cir. 1969).

Illustrative Case

Grumman Aircraft Engineering Corporation sought copies of opinions and orders of the Renegotiation Board issued during the renegotiation of the contracts of fourteen competing companies as well as the documents relating to its own renegotiations. The Board released to Grumman "clearance notices" and "unilateral orders" concerning the fourteen competitor companies and a "statement of facts and reasons" relating to one of the other companies. At the same time the Board released "performance reports" relating to Grumman. The Board considered this action to be full compliance with the FOIA. Grumman alleged that there were other documents which should be released. The court determined that the Board must release all documents which constituted final opinions. The court considered "all documents which state conclusions and reasons upon which the Board has acted, as well as any dissents and concurrences thereto" to be final opinions. It went on to list all the documents which might be included in this category. A final opinion might be a summary of facts and reasons when no subsequent statement of facts and reasons was prepared, it might be a report and recommendation of a division which did not result in a clearance, it might be the report of a regional board which did result in a clearance, or it might be the report and recommendation of a division which resulted in a clearance. The determining factor was whether it represented the conclusion and reasoning on which a final determination of the Board was made, and if it did, it must be released.[30]

The government collects its own information and compiles its own records about businesses for many different reasons. As one example, it maintains complete files on businesses with which it does business. Not only are government contractors required to submit many reports and statements, but the government also collects information for other records. The government maintains records concerning the bidding process, renegotiation of contracts, and performance reports on a particular contractor.

INVESTIGATIVE FILES

Businesses other than those involved in the procurement process may be very much interested in what government files contain pertaining to them. In particular, a business being investigated by the government or involved in a dispute with the government has an obvious reason for interest in government files. There is an exemption under the FOIA which may apply to prevent a business from obtaining records that the government has compiled. The b(7) exemption for investigatory records applies even before there is an actual dispute or before an actual charge is filed against a company. The only requirement is that the investigation might end in some kind of sanction against the company. The sanction may even be cancellation of a contract or withdrawal of funds; it is not restricted to prosecution. General agency audits or reviews not aimed at punishment are not covered by this exemption.

Before 1974 the FOIA had granted to agencies broad discretion to withhold "investigatory files compiled for law enforcement purposes except to

---

[30] *Grumman Aircraft Eng'r Corp. v. Renegotiation Bd.*, 325 F. Supp. 1146 (D.D.C. 1971).

the extent available by law to a party other than an agency."[31] No further limitation was placed on the information's qualification for exemption. The exemption was used by many agencies to withhold almost all agency files used in connection with the enforcement of any statute. For example, in an action under the FOIA to obtain records relating to the investigation of safety defects in new cars, the court withheld the records under Exemption b(7).[32]

In response to this interpretation of the scope of the exemption Congress amended the b(7) exemption in 1974. The exemption now contains a number of limitations. However, courts and agencies have proceeded to follow a very conservative approach. Cases following the 1974 amendment have generally permitted the withholding of investigatory records until the investigation has ended and the dispute has been completely resolved. Although the Supreme Court has also given the exemption a broad construction, it hinted that there was a limitation on this exemption. In *NLRB v. Robbins Tire & Rubber Co.,*[33] the Court stated that Congress did not intend to make investigatory material "endlessly" exempt but intended only that "with respect to particular kinds of enforcement proceedings, disclosure of particular kinds of investigatory records while a case is pending would generally interfere with enforcement proceedings."

In addition to a business under investigation by the government, a business that is engaged in an active dispute with the government or is the object of an enforcement proceeding by the government might be interested in government records on that matter. The exemption for investigatory records compiled for law enforcement purposes applies also in an open enforcement proceeding. A major problem for the government arises out of the use of Exemption 7(A) in connection with an active enforcement proceeding. Some courts have required the government to publish a detailed index in justification of its use of the exemption. Called a *Vaughn*-type index, this index is a relatively detailed justification specifically identifying the reasons why a particular exemption is relevant and correlating those claims with the particular part of a withheld document to which they apply.[34] When a *Vaughn*-type index is required to be filed in connection with an open case, the index itself could disclose the details of the government's case to the plaintiff because it offers such a detailed description of the disputed documents. For this reason, some courts have allowed the government to file its index in camera, which means that it is examined privately by the judge in chambers instead of publicly in court. Even an in camera filing of an index can pose problems for the government in an enforcement proceeding. As is true whenever an FOIA request is made to the government, the employees most familiar with the documents must attend to an examination of the documents.

---

[31] 5 U.S.C. § 552b(7).

[32] *Ditlow v. Brinegar,* 494 F.2d 1073 (D.C. Cir. 1974).

[33] 437 U.S. 214 (1978)G.

[34] *Mead Data Central v. U.S. Dep't of the Air Force,* 566 F.2d 242, 251 (D.C. Cir. 1977).

When a *Vaughn* index is required, agency employees involved in the dispute must take time from their preparation for the enforcement action to prepare the index. This diversion of agency resources to the handling of an FOIA request or the preparation of an index necessarily interferes with the government's preparation of its case. Therefore some courts have refused to require the government to prepare an index and instead have allowed it to make more general justifications for its use of the exemption. Other courts still require the preparation of a detailed index.

Illustrative Case

Bristol-Myers Co. brought suit under the FOIA for the release of documents prepared by the Federal Trade Commission (FTC) in the course of an enforcement proceeding. Bristol-Myers was contesting a complaint issued by the FTC charging that the company had falsely advertised Bufferin, Excedrin, and Excedrin PM. Pursuant to discovery rules, Bristol-Myers had been able to obtain copies of various studies prepared by or for the FTC concerning consumer awareness and perceptions of analgesic products and copies of scientific studies concerning the properties of these products. The company sought still other documents through resort to the FOIA. The court of appeals held that a decision by the FTC to terminate an adjudicatory proceeding or not to include a proposed charge in a complaint is a decision in a case, and if the commission prepared a memorandum explaining the reasons for the decision, it would qualify as a final opinion and be subject to the indexing requirements. The FTC responded by releasing a detailed index and affidavit describing with particularity the nature and contents of the documents withheld. The court stressed that the government was required under the FOIA to prove that it was entitled to the exemption claimed.[35]

FOIA requests are often made by employers defending charges of unfair labor practices. Some records concerning the dispute may be released, while agencies have been upheld in withholding other documents.

Illustrative Cases

Marathon sought disclosure of certain information from the NLRB in response to the filing of unfair-labor-practice charges against it. The regional director of the NLRB denied most of Marathon's requests, finding that the material requested was exempt from disclosure. The court found that file notes, investigative reports, and recommendations which reflected the deliberative processes of the Board were exempt from disclosure. Also exempt from disclosure, were file notes and investigative interview reports and recommendations which contained details of the NLRB's investigative techniques and strategies. The court did order disclosure of all the purely factual affidavits and statements which were not deliberative or advisory. In addition, it required disclosure of the NLRB's "confidential sources" whose identities would ultimately be disclosed when they were called to testify. Weighing their interest in retaining their confidential status for a longer period of time against the FOIA's policy of disclosure, the court found no basis to protect their identities.[36]

[35] *Bristol-Myers Co. v. FTC*, 598 F.2d 18 (D.C. Cir. 1978).
[36] *Marathon Le Tourneau Co., Marine Div. v. NLRB*, 414 F. Supp. 1074 (S.D. Miss. 1976).

In a companion case, Sealand Terminal Corp. sought to compel the disclosure of information from the NLRB relating to unfair-labor-practice proceedings against Sealand. The court held that certain correspondence and documents contained in the materials were exempt but ordered disclosure of other materials which had been requested. The court found that all correspondence and documents sent or received by the NLRB and addressed to or signed by Sealand or its attorneys, as well as all documents of public record, did not fit into any exemption and therefore had to be released to Sealand.[37]

Discovery entails the disclosures which parties to a lawsuit can be compelled to make. It was not intended that the FOIA be used as a substitute for or an extension of traditional discovery. In fact, the Supreme Court enunciated this view in *Renegotiation Bd. v. Bannercraft Clothing Co.,*[38] stating that the "FOIA's stress was on disclosure to be sure, but it was on disclosure for the public, *EPA v. Mink,*[39] . . . and not for the negotiating self-interested contractor. . . . Discovery for litigation purposes is not an expressly indicated purpose of the Act." The Court in that case held that the corporation, because it was seeking a disclosure which served its own interest, was not entitled to the materials. However, there was strong dissent to the Court's enunciation of this idea. Four justices stressed that, contrary to what the Court said in its opinion, the FOIA had as one of its purposes "discovery for litigation purposes." They cite the Senate report, which stated that the "FOIA was designed in part to prevent a citizen from losing a controversy with an agency because of some obscure and hidden order or opinion which the agency knows about but which has been unavailable to the citizen simply because he had no way in which to discover it."[40]

The lower courts have not seemed to follow the Supreme Court's position in *Bannercraft* but have relied instead on the language of the act to order disclosure. The FOIA requires records to be made available to "any person," and this does include someone who is self-interested. The act did not intend that the agencies examine the interests of a person seeking release; in fact, it was expressly worded so that personal interests of requesters would not enter in. Although the FOIA was not intended to expand discovery, neither should discovery rules be allowed to limit the FOIA. The litigation status of a requester should not even enter into a decision for disclosure of records under the FOIA. The fact that a person does have a personal interest in receiving records doesn't diminish or increase the right to obtain information under the FOIA. Access to agency documents must be determined by the public's right to obtain them.[41]

Irrespective of what the Supreme Court said in *Bannercraft,* the FOIA

---

[37] *Sealand Terminal Corp. v. NLRB,* 414 F. Supp. 1085 (S.D. Miss. 1976).

[38] 415 U.S. 1, 22 (1973).

[39] 410 U.S. 73, 80 (1973).

[40] S. Rep. No. 813, 89th Cong., 1st Sess. (1965).

[41] *Deering Milliken, Inc. v. Irving,* 548 F.2d 1131 (D.C. Cir. 1977).

has been used as a means of discovery in connection with lawsuits. It has been employed in lawsuits when the government is a party to get information which is not generally subject to discovery, such as agency reports which contain evidentiary data but which may not be in the investigatory file. It has also been used extensively to obtain records at a time that discovery rules would not permit. Persons involved in lawsuits with the government have also found that they can use the FOIA to delay litigation by making requests which tie up the files and require the time of personnel who are intimately familiar with the case to fill the requests. The act has also been used extensively in litigation between private parties when the government is not a party to obtain information about an opposing party which would not be available under traditional discovery rules. A litigant may also be able to obtain records concerning government activities and policies relating to the subject of the lawsuit which may be helpful in litigation.

Some records pertaining to a dispute can be withheld because they are "investigatory files compiled for law enforcement purposes" (Exemption 7). In this context courts have also chosen to rely on another exemption (Exemption 5) to withhold documents involved in a dispute between the government and a private entity. Exemption 5 protects "inter-agency or intra-agency memorandums or letters which would not be available by law to a party other than an agency in litigation with the agency."[42] In formulating this exemption it was recognized that agency employees must be allowed some freedom to exchange ideas and discuss matters frankly without fear of those discussions being made public. At the same time, it was noted that some limitation on the exemption was necessary to prevent "indiscriminate administrative secrecy."[43] The limitation on this exemption came partially through another provision of the FOIA which requires public accessibility to "final opinions, including concurring and dissenting opinions, as well as orders, made in the adjudication of cases."[44] Another provision requires that "statements of policy and interpretations which have been adopted by the agency" be made available to the public. [45]

The interplay of Exemption 5 and the two provisions quoted above is accomplished by distinguishing between predecisional memoranda and post-decisional memoranda. Memoranda which are prepared prior to a decision of an agency and which reflect the "deliberative or policy-making processes" of the agency are generally exempt from disclosure. By contrast, memoranda which are prepared after a decision has been reached by the agency and which explain the agency decisions are not exempt from disclosure. The substantive law must be made available to the public, for it cannot be expected to abide by indefinite and indeterminant standards of compliance.

---

[42] 5 U.S.C. § 552b(5).
[43] S. Rep. No. 813, 89th Cong., 1st Sess. 9 (1965).
[44] 5 U.S.C. 552a(2)(A).
[45] 5 U.S.C. 552a(2)(B).

Illustrative Case

Sears, Roebuck sought disclosure of advice and appeals memoranda issued by the NLRB in connection with unfair-labor-practice charges. Advice and appeals memoranda are documents generated by the office of the general counsel of the NLRB in its determination whether to allow the filing of unfair-labor-practice charges. The Supreme Court held that the memoranda which explained decisions not to file suit were "final opinions" and were not exempt from disclosure under the FOIA. However, when the general counsel decided to allow the filing of an unfair-labor-practice complaint, the memoranda were not disclosable as "final opinions" but fell within the protection afforded by b(5) to intraagency memoranda. The court also added that documents incorporated into the final opinions by reference do not necessarily become disclosable. [46]

In addition to distinguishing between predecisional memoranda and final opinions, many courts also distinguish between deliberative and factual materials. Agency-generated information containing factual material is not generally afforded b(5) protection. This is in accord with discovery rules which generally mandate disclosure of factual materials to a party involved in litigation with the government.

Illustrative Case

Ethyl Corp. made a request under the FOIA for the disclosure of documents containing medical and scientific data considered by the Environmental Protection Agency (EPA) in connection with the issuance of proposed lead regulations under the Clean Air Act. The administration resisted the request, claiming b(5) protection and executive privilege. The court held that the claim of executive privilege for matters of "official information" in this instance was merely a restatement of the b(5) exemption for deliberative or policymaking processes. Neither b(5) nor executive privilege extended to the purely factual portions of government documents. The court then held that the purely factual portions of the documents must be disclosed because they were severable from the "deliberative or policy-making" portions and would not compromise the secrecy of the rest of the documents. [47]

Staff Manuals and Guides

Not only might a company have a real interest in government records which pertain to or directly affect its particular business, it might also have a real interest in more general government records which at some time might affect that business. Among these records are staff manuals, guides, and other materials which set forth the policies and practices of an agency. These materials are made available to the public under a provision of the FOIA requiring disclosure of "administrative staff manuals and instructions to staff that affect a member of the public." [48] At the same time the provision is limited by exemptions. One exemption allows the withholding of "inter-agency or intra-agency memorandums or letters." [49]

---

[46]*NLRB v. Sears, Roebuck & Co.,* 421 U.S. 132 (1975).

[47]*Ethyl Corp. v. EPA,* 478 F.2d 47 (4th Cir. 1973).

[48]5 U.S.C. § 552a(2)(C).

[49]5 U.S.C. § 552b(5).

Another potentially overlapping exemption allows the withholding of "investigatory records."[50] The disclosure requirement might also conflict with Exemption 2, which exempts from disclosure matters "related solely to the internal personnel rules and practices of an agency."[51] Unresolved conflicts concerning disclosure of staff manuals, guides, and other materials in particular instances remain. For example, a staff manual may contain the investigatory techniques and procedures of an agency. The first section of the FOIA requires disclosure, but Exemption 7 requires withholding. The act does not resolve the conflict by specifying which provision should prevail.

Investigative and enforcement manuals can be very useful to a business for a number of reasons. They can provide insight into agency plans for enforcement. At the same time agency manuals set forth guidelines for agency personnel to use in administering rules and regulations, enabling a business to "conform its actions to the agency's understanding of the law."[52] The exemption for "investigative techniques and procedures" was intended only to protect matters which would interfere with law enforcement efforts. Some courts have applied the protection of Exemption 7 only to information which would provide an individual with the knowledge of how to break the law and avoid detection. Information which if released would merely provide an individual with the knowledge of how to conform to the law ought to be released.

Illustrative Case

Stokes and Barbe requested from the government the *Training Course for Compliance Safety and Health Officers,* including all instructor and student manuals, training slides, training films, and other visual aids and materials used in training Occupational Safety and Health Administration (OSHA) inspectors. The government denied the request, contending that the manual was a law enforcement manual and thus was exempt from disclosure. Stokes and Barbe instituted an action pursuant to the FOIA, seeking injunctions to prohibit the secretary of labor from withholding the materials. The plaintiffs contended that the manuals were administrative manuals and were subject to disclosure. The court of appeals held that the manuals were administrative in nature and did not come within the exceptions for law enforcement materials, intraagency or interagency memoranda, or materials relating solely to the internal personnel rules and practices of an agency. The court thus ordered release of the materials to the plaintiffs.[53]

PROCEDURAL GUIDE TO USING THE FOIA

In accordance with agency rules, the FOIA provides that each agency shall make records available to any person upon a request which reasonably describes those records and is made in accordance with published rules and procedures. Each agency issues its own procedural regulations which contain instructions on making FOIA requests to that particular agency. Almost all

---

[50] 5 U.S.C. § 552b(7).

[51] 5 U.S.C. § 552b(2).

[52] *Hawkes v. IRS,* 467 F.2d 787, 795 (6th Cir. 1972).

[53] *Stokes v. Brennan,* 476 F.2d 699 (5th Cir. 1973).

agency rules prescribe to whom the request should be directed. Most agencies will reroute a misdirected request, but the time limits of the act will not start to run until the request is in the proper hands. It is a good idea to talk informally with an agency first to determine which record is actually wanted and where it is, but the request itself should always be written and ought to state that it is made pursuant to the FOIA. This may save time and avoid delays even with agencies which have not made mention of the act a prerequisite to release of records. Compliance with a particular agency's published procedures is a prerequisite to the triggering of other provisions of the act. Failure to follow an agency's regulations may result in dismissal of a later lawsuit on jurisdictional grounds.

Illustrative Example

Tuchinsky, an adviser to draft registrants, was seeking to obtain certain information from a state Selective Service System. Selective Service regulations provided that the local board had discretion to release the type of information sought by plaintiff. Tuchinsky did not even request this information from the local board but instead had gone to the state board. The court decided that it would not even look at the issue of release of these documents because plaintiff had "leapfrogged over a substantive step in the administrative process."[54]

The request need not state any reason why the records are sought. One of the most novel things about the FOIA is that an individual does not have to demonstrate a need for records or even a reason for wanting them. Records are to be released without consideration of the status of the individual. In some circumstances it might be advantageous to explain the reasons behind a request. The exemptions are not mandatory, and an agency official may release information which might otherwise be withheld if there is a good reason for the release.

In addition to compliance with agency procedural regulations, the FOIA requires that the request "reasonably describe" the records which are desired. Although the standard is strict enough that the description must enable the records to be "located in a manner which does not involve an unreasonable amount of effort,"[55] it is not to be used by the agency to obstruct public access to records. Generally, a description is considered sufficient if a professional employee of an agency who is familiar with the subject area of a request could find the record from that description. The attorney general's memorandum emphasizes that the agencies should use their knowledge of the contents of the files to facilitate the processing of requests. If documents are identified from a request, the request cannot be denied merely because of the sheer quantity of the materials requested.

The costs of search and copying may be assessed against the requester, and it therefore makes sense to narrow a request to save on the payment of fees. The act provides for agencies to issue regulations setting out a uniform

---

[54] *Tuchinsky v. Selective Service Sys.*, 294 F. Supp. 803 (N.D. Ill.), *aff'd*, 418 F.2d 155 (7th Cir. 1969).

[55] Attorney General's Memorandum of 1975, p. 23.

fee schedule and specifies that the fees are to be limited to reasonable charges for the actual search and copying. An agency may provide in its regulations that the initial request contain an offer to pay the search and copy fees. The request itself should also place a ceiling on the fees which the requester is willing to pay. Agency regulations may also require that the requester pay an advance deposit when the costs of search and copying are going to be substantial. The FOIA also provides for a waiver of fees when disclosure of documents would primarily benefit the general public.

Freedom of Information Act requests are relatively simple and do not normally require extensive legal-type demands. All that is required is a simple letter which specifically describes the records sought, such as the following sample FOIA request:

Illustrative Example

Name of agency
Address of agency
City, state, and zip code

Re: Freedom of Information Act Request

Dear _____ :

Pursuant to the provisions of the Freedom of Information Act, 5 U.S.C. § 552, I am requesting the release of [identify the records as clearly and as narrowly as possible].

I am willing to pay any fees incurred by the search for or copying of these records if they don't exceed $_____ . If the fees are in excess of that amount, please inform me before you fill this request. [*Optional:* I believe that the release of this information would primarily benefit the public and therefore request a reduction or waiver of any fees to be charged.]

If you consider any portions of this material to be exempt, please release any separable portions which do not fall under the exemption. In addition, if you think it necessary to withhold any records, please inform me of the applicable exemptions which you think justify the withholding and inform me of available appeal procedures.

I would appreciate your handling this request as quickly as possible, and I look forward to receiving your response within 10 days.

Sincerely,

Signature
Address
City, state, and zip code

Under the FOIA any requests made become a matter of public record. To avoid being identified as the requester of specific information it may be necessary to have someone else make a request. An attorney outside a company can make a request in the attorney's name. In addition, there are private firms which will make FOIA requests for someone who wishes to remain anonymous.

Agency Response

An agency must determine within 10 working days after a request has been received at the proper agency office whether to grant or deny the request. The agency may extend the time limit for another 10 days under extraordinary circumstances and upon notice to the requester. Otherwise, the requester may sue if the time limit has been violated, treating the delay as a denial. A court may then enjoin the withholding of the documents, or it may accept an excuse by the agency that it is exercising due diligence but that exceptional circumstances have caused the delay. The court may then grant the agency more time.

Illustrative Case

The plaintiffs had requested from the Attorney General and from the Federal Bureau of Investigation (FBI) all documents relating to the role of Patrick Gray in Watergate. At that time the FBI had 5137 requests waiting to be processed and not enough resources to deal with them. At FBI headquarters, 191 employees were already working on FOIA requests. The court found that the plaintiffs' request was a difficult one and that the FBI was using due diligence in responding to it. So the court granted the agency additional time to respond.[56]

If an agency decides to grant a request, the records should be made promptly available for inspection and copying. If the request is denied, a reason must be given for the denial. The requester is to be given the name and title or position of the person responsible for the denial and must be informed of the right to appeal to a higher official in the agency.

Administrative Appeal

The FOIA itself doesn't explicitly require a requester to appeal within an agency before bringing an action in court, but courts may treat the lack of an agency appeal as a failure to exhaust administrative remedies and dismiss a suit for that reason. Although the act doesn't set any time limit for an appeal, agencies have established such limits by regulation. Usually, when a denial is received, there are 30 days within which to appeal that decision. If the applicable time limit passes, the requester can simply make another initial request and then appeal within the time specified.

An appeal also must comply with the agency regulations which set out the procedure to be followed. It should contain a request that at least any segregable portions of the documents which don't fall within an exemption should be released. The segregable portions may contain what the requester is seeking and so eliminate the need for resort to the courts. Again, a letter such as the following sample will normally suffice to appeal a denial of an initial FOIA request.

[56] *Open America v. Watergate Special Prosecution Force,* 547 F.2d 605 (D.C. Cir. 1976).

Illustrative Example

Name of agency official
Title
Name of agency
Address
City, state, and zip code

Re: Denial of FOIA Request

Dear _____:

I wish to appeal your denial of my request of [date] made pursuant to the Freedom of Information Act, 5 U.S.C. § 552, for the release of information.

I received a letter from your agency on [date] denying my request for access to [description of records requested]. I am enclosing a copy of my request and your denial. I am certain that upon reexamination of these letters you will determine that the records I am requesting should be released.

I would appreciate your handling this appeal as quickly as possible, and I expect your decision within 20 days.

Sincerely,

Signature
Address
City, state, and zip code

The agency must then act on the appeal within 20 working days. If on appeal the request is again denied, the notification must set out the name and title or position of the person responsible for that denial and inform the requester of the provisions for judicial review of that decision. Segregation of exempt material or deletions from released documents also act as a partial denial and afford the basis for a suit. The FOIA also requires the agency to specify the reasons for the deletions and to inform the requester of the availability of judicial remedies.

Judicial Review

Upon denial of an appeal, the requester can file suit in a district court. Once suit has been filed, the agency must answer within 30 days of service of process. Show-cause court orders may be used to shorten the time for a preliminary hearing to less than 30 days. FOIA cases take precedence on a court's docket over all cases except for those that the court considers of greater importance. This system of docket preference has worked to expedite FOIA cases through the court system and has forced the courts to grant more attention to those cases.

The district court has jurisdiction to review a decision by an agency in a de novo proceeding and to determine whether the agency ought to release the documents required. De novo review by the court means that the matter is tried anew by the court as if no decision had been previously rendered by the agency. De novo review was provided so that an agency couldn't merely assert an exemption and then request that the court defer to its "expert" decision. In these proceedings the agency bears the burden of proving that an exemption applies because it has control over the documents and the requester can't really make the argument that the exemption doesn't apply without an examination of the documents themselves. When a court is considering whether to require disclosure of the records, it may examine the contents of the records in camera to determine whether they should be withheld under any of the exemptions. A private examination of the documents by the judge, the in camera inspection is an attempt to counter the hardship caused by complete agency control of the documents.

The issue of whether the court retains its equitable powers to withhold documents even though they fall outside the exemptions has not been decided. Arguments can be made that equitable discretion remains in the courts. One argument is that the act merely confers jurisdiction on the courts to enforce the act: it doesn't mandate enforcement. The words used are "shall have jurisdiction to enjoin." There is no mandatory provision for enforcement by the courts. The district court, as an equity court, seems to have the discretion to refuse to order disclosure even if the literal terms of the act would require disclosure when the documents really should be protected. The Supreme Court has said in dictum that the FOIA does not reflect a congressional decision to "limit the inherent powers of an equity court."[57]

On the other side, however, there is an argument to be made that the district court lacks the equitable power to withhold documents which don't fall into one of the specific exemptions. The argument against the equitable power to withhold also rests on a statement by the Supreme Court that the exemptions are "explicitly made exclusive . . . and are plainly intended to set up concrete workable standards" for decisions on withholding.[58] It is also true that the mandate that documents be released to "any person" without consideration of needs or interests works against the argument that a court should engage in an equitable balancing of interests.

Costs and Attorneys' Fees

A court may assess court costs and attorneys' fees to a litigant who has substantially prevailed against the government. A plaintiff substantially prevails if the suit could reasonably have been regarded as necessary and if plaintiff's action had a substantial causative effect on disclosure of the information.[59]

Illustrative Case

After the plaintiff, Nationwide Building Maintenance, Inc., had filed a suit under the FOIA, the government abandoned its exemption claims and released the requested information before the court had made any finding. The District Court for the District of Columbia denied the plaintiff's request for attorneys' fees and court costs, con-

[57] *Renegotiation Bd. v. Bannercraft Clothing Co.,* 415 U.S. 1 (1974).

[58] *EPA v. Mink,* 410 U.S. 73 (1973).

[59] *Vernon & Low Income Advocacy Council v. Usery,* 546 F.2d 510 (2d Cir. 1976).

cluding that the plaintiff had not substantially prevailed because the government had disclosed before the court made any findings. The Court of Appeals for the District of Columbia reversed, holding that the plaintiff had substantially prevailed and was entitled to a discretionary decision by the court as to whether attorneys' fees ought to be awarded.[60]

The FOIA does not provide, however, for an award of attorneys' fees whenever the plaintiff substantially prevails. The legislative history of the act stresses that this provision was not included to reward a litigant who succeeds against the government but to provide a practical means for the average citizen to pursue a request through judicial review. Criteria were set out for the court to consider in its awarding of fees. In exercising its discretion, the court should consider the benefit to the public, the commercial benefit to the plaintiff, the nature of the plaintiff's interest in the records, and also the reasonableness of the government's withholding. [61] The greater the public interest in and benefit from a disclosure, the more likely it is that attorneys' fees will be awarded to the litigant.

The act also provides that whenever a court finds that agency action was arbitrary and capricious, the responsible agency employee may be subject to disciplinary action. When the court finds that there are questions as to arbitrariness, the U.S. Civil Service Commission (since 1979, Merit Systems Protection Board) is to initiate a proceeding to determine whether disciplinary action is appropriate. Then the responsible agency is to impose promptly the sanctions which the commission directs. The standard imposed is that the action be arbitrary and capricious, amounting to bad faith, and applies when the employee either ignores or refuses to follow the law, not when there is any colorable claim for withholding. Unlike the award of costs and attorneys' fees, this procedure can be initiated only when the court has actually ordered release of the documents.

A judicial appeal also is to be expedited on the docket ahead of other cases except those which the court considers of greater importance.

PRIVACY ACT

While the FOIA attempts to open government files and records to the public, the Privacy Act attempts to provide a balance so that release of records won't invade an individual's privacy. The Privacy Act is concerned with the confidentiality of the records of individuals. It is intended to give an individual some degree of control over the collection, release, and maintenance of records about that person and is designed to provide the individual with judicial remedies to ensure the protection of his or her rights.

The scope of the Privacy Act is narrower than that of the FOIA. While all agency records are subject to the FOIA, only those records contained in a "system of records" are subject to the Privacy Act. A system of records is

---

[60] *Nationwide Building Maintenance, Inc. v. Sampson*, 559 F.2d 704 (D.C. Cir. 1977).

[61] 120 Cong. Rec. 17014 (1974).

defined as a group of records under the control of an agency from which information is retrieved by means of an individual identifier, such as a name, number, or other symbol assigned to a particular individual.[62]

The Privacy Act provides that no records shall be disclosed without the consent of the individual except as required by the FOIA. The FOIA, then functions as an exemption to the restrictions on disclosure contained in the Privacy Act. The FOIA is clearly a disclosure statute, and records in the possession of an agency, except for certain exempted records, must be disclosed.

For example, one exemption to the FOIA includes "personnel and medical files and similar files the disclosure of which would constitute a clearly unwarranted invasion of personal privacy." [63] Whether information is protectible under the Privacy Act depends on whether it comes within an exemption to the FOIA. If disclosure of certain records would not constitute a clearly unwarranted invasion of personal privacy, those documents are required by the FOIA to be disclosed and aren't subject to the restrictions of the Privacy Act. However, if the documents fit under that exemption, the Privacy Act takes away the discretion of the agency to release those documents and makes the FOIA exemption mandatory. The other FOIA exemptions are not mandatory, but in conjunction with Privacy Act materials which would constitute an unwarranted invasion of personal privacy they must be withheld because they are not required to be disclosed under the FOIA. This makes "clearly unwarranted invasion of personal privacy" the standard of disclosure for the Privacy Act as well as the FOIA.

The Privacy Act is intended to give an individual control over the release of records maintained by agencies which pertain to that individual. Its protection is limited to individuals and does not extend to corporations.

Illustrative Case

Shermco Industries was a contractor overhauling the Air Force's airborne generators pursuant to a 5-year contract with the Air Force. After the completion of 2 years of the contract, the government terminated the contract and solicited bids from a number of contractors. The government awarded the new contract to Tayko Industries, and Shermco filed a protest. After a great deal of correspondence between Shermco and the Air Force by which Shermco attempted to obtain documents concerning the termination of its contract and the award of the new contract, Shermco filed suit against the Air Force. Shermco sought the release of documents concerning the contract under the FOIA and the Privacy Act. The government alleged that the plaintiffs didn't have standing to sue under the Privacy Act. The court held that the Privacy Act grants access to records to individuals and only to individuals. An "individual" is defined as "a citizen of the United States or an alien lawfully admitted for permanent residence."[64] A corporation is not an individual under the definition and so lacks standing to gain access to records. In addition, the Privacy Act grants access only to information about individuals. The act specifies that "each agency that maintains a system of records shall upon request of an individual to gain access to his record or to any infor-

---

[62]5 U.S.C. § 552a(a).

[63]5 U.S.C. § 552b(6).

[64]5 U.S.C. § 552a(a)(2).

mation pertaining to him which is contained in the system, permit him . . . to review the record."[65] A "record" means information about an individual that is maintained by an agency. Since plaintiff was seeking information about Shermco Industries, he couldn't use the Privacy Act to attempt to gain those records. And the Air Force maintained no system of records on the plaintiff, Peter Shermco, the president of Shermco Industries. The court held that plaintiff thus lacked standing to seek access to records under the Privacy Act.[66]

By contrast to the FOIA, the Privacy Act deems the character of the requester pertinent. Since access to records is available only to an individual, it is important in what capacity a person makes a request. Congress intended to create a distinction between persons making a request in a personal capacity and those acting in an entrepreneurial capacity.[67] Therefore, only individuals making a request for records in a personal capacity will be granted access to records.

The act provides that agencies shall not release any records about an individual without that person's consent.[68] This provision is subject to a number of exceptions, one of which is that disclosures required by the FOIA are exempt from the restrictions of the Privacy Act.[69]

The Privacy Act also gives individuals a right of access to records contained in an agency's system of records which pertain to that individual. The act then gives that individual a right to seek corrections of any mistakes contained in those records. The agency must reply within 10 days either by correcting those mistakes or by informing the individual of its refusal to amend the records, the reason for the refusal, and the procedures for review of that decision. An agency has 30 days from a request for review to make a final determination unless good cause is shown for an extension. If the request is again denied, the individual may file with the agency a statement explaining the reason for disagreement with the record, and this statement becomes part of the file. Individuals then have the right to judicial review of any adverse decision.[70]

Provisions of the Privacy Act also govern the gathering and maintenance of personal information by agencies. The act limits the information which an agency may have in its files to that which is relevant and necessary to accomplish the agency's purposes.[71] The act also provides that the records which are kept must be accurate, complete, timely, and relevant.[72]

The act also provides that when information is requested from an individual, the individual must be informed of the authority which authorizes

---

[65]5 U.S.C. § 552a(d)(1).

[66]*Shermco Industries, Inc. v. Secretary of the Air Force,* 452 F. Supp. 306 (N.D. Tex. 1978).

[67]OMB Guidelines, 40 Fed. Reg. 28,591 (1975).

[68]5 U.S.C. § 552a(b).

[69]5 U.S.C. § 552a(b)(2).

[70]5 U.S.C. § 552a(b)(2).

[71]5 U.S.C. § 552a(e)(1).

[72]5 U.S.C. § 552a(e)(5).

the seeking of that information, whether disclosure to the agency is mandatory, the purpose for which the information is sought, and the uses which may be made of the information obtained. In addition, the agency must inform the individual of possible consequences attaching to a refusal to provide all or part of the information sought.[73]

The act then goes on to ensure that its provisions will have some meaning by requiring agencies to publish notices of all of their systems of records in the *Federal Register*. A notice must include the names and locations of all systems of records, the types of records maintained in those systems, and the categories of individuals on whom records are maintained. The notice must then set out agency procedures concerning these records, including how to discover whether an individual is included in those records and how the individual can gain access to the records.[74] Furthermore, agencies are required to keep an accounting of disclosures made and to notify an individual when any record on that individual is made available to any person.[75]

Both civil remedies and criminal penalties are available to an individual under the Privacy Act. The act requires that administrative procedures must be exhausted before resort is made to litigation. An individual may bring a civil action against an agency in a district court for an order to permit access to records, for amendment of those records, or for expungement of any material that is not accurate. In addition, there is a civil action granting relief for failure of an agency to comply with any other provisions of the act or of the regulations promulgated pursuant to the act if that failure of the agency has had an adverse effect on an individual.

Attorneys' fees and litigation costs are available to the plaintiff for any of the actions permitted by the act in which the complainant substantially prevails. If an agency fails to maintain accurate records or fails to comply with any of the other provisions of the act and this failure has an adverse effect on an individual, damages are available in addition to court costs and attorneys' fees. However, in a damage action the plaintiff must show that the agency's action or failure was intentional or willful, and even upon this proof damages are limited to actual damages, with a minimum damage recovery of $1000. Furthermore, the damage action must be against the agency itself; no individual liability is provided for.

Criminal actions are established only for knowing and willful violations of the act. The provisions set a maximum penalty of a $5000 fine for any agency officer or employee who willfully discloses any information on an individual, knowing that disclosure is prohibited, or who willfully maintains a system of records covered by the act without publishing the required notice in the *Federal Register*. It also provides criminal penalties for any person who knowingly and willfully requests or receives an individual's records from an agency under false pretenses.

[73]5 U.S.C. § 552a(e)(3).
[74]5 U.S.C. § 552a(e)(4).
[75]5 U.S.C. § 552a(e)(8).

GOVERNMENT IN THE SUNSHINE ACT

The Government in the Sunshine Act represents a further, logical step in the continuing process of opening governmental decision making to the public.[76] The act is another manifestation of the post-Watergate concern that the government be held accountable to the public. The sunshine concept reflects the feeling that greater accountability will restore the public's faith in the government and increase public understanding of government operations while serving as a practical check against government abuse.[77]

Under the act, federal agencies headed by a collegial body of two or more individuals must conduct their meetings in public, subject to certain exemptions. Meetings are defined in the act to include any gathering of at least the minimum number of individual members of an agency required to take action who deliberate or conduct or dispose of agency business. A meeting does not occur unless that group has the power to act, but the definition of "meeting" is being broadly construed to avoid any attempts at evasion.

The Sunshine Act grants to individuals the right to attend public meetings of agencies covered by the act. To ensure that this right can be exercised, notice must be provided, generally by publication in the *Federal Register* or other public posting, of the time and place of an upcoming meeting and the subject matter to be discussed. The act does not give individuals a right to participate in meetings, merely a right to attend. Minutes of the meeting should then be made available to the public.

The Government in the Sunshine Act provides for ten exemptions from the openness requirements. The first eight exemptions correspond to the first eight exemptions of the FOIA, with the exception of the FOIA's exemption for interagency and intraagency discussions of policy since those are crucial to the openness principle. Instead, in the Sunshine Act Exemption 5 covers the right to close meetings which would accuse a person, including a corporation, of a crime or formally censure a person. Two additional exemptions protect against premature disclosure of information or releases which concern the agency's issuance of a subpoena or its participation in an adversarial proceeding.

Prior to the holding of a meeting, an agency may find that the meeting is likely to disclose an item covered by one of the exemptions and that the public interest does not require that the meeting be opened. The agency must then vote by absolute majority and without proxies to close the meeting or a portion of it. The meeting must still be announced in advance along with the fact that it is closed and the reasons for the closing. A transcript must then be made of the proceedings, and the public has a right of access to nonexempt portions of the transcript. The rest of the transcript is available in case the decision to close the meeting is challenged. A court can then release the transcript of the wrongfully closed portion.

Since the purpose of the act is to open government processes to the public,

[76]H.R. Rep. No. 880, pt. 1, 94th Cong., 2d Sess. 4 (1976).

[77]S. Rep. No. 354, 94th Cong., 1st Sess. 4-5 (1975).

the provisions strongly encourage open meetings. In addition, the presumption in favor of open meetings is so strong and administrative obstacles to closing a meeting are so burdensome that it is generally in an agency's best interest to keep meetings open. This poses a problem for conflicting interests which are threatened by a strict rule of openness. Although a person can request closure of a meeting, the exemptions are not mandatory and nothing in the act mandates closure. Some interests may be protected by other statutes; for example, 18 U.S.C. § 1905 prevents the disclosure and use of trade secrets. There is, however, other business information which can't be classified as a trade secret but which a person would desire to keep confidential. Even though confidentiality is justified by the inequity of allowing a competitor to gain access to procedures and developments of a business, the presumption weighs strongly in favor of keeping a meeting open. A person can request that a meeting be closed if the meeting is likely to involve accusing a person or a corporation of a crime, disclosure of information which is compiled for law enforcement purposes, or disclosure of other information which would constitute a clearly unwarranted invasion of personal privacy. The agency, upon request of any of its members, shall then vote on whether to close the meeting.

Even if a meeting is closed, there are costs to the individual of that decision. The identities of those attending and the reason for closure of the meeting must be made public. This can lead people to draw some conclusions which in themselves may be harmful. For example, officers of a certain corporation attend a meeting which is closed pursuant to Exemption 5 (which covers the right to close meetings which are likely to involve accusing any person or corporation of a crime). The release of this information might well cause a drop in the price of stock in that particular corporation.

Sunshine Act disputes may be pursued directly to the courts. No administrative appeals are provided by the act. The district courts have jurisdiction to enforce the provisions of the act. When a meeting is closed by an agency, the court is authorized to conduct a review in advance of the scheduled meeting and may enjoin the meeting from being held before the hearing and then may enjoin the closing.

After a closed meeting has been held, a person must bring an action for equitable relief within 60 days of the public announcement of the meeting. The court may grant whatever relief it deems appropriate, including granting an injunction against all future violations of the act and ordering the disclosure of transcripts which are not authorized to be withheld. In addition, any other federal court which is authorized by law to review agency actions may afford relief mandated by the Sunshine Act in proceedings pursuant to other laws. The burden is on the agency in these actions to defend its closure.

The court may assess attorneys' fees and court costs against the agency when the plaintiff substantially prevails in an action. The U.S. Treasury is actually liable for any costs assessed against an agency. Furthermore, when the plaintiff brings an action for dilatory or frivolous purposes, costs may be assessed against that plaintiff.

5 LOBBYING THE AGENCIES ON RULE MAKING

JEFFREY H. JOSEPH
Manager, Business-Government Affairs Division
Chamber of Commerce of the United States

Once upon a time, businesses had an easy time in determining whether they had regulatory problems. In those good old days, certain industries, most notably transportation, utilities, and banking, were commonly referred to as "regulated." However, the political decisions of the late 1960s and early 1970s changed the old rules of thumb. In fact, the establishment of a number of new federal regulatory agencies over that period caused the distinction between regulated and nonregulated industries to disappear. The new agencies, dealing with broad issues like workers' safety and health, environmental protection, equal employment opportunities, and consumer product safety, created a new breed of regulator, one whose expertise was no longer based on a thorough understanding of the workings of a single industry. Instead, these agencies were staffed with generalists, empowered by the Congress to pursue broadly stated, long-range societal goals.

As time passed, the federal agencies began to develop hearty appetites continually to expand their bounds. For example, the life insurance industry, which had always been regulated at the state level, now found itself under constant scrutiny in Washington, both by federal regulatory agencies which wanted to enlarge their domains and by certain elected officials, who saw regulation as the only answer to problems in the marketplace.

It was, to a great extent, in response to the myriad of agencies and the promulgation of numerous rules and regulations deemed excessive by the business community that corporate attitudes toward the importance of government relations began to crystallize in favor of substantial involvement.

Strategically speaking, there are three obvious targets for involvement in corporate-government relations: the Congress, the executive branch, and the independent regulatory agencies. While this chapter will deal with working relationships with the regulatory agencies, it is important to note that there is a clear interrelationship between the three sectors. At all times, regulatory agencies are pursuing congressionally mandated directives, and it must not be forgotten that the Congress can change the parameters of its original assignment to an agency at any time. Second, the executive branch can play a very important role in the formulation of regulatory agency proposals as it pursues its own broader objectives of fighting inflation, balancing the budget, or promoting specific policy directives. Therefore, successful regulatory relations will require a careful mixing of all Washington government relations functions. Experienced Washington watchers have come to learn that one cannot assume the war has been won when legislation passes the Congress in a relatively satisfactory form; many have experienced the shock of seeing regulatory agencies interpret new statutes as they choose to see them, raising again, in the form of regulations, issues thought to have been resolved in Congress.

A good regulatory relations program relates closely to successful programs for legislative liaison. The importance of a good relationship between a company and agency personnel, at both the federal and the state level, cannot be overstated. Specifically, businesses will find it necessary to encourage their technical people to meet regularly with agency officials to maintain a dialogue on the specific issues at hand. Some corporations will see this as an opportunity for the regulators to witness firsthand the potential effects of a proposed rule and will invite the agency staff to a corporate facility. At times some agencies will be very receptive to overtures from business, but at other times the same agencies will feel compelled to keep their distance. The politics of the situation will dictate the scenario.

While most major corporations rely on a government relations staff or a Washington counsel to advise them and coordinate their regulatory agency relations, average American business executives are not foreclosed from doing the same and can find their way through the bureaucratic maze and achieve results in this area. But first, one must know how the process works, what the tools of the trade are, and who potential allies may be. Once these criteria have been established, a successful regulatory relations program can become a mechanical process.

However, business executives should understand that they must consider all possibilities. They must come to learn that their participation in the regulatory process is essential to protect their basic interests. Disregard for the process or for full utilization of available options can be disastrous.

Illustrative Example

Rolls-Royce has had a problem in the United States ever since Congress empowered the National Highway Traffic Safety Administration (NHTSA) to set average fuel economy standards for automobile manufacturers. The NHTSA indicated that the standard for the 1978 model year would be 18 miles per gallon. Accordingly, the company petitioned for an exemption from the standard. The law allows the NHTSA to exempt low-volume producers (Rolls-Royce sold a mere 1129 cars in the United States in 1977), but the agency has a lot of discretion about what standards to apply in such cases.

The Rolls-Royce petition was filed originally in July 1977. The NHTSA demanded more information, however, and so an amended petition was filed in October 1977. It was published in the *Federal Register* in December of that year, accompanied by a lengthy NHTSA exposition of all the possible rulings that might be issued in the case. The American people were invited to comment and were given until January 18, 1978, to make any points they deemed relevant.

On July 13, 1979, the NHTSA finally published its preliminary evaluation of the issues presented by the case and of the people's comments. It turned out that, of all the 218 million eligible commentators, only 1 individual had weighed in. He said that Rolls-Royce should be exempted "in the name of common sense." Seemingly shaken by this position, the agency has now in effect exempted Rolls-Royce. It has proposed for the company a standard of 10.7 miles per gallon, which should be met easily.

The moral to this story is not that a corporation could see its vital interests affected by a mere handful of individuals through rule making but rather that the process allowed interested parties to work to protect their interests. Rolls-Royce should have encouraged all its dealers to comment on the *Federal Register* notice. For all it knew, an anti-big-car group was organizing around the country to generate comments in opposition to big cars.

KEEPING INFORMED OF GOVERNMENT REGULATIONS

Until 1935 individuals who tried to keep track of government regulations had to scour through agency proposals buried deep in the files of individual agencies. There was no central clearinghouse or standardized sequence, only a process of trial and error until an individual tracked down a specific regulation by chasing its paper trail through an agency's bureaucracy. In 1935, however, Congress passed the Federal Register Act, setting up the basic centralized system which is still in existence today.

Times have changed since 1935, however, and an important difference exists in the design and usage of the *Federal Register*. The enactment of another major law added an important dimension to the *Register*'s purpose. Passage of the Administrative Procedure Act (APA) in 1946 added to the *Federal Register* system an opportunity for interested persons to comment on agency proposals prior to the issuance of federal regulations.

The *Federal Register* serves as the road map for the rule-making process. It contains three types of documents: proposed rules, final rules, and notices, which are not rules but documents of general interest to the public. The *Federal Register* also prints a schedule of meetings called by the various regulatory agencies.

The General Services Administration (GSA) publishes the *Federal Register* on a daily basis, as well as the *Code of Federal Regulations* (CFR), a compilation of all the federal regulations, which has been expanded to approximately 140 volumes. The Office of the Federal Register in the GSA for the last several years has encouraged regulatory agency officials to be more deliberate in the promulgation of rules and at the same time has promoted the use of plain English instead of "legalese."

In spite of management efforts to hold back the overkill associated with proposals in the *Federal Register,* the number of pages of small print continues to multiply on a yearly basis. A few years ago, business executives would note with amazement, "Did you know the *Federal Register* contains more than 50,000 pages of rules, regulations, meetings, and orders this year?" The numbers have continued to escalate to the point at which the *Federal Register* runs to more than 87,000 pages per year.

The initial portion of the *Federal Register* entry contains basic information. The following example illustrates the standardized sequence.

Illustrative Example

Name of agency   Department of Health, Education, and Welfare.

Name of subunit   Food and Drug Administration.

Descriptive title for the action   Reimbursement for Participation in Administrative Proceedings.

Agency proposing the rule   Agency: Food and Drug Administration.

Type of action   Action: proposed rule.

Summary   Summary: This document proposes a demonstration program for providing financial assistance to participants in certain administrative proceedings of the Food and Drug Administration (FDA). The agency invites public comment (1) on where a demonstration program providing financial assistance to participants in administrative proceedings, under appropriate circumstances, should be established and (2) on the applicable scope, criteria, and procedures for such a program. The program would be established to determine whether the process of administrative decision making would be enhanced by reimbursing participants whose participation in agency proceedings would contribute or could reasonably be expected to contribute to a full and fair determination of the issues but who otherwise would be unable to participate effectively.

Relevant dates   Dates: Comments by June 18, 1979; the proposed effective date of a final rule based on this proposal is 30 days after date of publication of the final rule in the *Federal Register.*

Address for comments   Address: Written comments to the Hearing Clerk (HFA-305), Food and Drug Administration, Room 4-65, 5600 Fishers Lane, Rockville, Maryland 20857.

Supplemental information   For further information contact: Alexander Grant, Office of Consumer Affairs (HF-7), Food and Drug Administration, Department of Health, Education, and Welfare, 5600 Fishers Lane, Rockville, Maryland 20857; 301-443-1547.

People may have some basic questions after seeing the *Federal Register* for the first time. After being overwhelmed by the many, many proposals in each daily edition, they may ask, "How can the agency get into things like this?" and "Why does anyone care about this?" The public must understand that the authority for agencies to promulgate rules is delegated by Congress. To some extent the only check on what the regulators do comes in the form of congressional oversight. However, federal agencies continue to break new ground on a daily basis.

Agencies implement the broad policies that Congress has delegated to them by issuing rules. In the past, Congress took greater care in specifying the details to agencies so that they could implement the policy objectives it had anticipated. However, in the more politically volatile world of the late 1960s and early 1970s, the quantity of legislation and the complexities of the many social, technical, and economic issues associated with them led to ambiguous statutes containing agency delegations.

Once an agency determines what it feels the original congressional intent was, the rules it promulgates have the same effect as laws. However, the agency must promulgate those rules in a certain fashion; that is, it must follow certain procedures. These procedures will be spelled out in the next section of this chapter, dealing with the rule-making process.

HOW BUSINESS CAN RESPOND TO PROPOSED RULES

Notwithstanding exemptions found in the APA which will be dealt with later in this chapter, all substantive rules must be made public in a "proposed" form before they become final. Accordingly, this requirement is satisfied as rules are presented to the public in the *Federal Register.*

The public is invited to respond to the agency proposal through a rebuttal submission referred to as a "comment." The typical comment period for most agency proposals is 30 to 60 days. The APA does not specify a required minimum number of days for an agency to accept comments, but many agencies resolve this ambiguity by establishing their own procedural rules.

From that standpoint, once an agency begins to work on a specific proposal, it will assign a docket or file number to the proceeding to make it easier for the public to obtain information quickly on specific agency actions. The dockets are made available for inspection and copy through public information offices.

Business executives should know that the date published in the *Federal Register* as the final date on which comments will be accepted often is not absolutely final. Many times, an agency will extend a comment period if enough groups ask for an extension. However, an agency will not grant an extension until those who request it state the reasons why it is impossible to comply with the original comment deadline. Upon determining that a request is reasonable and that a delay in the procedure will not have an adverse effect on the outcome of the decision, an agency will usually grant the request to extend the comment deadline. After granting the extension, the agency will publish the new deadline in the *Federal Register.* Once this has been done, all affected parties are on notice of the new timetable.

In some instances, agencies will allow informal extensions. That is, the agency will continue to accept and consider comments after the published deadline. Quite often, an extension will not be granted until the last possible moment.

So that agencies are not forced into a situation which seemingly catches the public off guard and forces affected groups to ask for extensions to prepare comments, an increasing number of agencies are warming to the idea of advance notices of proposed rule making. Although this step is not required by the APA, it is being used increasingly when a regulatory agency is not sure in what direction it should proceed. However, it is a requirement found in Executive Order 12044, *On Improving Government Regulation,* which will be explained later in this chapter. Polling the public can provide an agency with helpful ideas and options which it can use as the basis for promulgating a rule.

The APA does require that agencies give 30 days' notice in the *Federal Register* that a new rule has been adopted. This provision is designed to give the public notice that a particular practice or procedure has been changed. A number of agencies now give up to 60 days' notice, as found also in Executive Order 12044 and in numerous legislative proposals which continue to attempt to codify the new, longer comment period.

When agencies so desire, it is not difficult for them to get around this requirement. All an agency need do is to identify its proposal as either an interpretive rule, a statement of policy, a substantive rule which recognizes an exemption or relieves a restriction, or a rule for which an agency finds that "good cause" exists for not providing 30 days' notice. It then publishes the reason in the *Federal Register.*

Illustrative Example

Clothed in the obscure garb of an administrative interpretation involving mobile homes, a 1979 ruling by the Federal Trade Commission (FTC) posed a serious threat to all manufacturers and retailers of consumer products. The ruling, if allowed to stand, would force all those associated with consumer products carrying written warranties to tack dozens of different warranties on goods sold across state lines. The ruling was made in an interpretative letter to the Wisconsin attorney general, which the FTC then circulated to all states and many consumer groups throughout the country.

Under the Magnuson-Moss amendments of 1975, the FTC was given additional powers to require companies to disclose certain warranty information. The intent of the Congress was to limit the paperwork that companies would be required to perform. Legislators intended that the FTC's new warranty disclosure powers should preempt, where possible, the disclosure requirements of the individual states. "This was designed," according to the Senate report, "to insure that suppliers of consumer products would not have to print warranties in conformance with the many possible State or Territorial disclosure formulas or labeling procedures." Instead, the FTC's interpretation of the Magnuson-Moss amendments would cut this preemption device and force companies to print dual notices in every state whose disclosure laws differed from the federal Magnuson-Moss provision.

Critics of the interpretation point to the considerable expense that the interpretation would generate. Companies would have to hire staffs to monitor all changes in state warranty laws. Lawyers would have to be hired to update printed warranty disclosures constantly. And consumers would be burdened with a lot of technical warranty information that they had not asked for and that they might not even understand. In essence, if left unchecked, the FTC would be making a rule without having to conform to the procedural requirements of the APA or the FTC Act. The FTC would be effecting trade rules by interpretation of law on its own.

To go more deeply into the merits of the issue, the business community argued that the FTC was overly narrow in its interpretation of the disclosure requirements in the Magnuson-Moss warranty amendment which Congress had attached to the FTC Act. This amendment stipulates that a federal warranty disclosure requirement may preempt a similar state disclosure requirement when the two are not precisely identical.

The congressional policy objective in allowing federal preemption of state warranty disclosure requirements was to lift an otherwise severe labeling burden from the shoulders of consumer products manufacturers whose goods are marked in different states. The FTC, however, had interpreted the "not identical" proviso to achieve the opposite result. The agency would require a manufacturer to disclose the details of both state and federal warranty laws even though they might differ only slightly from one another. Members of the business community objected that this dual warranty disclosure was expensive, produced no genuine benefit, and flied in the face of the clear intent of the legislators.

In response to a petition from members of the mobile home industry, the FTC published a *Federal Register* notice of September 6, 1979, requesting comments on the FTC's interpretation. The deadline for comments was set at November 5, 1979. Unfortunately, the important issues at stake were thoroughly obscured in the technical language of the announcement itself. A number of business groups, upon learning of the hidden meaning of the mobile home interpretation, requested that the FTC extend the deadline of comments until January 4, 1980. In response to these petitions, the extension was granted.

When an agency publishes a final rule in the *Federal Register,* it is required to include a summary of the comments received in response to the proposed rule and to state whether the changes recommended and the comments offered have been incorporated in the final rule. Normally, an agency must explain why it has decided not to incorporate any suggestions made.

On occasion, an agency will adopt a final rule and yet, at the same time, request comments that are not due at the agency until after the rule becomes effective. On other occasions, when the issue is controversial, an agency will adopt a final rule but announce to the public that it will not implement the rule until it gets a clear go-ahead from the Congress or the requisite oversight or appropriations committee.

Finally, agencies sometimes use what they identify as "interim final rules." These actions fall somewhere between a "proposed rule" and a "final rule with an opportunity for comment." An agency usually adopts an interim final rule when it feels intense pressure yet is not sure what it should do. The publication of an interim final rule will provide an opportunity for public comment but does not force an agency to do anything with the comments.

RULE MAKING

Federal regulatory agencies have three basic functions: rule making, adjudication, and regulatory enforcement. In terms of inherent powers, a regulatory agency encompasses elements of legislative, judicial, and executive authority.

Administrative agencies have entered the age of rule making. To some extent, old-line regulatory agencies were forced to turn to this approach as the burden of existing responsibilities increased, and in the late 1960s and early 1970s the Congress spurred this trend by creating a number of new agencies with broad social mandates. Without a tool like rule making, most commentators concede that these new agencies could not possibly carry out their broad congressional mandates.

Rule making, the process of formulating, amending, or repealing rules, is complex and encompasses a number of sophisticated concepts. The Administrative Procedure Act of 1946 is the basic road map through the regulatory process; in essence, it is a rule-making bill of rights. The APA addresses the procedures required for rule making and adjudication, and with the exception of informal adjudication it specifies minimum procedures to be followed by agencies in such proceedings.

The APA requires that agencies follow certain prescribed steps; it emphasizes the right of individuals to have an opportunity to know of a proposed rule prior to its final adoption and to comment on its potential effect on an individual or a group.

In addition, new protections for small businesses and local governments have been guaranteed by the Regulatory Flexibility Act. This act requires agencies to tailor their rule making to the problems of small businesses. The agencies must publish semiannually a notice of all proposed regulations which would have a significant impact on small businesses. The notice must describe the basis and purpose of the rule as well as provide an agency contact. The agency must prepare a regulatory flexibility analysis explaining the reason and basis for the rules, estimating the reporting and record-keeping burden on small businesses, and proposing less burdensome alternatives. Following adoption of a final rule, the agency must prepare a second analysis explaining the comments received in response to the proposed rule along with the reasons for adopting the rule as written. Agencies are also required to review systematically existing regulations in order to identify those which are especially burdensome to small businesses.

The APA also establishes the duties of administrative hearing officers as it seeks to guarantee the right to an impartial tribunal, a fair hearing, and a right to counsel. Finally, the APA establishes legal standards for judicial review of administrative action: a check by the judicial branch on policy-making proposals delegated to the "fourth branch" of government by the legislature.

As mentioned, the APA does not provide an exclusive source of administrative law; the act calls only for minimum requirements and expressly provides that it does not limit or repeal additional requirements imposed by statutes or otherwise recognized by law. Individual agencies elaborate on APA requirements in their own procedures, but these can be found only on an agency-to-agency basis in the *Code of Federal Regulations*. Quite often, specific statutes may describe and require particular procedures applicable only under those statutes. Unless a specific piece of legislation preempts the use of the APA, it must be followed by the agency. However, one must be aware that certain agencies, such as the FTC, have their own specific statutes establishing hybrid rule-making procedures.

Federal agencies can make three kinds of rules: (1) implementing or substantive, (2) interpretive, and (3) procedural. Implementing or substantive rules constitute the most important quasi-legislative activity of an agency because they have the force of the law. When Congress expressly confers on an agency the power to enact rules having the force and effect of law, the agency cannot promulgate a rule which conflicts with a statute.

Although interpretive rules do not have the force of law, they do express the view of the enforcing agency, which is regarded as having expertise and knowledge of specific subjects. As a result, these interpretations are afforded great weight when they are reviewed by the courts. However, because of the lesser status of the interpretive rules, agencies are not required to follow in their formulation the complete procedures that are required for substantive or implementing rules. The difference between implementing and interpretive rules depends on whether a rule fulfills a statutory mandate or whether the agency is only informing the public of its views of the statute's meaning. Because the differences between these two types of rules is very important, that is, because substantive rules are legally binding and require more finely detailed procedures for promulgation, business entities should carefully examine through corporate or trade association counsel those proposals which may affect them.

Procedural rules are what they sound like, that is, guidelines on the issuing agency's procedures. In essence, they represent the laws of the agency, simply because an agency's rules regarding its own affairs are binding on all persons dealing with that agency. Generally, the promulgation of procedural and interpretive rules does not require compliance with all procedural requirements for implementing rules.

Basically, the purpose and effect of a rule determine the procedures that an agency adopts in formulating the rule. If an agency attempts to promulgate a rule that a business group feels will have a "subsequent impact" on the rights or activities of affected businesses, they should demand that the agency grant those businesses the procedural rights guaranteed by the APA.

PRESIDENTIAL EXECUTIVE ORDERS

In 1978, President Carter issued an executive order to improve government regulation that technically applies to all executive branch agencies. The order is comprehensive. It applies to all existing and future "significant" regulations. While agencies are required to develop their own definition of significant, certain criteria are mandatory, and if an agency concludes that a regulation is not significant, it must so state when the regulation is proposed.

The order creates early opportunities for public participation in the development of regulations. At least twice a year, agencies must publish in the *Federal Register* an agenda of significant regulations. At a minimum, this agenda must identify significant regulations being considered by the agency, the need and the legal basis for the actions being taken, and the status of regulations previously listed on the agenda. The agenda shall also include existing regulations that are scheduled to be reviewed.

Before rules are proposed, agencies are to encourage public involvement by using advance notices of proposed rules, public conferences, and other means of involving those likely to be affected by the regulations. The order specifies that the agencies must give the public at least 60 days to comment on proposed significant regulations.

Agency administrators are directed to exercise close control over the development of significant new regulations. Before an agency proceeds to develop a new regulation, its head shall have reviewed the issues, the alternative approaches to be considered, the plan for obtaining public comment, and the target dates for development of the regulation. Then, before a significant regulation is proposed in the *Federal Register,* the agency head must approve it. Among the requirements that this official is expected to determine are that the regulation is needed, that its direct and indirect effects have been adequately considered, and that alternative approaches have been considered and the least burdensome of the acceptable alternatives has been chosen.

Early in the decision-making process the agency must prepare special regulatory analysis that carefully examines alternative approaches in cases in which a significant regulation may have major economic consequences for the general economy (a major increase in cost or prices for individual industries, geographic regions, or levels of government or an annual effect on the economy of $100 million or more). The regulatory analysis must identify the alternatives that were considered, the economic consequences of each one, and the reasons why one was chosen over the others. The notices of proposed rules must explain the approach that is favored and describe the others that were considered. The notice shall also tell the public how to obtain a copy of the drafted regulatory analysis. And, when the final rule is published, the final regulatory analysis must be made available to the general public. In addition, a regulatory analysis review group, chaired by the Council of Economic Advisers, was created by President Carter to review the regulatory analyses prepared by the agencies.

Agencies must periodically review their existing regulations in light of Executive Order 12044. This review is to follow the procedural steps outlined within the order for the development of new regulations. Agencies must establish the criteria that they will apply to select regulations for review, which can be found in the executive order.

In 1978, each agency affected by the order published in the *Federal Register* a draft report which outlined its process for developing regulations. The reports included changes made in response to the President's order; proposed criteria for defining "significant" agency regulations; proposed criteria for identifying regulations which would require "regulatory analyses"; and proposed criteria for selecting existing regulations for review and a list of regulations that the agency would consider in its initial review.

By and large, most commentators have not been satisfied with the initial efforts of the agencies affected by Executive Order 12044. In mid-1979, all agencies were asked by the U.S. Regulatory Council again to go through the process of complying specifically with the full intent and objectives of the executive order. However, because the executive order did not create new grounds for judicial review and because there was uncertainty about the success of a self-regulatory program of federal regulators, legislative proposals continued to capture much attention in the Congress. The thrust of most of these proposals would codify and, in some instances, even strengthen many of the basic concepts touched upon in Executive Order 12044.

As one of his first actions in office, President Reagan issued Executive Order 12291. This order set up the Presidential Task Force on Regulatory Relief, which requires that federal administrative rules and regulations be subjected to cost-benefit analysis. The new standard precludes regulatory action unless "the potential benefits to society from the regulation outweigh the potential costs to society." In addition, when more than one alternative is available, the regulation "involving the least net cost to society is to be chosen." The potential impact of Executive Order 12291 on existing and future rules and regulations is significant.

TRADE ASSOCIATION PUBLICATIONS AND OTHER SOURCES

The *Federal Register*'s staff knows only what the various agencies tell it when they need something printed in the *Register*. On occasion, a well-connected reporter will scoop the *Federal Register* with advance notice of public rule making. Accordingly, this information will appear as a straight news story, buried in the national news or in the business and financial sections of daily newspapers. Therefore, one cannot count on the press to provide regularly the kind of information business executives need to know concerning agency rule making.

A number of specialized trade publications can be very helpful. These sources usually are in the form of newsletters or loose-leaf subscription services dealing with very specific subject matters. The publishers of these news services have reporters covering very narrow beats of particular agencies or statutes. Each trade publication has its own style; some are almost too straightforward and factual, while others mix fact, rumor, and irreverence.

Illustrative Examples

Holder in due course   What, me hire an expert? That is the gist of the FTC's denial of a request for an extension of the 30-day public comment period announced when the FTC dumped thousands of additional pages on the rule-making record. An August 8 letter to lawyers for the American Bankers, Consumer Bankers and Independent Bankers Associations describes the kinds of materials added to the record, specifically noting the controversial survey report on "holder" compliance, done some time ago but only recently unearthed from staff files. The whole purpose in reopening the record, said the response, was to receive the results of the compliance survey and of the staff's enforcement experience.

"None of these materials require subtle evaluation," explained the Commission letter. *"These documents do not necessitate the type of scrutiny and rebuttal they might if*

they constituted expert opinion . . . [emphasis added]." Get your comments in by August 17.

How much did that survey cost??[1]

Railroads: DOT favors exemption from ICC regulation for railroad grain shipments The Department of Transportation is seeking a relaxation of Interstate Commerce Commission rules on rail shipments of grain, a move which farmers vigorously oppose.

DOT filed a brief with the commission August 24 in response to a request for comments on proposed changes in setting grain rates. The ICC was urged by DOT to permit railroads more flexibility in setting rates for hauling grain. DOT argued that competing truck and barge shipments of the commodity are not restricted by ICC regulations.

DOT recommended the commission begin a legal proceeding that could result in exemption from regulation of grain shipments. The commission voted in March to exempt rail shipments of fresh fruits and vegetables, and DOT said that as a result, the railroads have developed the means to adjust prices to keep pace with changes in the market.

Although setting more flexible rates for grain prices could be more complicated, DOT conceded, the experience with perishables encourages us to believe it can be done. One recommendation is to permit a two-tier pricing similar to that used by trucks and barges. Under the system, a shipper can sign a freight contract in advance or wait to take advantage of the spot market, where freight rates fluctuate.

Pricing flexibility would permit railroads to raise prices quickly during peak periods, according to DOT. The financially ailing rail lines would be in a better position to buy additional rail cars for hauling grain and help to avoid car shortages, DOT continued.

Largely because of the prospects of increased rates, farmers strongly protested last March an exemption from regulation for grain rates at the time the exemption for fresh fruits and vegetables was proposed.

DOT also recommended maintaining the present policy of allowing railroads to set different freight rates for domestic grain shipments and grain for export, noting the fluctuations of demand are greater in the export market.[2]

The Regulatory Council has its eye on coal Charged with spreading the regulatory reform gospel, the Council so far has deftly avoided specifics. But that may change. The Council has tentatively chosen coal as an example of the industry beset with overlapping state and federal regulations that could be streamlined. The strategy will be to identify the overlaps, asking state and federal agencies to then find other examples.[3]

While industry-specific trade associations will keep their members informed of agency actions which affect them, not many are geared to covering all the agencies in Washington. However, the Chamber of Commerce of the United States has established a program designed specifically to keep business executives informed of, and poised to react to, federal rule making in most regulatory agencies. The chamber, recognizing the pressing need for

[1]Reprinted from *FTC: Watch,* no. 78, Aug. 19, 1979.

[2]Reprinted from *Daily Report for Executives,* Bureau of National Affairs, Inc., no. 164, Aug. 27, 1979.

[3]Reprinted from *Legal Times of Washington,* vol. 11, no. 7, July 23, 1979.

greater action and improved communications to those affected by federal regulation and for a flexible mechanism through which people can work together, has developed its Regulatory Action Network. This is designed to be a communications and action network of business executives of all types who are interested in reforming the regulatory process and changing the impact of specific regulatory agency rules and regulations. The Regulatory Action Network is designed, in essence, to provide a needed early alert to allow those affected to have meaningful input into the regulatory process as specific proposals weave their way through the federal bureaucracy.

The Regulatory Action Network has developed a number of publications and communications techniques to keep grass-roots business executives informed. Among them are *The Regulatory Action Network: Washington Watch,* a monthly newsletter which alerts executives to regulatory developments that are pending in agencies and are ripe for business involvement; and a series of publications which provide short analyses of major regulatory issues, as well as detailing the specific workings of various statutes or enforcement mechanisms, present regional issues of concern to the American public, and a quaint business executives with methods of dealing with the federal regulatory process.

HOW TO DEAL WITH THE REGULATORY AGENCIES

Rule making does not begin with the publication of the notice of a proposed rule. It begins with the perception that a new rule may be desirable or that an existing rule should be modified or repealed. Under Section 4 of the APA, any person may petition for the issuance, amendment, or repeal of a rule. However, initial action is usually taken as an outgrowth of recommendations from the agency's staff, resulting from a specific legislative mandate or from recognition that a rule can implement or interpret a legislative mandate. But the past several years have seen important rules proposed initially by private sources. Business groups must be aware, therefore, that petitions can be the source both of beneficial rules that they propose and of detrimental rules proposed by adverse interest groups.

Illustrative Example

In 1979, the Securities and Exchange Commission (SEC) decided to publish for comment in the *Federal Register* a petition filed by the Georgetown University Law Center Institute for Public Interest Representation which had broad consequences for the business community. The law students suggested to the SEC that it require public corporations to file with the agency details of any arrangements between corporate directors and corporate counsel for reporting any "possible illegal" activities discovered by the attorney. In addition to filing arrangements for corporate attorneys, the petition would require corporations to make the following specific disclosures:

- A certification that the corporate board of directors has instructed its counsel to report possible violations of law and other possibly illegal corporate behavior

- Written retainer arrangements and all other written agreements between the board and the corporation's outside counsel dealing with, among other matters, the

nature and frequency of their contacts and the attorney's obligations upon discovering a supposed illegal act

● **The resignation or dismissal of corporate counsel, along with the reasons**

The issue is still unresolved, but it illustrates the potential responsiveness of agencies to place such issues before the public for comment.

Regardless of whether a proposed rule is initiated within or outside an agency, a process of intraagency consideration necessarily precedes publication. During this period, it is desirable and proper for business groups that would be affected by the rule to consult informally with the agency to inform it of potential ramifications. It is important to offer the agency technical data to prove one's case whether a business group is urging the agency that a proposed rule be modified by reflecting the interest of those affected or that a rule be dropped from consideration. Providing impact analyses, cost-benefit ratios, employment results, and other statistics before the proposal of a rule can be an important first step in arriving at an acceptable final rule. Agencies generally are receptive to such information.

Obviously, a business executive or business group will have greater success in working with an agency if the executive or group has some familiarity with that agency and its staff. Therefore, business groups, through their trade associations and Washington counsel, should undertake long-range programs to establish a dialogue with the regulators. At a bare minimum, business groups must understand the basic content of the APA as well as any rules and regulations which are directly applicable to any specific government unit. Beyond this requirement, a few useful pointers in establishing and maintaining agency contacts follow:

● As a general rule, contacts should be initiated and developed at the working-staff level. Subsequent contacts with higher-echelon staff may be necessary, but it is essential to start at the working level. Ideally, initial contact and development of a working relationship should occur when there is no immediate problem to solve.

● Cultivating contacts with key working-staff people is crucial in establishing a mutually beneficial and effective liaison. An effective liaison means a continuous informational and working relationship on relevant matters. It does not mean continuous contact at times when there is nothing truly relevant to discuss.

● Avoid "leapfrogging" within an agency or department. In this respect, it is probably advisable to follow excessive protocol rather than to alienate helpful contacts and possibly damage future working relationships. However, if the lower-echelon executives cannot be of adequate assistance, move on. This must be done tactfully to ensure that the liaison at the working level is kept intact. It is important to remember that top officials often refer a matter back to the working level. Make sure that the lower-echelon executives are aware of the particulars and are prepared in advance. Such assistance aids the staff in performing well for its superiors.

● Know who does what. It is important to identify the appropriate department or agency and staff person with whom to get in touch on a specific problem. This may require research. Consider these approaches: (1) Obtain the necessary information from existing staff contacts. (2) Some agency or department contacts are obvious; there are divisions or bureaus that are identified with and concentrate on specific industry problems. (3) Telephone directories of specific agencies or departments often provide information on staff and areas of responsibilities. There are also specialized publications which will furnish this information.

- It is recommended and generally advisable that concerned business executives work with their associations in establishing contacts with an agency or a department. However, it must be remembered that an association represents the views of an entire industry and cannot appear to be going to bat for a single member.

- Once rule making has begun in an agency, it is useful to generate pressure from other sources by mailing or presenting copies of the relevant comments to other key Washington people. Besides getting in touch with the agency, it is essential that your senators and representatives be copied in. The Regulatory Analysis Review Group, the White House's regulatory watchdog, should also be informed.

- In writing comments, keep the following thoughts in mind:

  1. Regulations are usually more technical than legislative. Product safety standards, environmental technology specifications, and many other regulations are intricate. If you have scientists or engineers on your staff, enlist their assistance in writing comments.

  2. Regulators do not respond to some of the arguments to which politicians do. They are not elected to their positions and consequently do not respond to emotionalism. Try to use statistics or other supporting facts for your arguments.

  3. Try to quantify what a proposed regulation will mean to your business in terms of staff time and money spent to conform to the substance of the regulation and to meet paperwork requirements.

  4. If keeping up with regulatory requirements will cause you to lay off employees or otherwise reduce your productive capacity, try to quantify these problems.

  5. Ask your trade association for information. On major regulatory issues, associations and organizations like the United States Chamber frequently form working groups to pinpoint problem areas in proposed regulations and outline arguments.

While legal skills and touching all bases are important in dealing with proposed rule making, tactical agency maneuvering in the 1980s also calls for an understanding of politics and the use of the press. The interplay among politics, publicity, and law has become an increasingly important part of agency rule making. Business executives and lawyers must fully understand the interaction and learn to take advantage of it.

It has become increasingly clear that the agencies themselves are making full use of public relations tactics. Many agencies have forced themselves to this course through their pursuit of matters which raise significant public policy issues. The Occupational Safety and Health Administration (OSHA) is cloaked in the mantle of protecting worker health and safety. The mission of the Environmental Protection Agency (EPA) is to protect the environment; the Equal Employment Opportunity Commission (EEOC) promotes civil rights. The national press assigns reporters to these beats. Consequently, the agencies' issues get a constant public airing.

Accordingly, responders to these sorts of agency initiatives have learned to generate their own public and congressional interest and debate on a particular subject. Witness the 1979–1980 phenomenon in which the House and Senate voted to terminate a number of specific rule makings then in process at the Federal Trade Commission.

Those who must deal with regulatory agency initiatives must learn to utilize every possible resource and argument to prove their cases effectively.

Logic on a case-by-case basis will determine whether an argument to an agency centers on the point that the rule is not needed, or that it is illogical, or that the required cost-benefit analysis is incomplete or faulty. However, knowledge of the strengths and weaknesses of the agency's position is essential to achieve positive results. Combining this with knowledge of the agency's process can often pay large dividends.

Illustrative Example

On April 27, 1971, the secretary of labor promulgated a regulation, 29 CFR 1910.217(d), prohibiting the manual feeding of power presses and requiring, instead, that power presses be fed and unloaded automatically. After carefully studying the situation, the Chamber of Commerce of the United States filed a petition on November 28, 1972, seeking to revoke this subsection of OSHA regulations that prevented hand feeding and removal of material from mechanical power presses. The chamber cited the fact that OSHA rules already required mechanical guards that would automatically prevent injuries to employees as well as evidence produced by industry safety experts.

This action was taken pursuant to the rule-making provisions of the Williams-Steiger OSHA Act of 1970), which says that "any person may at any time petition the Assistant Secretary in writing to revise, amend, or revoke any provisions of this part." The effective date for the enforcement of the original "no hands in dies" requirement was set as August 31, 1974.

In January 1973, the secretary of labor invited interested parties to submit data on work injury experience with point-of-operation guards and also the result of no-hands-in-dies requirements. Information was submitted by 320 members of the chamber. On the other side of the case, which was led by the AFL-CIO and the United Auto Workers, only 5 witnesses appeared, and they acknowledged their failure to produce statistics, saying even that their material was "almost worthless." On May 13–15, 1974, the secretary of labor, in response to the chamber's position and to testimony, revoked the OSHA requirement.

Subsequently, the AFL-CIO went to court. The United States Chamber entered the case as an intervenor on the side of the secretary of labor. The U.S. Court of Appeals for the Third Circuit heard the case, which originated as *AFL-CIO v. Brennan, Stender, and Chamber of Commerce of the United States* and which subsequently became *AFL-CIO v. Marshall,* and the circuit court on September 17, 1976, gave a judgment order supporting the chamber's case.

JUDICIAL REVIEW

What happens if a group is dissatisfied with the results of an agency proceeding? As illustrated above, it must turn to the courts and seek judicial review of the decision. Therefore, a thorough understanding of the scope and procedures of judicial review of agency actions is essential. (See Chapter 10.)

The vast majority of review courts can consider only the agency's administrative record (testimony and evidence presented during the agency proceeding). De novo review, which calls for a completely new record, is provided for only in a few specialized statutes and under limited conditions in the APA. Therefore, the task of any group appearing before an agency is to use every procedural opportunity or entitlement to present a thorough case to the agency. If judicial review is necessary, the best possible administrative record will have been made.

A court can hold that a rule adopted through informal procedures is unlawful if the rule is "arbitrary, capricious, an abuse of discretion, or otherwise not in accordance wtih the law." This is known as the reasonableness standard, which governs informal rule making and informal adjudications. Additionally, if the agency action is held unconstitutional or in excess of jurisdiction or fails to follow the APA or specific statutory procedures, the agency action will be set aside.

"Reasonableness" is based on the agency's explanation of its action; the reviewing court will not go beyond this explanation in justifying reasonableness. However, the courts will demand that the agency demonstrate a sufficient record which provides a rational basis for the decision. The same standard of reasonableness is applied to decisions regarding possible abuses of discretion.

When an agency action arrived at by formal procedures is being reviewed, a substantial-evidence test replaces the reasonableness test. "Substantial evidence" requires that the court determine whether the evidence supporting the agency's decision is in fact substantial, that is, is based on the entire record. This of course infers that the record also contains evidence which contrasts with the agency's decision.

While substantial evidence in theory is more demanding than reasonableness as a standard of review, courts often have difficulty in separating the concepts. Usually, courts simply determine whether there is sufficient evidence to support a reasonable decision arrived at by the agency.

Regardless of the standards which have been enunciated for judicial review of agency actions, the judge's view of the merits of the particular case is more likely to govern whether the court will review the agency's action than is any theory of review. The courts, and not the agencies, are the final arbiters of agency authority. The courts are charged with reviewing the agencies' exercises of legislative discretion. When an agency abuses its power in issuing a regulation, the courts will generally find a way to strike it down.

Illustrative Case

OSHA promulgated a regulation requiring employers to pay employees for time spent accompanying OSHA inspectors during walk-around inspections. The regulation was challenged by the Chamber of Commerce of the United States, which argued that the regulation was adopted without compliance with the APA. The Court of Appeals for the District of Columbia Circuit found that the regulation was an attempt to supplement the act, not merely to construe it. The court held that it must therefore be treated as a legislative rule, which requires notice-and-comment procedures. In a critique of abuses of agency rule-making authority, the court held that the regulation was invalid.[4] It returned the case to the district court, which vacated the ruling. On May 29, 1981, OSHA withdrew the regulation.

---

[4] *Chamber of Commerce of the United States v. OSHA*, 636 F.2d 464 (D.C. Cir. 1980).

When an agency action does not meet the appropriate standard, the court can issue either a prohibitory or a mandatory injunction and declare the agency action unlawful. If the agency's error is in withholding rather than compelling action, the court can then require the agency to act.

As mentioned earlier in this chapter, it is critically important to raise all issues at the agency level because court review considers only those proceedings and the resulting record.

Business executives who do take the time and make the conscious decision that they want to learn more about participating in and consequently influencing the regulatory process can have success. But as all executives know, success is not easy.

6 PUBLIC RELATIONS AND THE REGULATORY PROCESS

ROBERT KEITH GRAY

Chairman, Gray and Company
and Former Vice Chairman, Hill and Knowlton, Inc.

> . . . I propose another affirmative and transcendental principle of public law, the formula of which is: "All maxims which stand in need of publicity in order not to fail their end, agree with politics and right combined."
>
> For if they can attain their end only through publicity, they must accord with the public's universal end, happiness; and the proper task of politics is to promote this, i.e., to make the public satisfied with its condition. If, however, this end is attainable only by means of publicity, i.e., by removing all distrust in the maxims of politics, the latter must conform to the rights of the public, for only in this is the union of the goals of all possible.
>
> Immanuel Kant, *Perpetual Peace*

Kant made publicity a virtue of republican government, in fact, a standard against which the actions of government were to be judged. He hardly could have envisioned the changes which were to take place over the next two centuries in our notions of publicity and of the distinction between the public and private realms of human affairs. Kant's explanation, that publicity removes distrust, seems woefully dated in a time in which publicity is regarded as a cheap trick and publicists are regarded as flacks.

Yet over the years and especially since World War II, there has been a growing and unfortunate tendency in government, for what has evolved in Washington (and in other capitals as well) is exactly the problem to which Kant reacted: the problem of "invisible governance."

Much as the kings and councilors of old met secretly to plan a nation's course, there is today a vast and impenetrable and invisible government in Washington. Its purpose is to administer the rules by which we live and do business—rules made in accordance with Congress but not by Congress. Its accountability is to Congress and the courts. Its name? The federal bureaucracy.

When a corporation or a trade association finds itself confronted by the invisible government, it must undertake a campaign of public education, because it becomes necessary, before any views are espoused or any stances taken on a given issue, to explain to the public why the issue is important and what the government *had done* (or, preferably, *is trying to do)*. When a company or an association needs help in this regard, it frequently comes to a public relations or public affairs firm.

The public relations–public affairs business has long been aware that as levels of public education and sophistication have increased, so too has the need to avoid traditional PR techniques. No longer is it either adequate or advisable to engage in the mere espousal of viewpoints or the promotion of products.

Consequently, since the early 1960s the traditional PR side of our business has waned as compared with the rising tide of public affairs–public education activities in which we engage. Hill and Knowlton began to give prominence to the phrase "public affairs" in 1961 (today it appears on their letterhead), because what is sought to be done is to turn the government's affairs into public ones; in today's political work the two far too frequently are not the same.

Often working hand in hand with a client's legal representative, public affairs counseling seeks to educate governmental decision makers. Public affairs appeals directly to the public, to that constituency whose well-being would be enhanced or threatened, shielded or exposed by the government's action. It seeks those constituencies, develops strategies by which to gain their attention, and makes them aware of the otherwise invisible actions which would impact upon them. It brings together those parts of the citizenry who might not realize they are potential allies, and it helps those who are so inclined to forge the political weaponry necessary to halt or hasten the now not quite so invisible hand of government.

And, much like other educators, we find that our basic tool, the most essential weapon, is straight, accurate, valid information.

INFORMATION

Perhaps the most steadily relied-upon tool of modern public affairs counseling is the constant, careful, politically informed monitoring of federal activities. This requires something a bit more intensive than carefully reading *The Washington Post*. In covering the full range of both visible and invisible governmental actions, public affairs stays in touch with issues and trends which affect not only present clients but future ones as well. When, for instance, a trade association or a firm needs help in redefining a particular regulatory requirement, the public affairs firm is usually on top of the issue before it arrives.

The "saccharin war" is a case in point. The U.S. Food and Drug Administration (FDA) is one of the nation's oldest regulatory agencies. For many, it epitomizes a regulatory agency's proper role in our form of government, having been created by Congress to protect the integrity of our food and drug supply. To others the manner in which the agency has performed its function in recent years is an increasing cause of concern.

It all started with the thalidomide controversy in the late 1950s. In response to growing public fear over the marketing of unsafe drugs, Congress passed what is now known as the Delaney clause. Authored by Congressman Jim Delaney of New York, who had recently lost his wife to cancer, this clause required the FDA to remove from the market any food additive which had been shown to cause cancer in laboratory animals.

On the surface, the clause seemed a reasonable approach to keeping our food supply free of carcinogens (substances which cause cancer). When it was passed, the Delaney clause made sense. But today many are questioning the rigid standard it imposes. Modern technology increasingly has enabled scientists to detect a significant number of carcinogens, but it has left the degree of risk to humans posed by such suspect substances still open to question.

Illustrative Example

In 1977, a Canadian study based upon laboratory rats showed that a few rats developed bladder tumors after having been fed large amounts of the artificial sweetener saccharin. Citing the Delaney clause, the FDA moved swiftly to ban the use of saccharin in all food and drugs. It turned out that the FDA had moved too swiftly.

Saccharin is the nation's only available nonnutritive (calorie-free) sweetener. It is used by millions of diabetics to control their intake of sugar and by millions of other Americans to help lose weight. Saccharin, in short, is a widely used and popular substance.

The proposed ban resulted in a classic confrontation between the FDA and millions of Americans who believed that saccharin contributed to their health. Congress eventually had to act as referee. The saccharin case provides one of the best examples of a situation in which government regulators have been stopped in their tracks by the public they seek to regulate.

However, the public's will, while immediately apparent from the public outrage expressed over the proposed ban, did not automatically prevail over the FDA. It required a massive and intense public education and legislative campaign to derail the FDA's proposed saccharin ban.

Within a few days of the FDA's announcement business leaders opposed to the saccharin ban organized under the auspices of the Calorie Control Council, an association of manufacturers and suppliers of dietary foods and beverages. The council, which had been organized for several years as a low-profile scientific group, suddenly was facing a significant public education challenge. The FDA was using the substantial resources available to it (its public information department is well staffed and financed) to flood the media with charges against saccharin, and the public was receiving only one side of the story. There were important scientific and public policy questions concerning saccharin which needed to be placed in proper perspective in the media. To organize and manage its public information response and later to support its legislative strategy, the Calorie Control Council turned to Hill and Knowlton. Within hours favorable spokespersons were placed in touch with key national and local media.

One thing the FDA had clearly managed to do was confuse the public. It had told the public saccharin was a dangerous substance, but in the same press release it admitted that it would require an equivalent consumption of over 1250 cans of diet soda before human consumption would equal the amount of saccharin provided to the rats. The public urgently wanted guidance on the relevance of the scientific data to its own personal health habits, and the FDA was not providing this information. The Calorie Control Council's public education program was launched to elucidate the questions concerning the safety of saccharin. This was an extensive communications program directed toward three audiences: the general public, third-party groups with a special interest in the issue (health groups, citizen groups, medical professionals, etc.), and, eventually, the Congress.

It became clear early in the campaign it would require intervention by Congress to prevent the FDA from banning saccharin. Only Congress had the power to suspend the authority it had granted to the agency.

The Calorie Control Council believed the saccharin ban was unwarranted as a matter of science and public policy. This was a view shared by many leading scientists, members of Congress, former government officials, and several private health groups. The public affairs assignment was to encourage the articulation of this point of view in the media and to develop a program for its communication to Congress and to the general public on a nationwide basis. It was not an easy task.

The scientific issues of the saccharin controversy were complex and not easily communicated. Scientists themselves were in sharp dispute over the scientific evidence. Few medical issues had been subjected to so much scrutiny with so little consensus resulting among the scientific experts.

If there had been consensus on the scientific evidence, there was none on the public policy consequences of the evidence. If saccharin were established to be a "weak carcinogen" (as one study suggested), was it sound public policy to disregard totally its benefits in determining an appropriate regulatory action? Many felt that the saccharin situation underscored the need for a revision of our food laws and the development of a more responsive drug regulatory policy.

The council's strategy was to identify and place spokespersons with media outlets who could effectively challenge the scientific and public policy basis for the FDA action. Hill and Knowlton counseled against using self-serving industry spokespersons. Publicity efforts were concentrated on the studies and statements of nonindustry scientists, medical authorities, and other third-party sources with qualified credentials and public credibility. It was important for the public to understand that scientific data are subject to diverse interpretations of the same "factual" information.

With the growing concern about the high incidence of cancer the public needed to be reassured that the scientific evidence against saccharin was inconclusive. Despite the one Canadian test the scientific evidence concerning saccharin's safety on balance weighed heavily in saccharin's favor. (This was confirmed 2 years later in additional tests.)

The public also needed to be informed about saccharin's benefits. Saccharin had an 80-year history of safe human use, including use by over 10 million American diabetics who must control their caloric intake. In recent years, saccharin has been widely used as an integral part of dietary management. With no substitute for saccharin available, the removal of popular and convenient saccharin dietary products such as diet sodas and beverages, canned fruits, noncaloric tabletop sweeteners, and other dietary foods was destined to make it more difficult for many to lead a normal life.

A primary objective of our public education program, therefore, was to direct information on saccharin to those individuals and groups who benefit most from its use. According to our research this included more than 44 million Americans. We targeted these individuals and groups for special communicative efforts.

Our goal was not only to get these groups to oppose publicly the ban but, more important, to communicate their views to Congress. We worked closely with such groups as the American Diabetes Association, American Medical Association, American Society of Internal Medicine, American Society of Bariatric Physicians, and the Diet Workshop, all of which opposed an immediate and total ban of saccharin.

As it became clear that Congress would intercede in the saccharin controversy, a communication program designed to convey our message to members of Congress, especially those serving on health subcommittees, was developed. Like most Americans, members of Congress are influenced by what they learn in the media. Media relations efforts were intensified in key congressional districts. And since members of Congress also rely heavily upon their staffs and constituents for information, keeping these individuals informed became a top priority.

It was critical to the campaign to sustain the public's interest in the saccharin controversy for several months. This required taking advantage of every news opportunity and utilizing Hill and Knowlton's nationwide network of offices to keep the issue alive not only in the national media but in the state and regional media as well. Since every member of Congress would eventually vote on the saccharin issue, it was important that this national media attention result in an outpouring of letters to Congress.

While only a handful of reporters attended the FDA's first press conference, over 200 reporters attended the second a month later. By now saccharin was a major story in all news media. While the FDA was announcing its proposed ban inside the building, a "counter" press conference by diabetics and others opposed to the saccharin ban was held on the steps of the FDA building and received equal coverage in the evening news telecasts. By the time of the FDA's public hearings a month later the press was giving major coverage to opposition groups coming to Washington to testify against the saccharin ban.

The public education program was helpful in moving the issue away from the FDA and into the halls of Congress. Initial reaction from many Washington Hill watchers was that Congress could not be made to go against the FDA. However, those observers failed to appreciate the enormous (and appropriate) influence which the media and constituent communications have upon Congress. When the votes were tabulated in Congress, only 30 of the 535 members voted in support of the FDA. Little more than 9 months after the FDA's original announcement, the President signed into law the bill which mandated an 18-month moratorium while further studies of saccharin safety were conducted.

Several essential guides to action can be seen by examining the public education campaign we undertook on behalf of the saccharin producers:

Publicize It

Kant, after all, knew what he was talking about. For in publicity, in the simple telling of what has occurred or will occur, is found the most potent weapon for combating regulators. The job becomes one that involves more than merely "getting ink" for a client's opinions and views. Rather, it must seek to inform selected publics about what is going on and how it will affect them. The publics are invited to respond not to us but to the political process itself. Every action taken in every office in Washington has ramifications that directly influence the way in which people live and earn their living. In this respect, public affairs does nothing more than "tell it like it is."

Enter the Process

Elaborate and often imperious rules govern the public's entrance into the regulatory process. For every notice of rule making appearing in the *Federal Register,* there are periods of time allotted for public comment about the proposed rule. Public affairs firms guide clients through this tangled forest of triplicate forms and allow them to make the strongest possible argument for their position. When it is advisable, we publicize their response, getting the message about the consequences of a regulation even more forcibly into the public mind.

Develop Allies

One of the most helpful strategies is to develop the allies upon whom a client can count for verbal, testimonial or political and financial support. Going over lists of potential allies, getting in touch with them, finding out their views, and developing media publicity and political input strategies for their points of view constitute one of the most time-consuming, ardous tasks of contemporary public affairs counseling. Yet this task is well worth the effort.

For once allies have been found and reached, they can have tremendous impact upon the legislators who oversee and fund the regulators. A rule change which seems to affect the steel industry, for example, may in turn affect the transportation, automotive, defense, and communications fields. These industries, as part of the basic task of doing business in an increasingly interdependent industrial environment, will be very much concerned about developments in fields related to their own. That concern should be allowed to work for the client: publicity, politics, and business health do go hand in hand.

Congress the Target

Congress becomes one of the most important tools for influencing the regulatory process. Public affairs efforts work through the offices of legislators whose states or districts are directly affected by proposed rule changes. The loss of jobs or taxable revenues in anyone's state or home district is a cause for grave concern. Public affairs endeavors should show the legislators just how extensive such losses might be. Moreover, when rule making reflects an avoidance of congressional directives or an unwarranted extension of authority, congressional thinkers are quick to spot the danger to the entire federal structure. The purse-strings control that Congress exerts over the regulatory structure is still the most effective deterrent to runaway regulation.

But here a caveat must be offered. Congress seldom acts against the public interest as it perceives it. This is not to say that there are no legislative mistakes. Rather, there are few senators or representatives for whom the serving of the public's interest is not a paramount motive. While there is disagreement about what the public interest is and what best serves it, the belief that it ought to guide action is real. *You never can succeed by advocating a position contrary to the perceived public interest.* Rather, try to demonstrate how a client's position is compatible with that interest.

The saccharin case study provides several graphic examples of the role that information plays in public education. Great quantities of information must be digested and retained for eventual usage. This information, which frequently would never be brought to public attention without the efforts of the public affairs specialist, is the basic building block of the work of public affairs counseling.

Developing that information and providing it to the media or to either the general public or a specific constituency—these are the arts in which public affairs counseling specializes.

THE TARGETS

Our work lends itself to the grammar of military strategy: we talk of campaigns and battles, of attack and defense. It becomes clear that our activities must be directed to two possible targets: the media or the Congress. Regulatory agencies can be influenced best through one of these forces; there is only a minimal opportunity to alter directly the actions of the invisible government.

Target 1: The Media

Despite the arguments of academic critics about the nature and scope of the media, the media are monolithic neither in purpose nor in outlook. For every conceivable audience or constituency there are several media outlets, and this diversity, along with the competition it creates, provides the public affairs specialist with the opportunity to try to bring a particular message to a particular audience.

The media, in addition, are absolutely voracious; they need a plentiful, daily supply of the one food upon which they thrive: news. The job is to bring newsmaker and news reporter together.

In Washington, two diverse types of news contacts are called for by clients. When a company devises a new product or a new service, it has in effect created news. Through the organization of press briefings, visits to editorial and reportorial offices, and a host of similar vehicles, endeavors are made to bring the news to the news media. They, of course, are free to reject the efforts. On a crowded news day, reporters are simply too busy to attend all the events in and around Washington. But, with a population of some 3 million, the Washington area is a major market of professionals, government employees, and political and thought leaders. So it is incumbent upon the public affairs specialist to try to make journalists aware of such product and service developments.

The other major focus is issue-oriented. Trade associations, businesses, and other groups must speak out on the issues which affect them. They want to talk to any of a number of audiences: governmental leaders, their own members, members of potentially allied groups, and the public at large. The media form the channel to these audiences. Extensive press coverage of an issue or an event tells these audiences that something important is happening, something which may directly alter their lives or livelihoods. The media animate political debate and change the flow of politics. Students of political journalism refer to this process as "agenda setting," and the public affairs role is to try to place an issue or a viewpoint on the press and public agenda in order to increase the likelihood that the issue will gain access to and prominence upon congressional and White House agendas.

An example of this approach to agenda setting can be seen in the Hides Action Program (HAP) though the goal here was legislative rather than regulatory action:

Illustrative Example

Problem Once the mainstay of small industrial towns throughout the central and New England states, the leather industry today is on the verge of extinction. The coup de grâce for the industry appeared to be the unregulated export of American hides to foreign shoe and leather goods manufacturers. Jobs were disappearing, and firms were going under. Upon assessing the scope of the problem, an amalgam of leather goods industries and trade associations approached us for help. A public education campaign was designed to bring the problem before the nation, and (although we were not involved in the lobbying) before the Congress.

Strategy The case was launched with the realization that, except for the most deeply interested workers and managers, there really was no awareness of the problem. What was needed was a campaign which would succeed in creating a public issue where none had existed before. The goal of this campaign? To establish in the public mind that it was essential to retain an equitable share of domestic hides within the United States. The natural constituency for the issue had to be molded into a cohesive, purposeful voice.

The Hides Action Program was created, and such a voice was found. Through HAP and its industry participants, newsletters, backgrounders, press briefings, and even rallies were generated. Because many of the issue's potential supporters were largely ignorant of the facts, much HAP communication was directed at the leather goods industry itself.

Implementation A threefold communications attack was organized. Constituent communications were designed to provide factual material and information about ongoing HAP programs. Direct contacts with key members of the press resulted in articles in major newspapers and in opinion-influencing magazines such as *Retailweek* and *Forbes.*

On the third level, mass rallies were staged in both Boston and Lewiston, Maine. These rallies received extensive play in the local print and electronic media (the Boston rally was covered in the evening news of all four Boston TV stations, for example) and thereby brought to the immediate attention of such influential political figures as Speaker Thomas P. O'Neill, Sen. Edward M. Kennedy, and Sen. Edmund S. Muskie. The Lewiston rally demonstrated how sheer legwork, when combined with a dose of creative madness, could produce results even under the most adverse circumstances.

Results A proposal to set formal export limits on hides was sponsored in the Senate, passed by the appropriate subcommittee and committee, but defeated on the floor by eight votes. On the House side, the proposal passed all tests except for the final vote.

These results appeared to spell defeat, but the publicity, interest, and primacy the issue had gained in Congress proved instrumental in forcing the White House to impose satisfactory restrictions upon the trade in hides and leather. Because the hides issue had grown from the provincial concern of a frightened industry to an issue of major national focus, presidential authority and responsiveness did what Congress was not quite able to do.

Target 2: The Hill

The need to reach the decision makers in Congress grows each day as new legislation broadens the role which the legislature plays both in the oversight of executive agencies and in making the policy by which the agencies operate. The United States Constitution mandated a legislatively dominated federal system, but over the years, and especially since the depression and World War II, an executive-dominated system has emerged. This trend seems likely to continue.

There are two primary emphases to our education campaigns once they are brought to bear on the Hill. The goal might be to influence the actual product of congressional activity, the language of legislation, or it might be to seek to encourage the Congress to overrule the policy direction of a regulatory agency or to step into the process to initiate a new direction. Each mode of legislative public relations takes on a distinctive character.

In the first instance, lobbying to achieve a particular legislative goal, our most effective means of moving the legislative process lies in direct contact with key lawmakers and congressional staff members. When a staffer writes a position paper for a legislator, it is the public affairs job to make sure that the staffer has heard and understood the client's views. It is preferable to work with the media within the representative's home district. This may involve feeding radio "actualities" to local stations. But always seek to educate the legislator about the impact that the issue has on the folks back home and the importance they ascribe to his or her actions. The quality of this sophisticated lobbying requires more than mere rhetoric and charm. It requires that the public affairs specialist instruct the client on how to make its case—how to use the facts, the information, and the knowledge for the greatest benefit. With such a method of persuasion, the client's chances are maximized while allowing the legislator ample opportunity to make up his or her own mind. This is exactly what the best consumer groups do; it is what the unions do; it is what the nature of politics in America calls for. The easy days of "booze and broads" are long gone. Lobbying today is blue suits and hard facts.

Illustrative Example

Problem The approach of the 1980 Olympics, the recommendations of President Ford's Commission on Olympic Sports, and the chaotic fragmentation of amateur sports authority in the United States prompted the U.S. Olympic Committee (USOC) to seek passage of the Amateur Sports Act of 1978. Designating the USOC as the coordinating body for amateur sports involving international competition, this bill provided a one-time federal grant of $30 million to the USOC for reaching, training, and supervising amateur athletics and administering this heightened effort. After comparatively easy passage in the Senate (May 8, 1978), the bill went to the House, where a donnybrook was brewing. For the public relations support necessary for the lobbying effort, the USOC turned to Hill and Knowlton.

Strategy House opposition was focused on two issues: the size of the financial authorization and the philosophical issue of government involvement in athletics. The public education strategy sought to cut through the opposition in two ways. First, a comprehensive public information campaign was organized. A series of media briefings, releases, and contacts with journalists was launched. While the media campaign continued, an intensive lobbying effort was under way on Capitol Hill. After three members of the House introduced the Senate-passed Amateur Sports Act, additional cosponsors for the legislation were sought.

Implementation The first test of the legislation occurred in a House Judiciary subcommittee, which reported the legislation without provision for federal financial assistance. USOC lobbyists went to work and had extraordinary success: the full Judiciary Committee reversed the action of its subcommittee.

At this point, only days remained in the 1978 congressional session, and adjournment before passage of the legislation would mean that the whole legislative process would have to be repeated in the next Congress. Therefore, the bill was brought to the House floor under an expedited proceeding which would require a two-thirds vote for passage. Some members objected to the procedure, and while the bill received 244 votes, a clear majority, it fell 25 votes short of the necessary two-thirds vote. Returning to the more favorable climate of the Senate, that chamber passed another version of the bill, providing for less financial assistance. This version was accepted by the House and was passed only 3 hours before it adjourned.

Results The unprecedented legislation provided a major boost to American amateur athletics. Federal financial assistance would be provided to amateur athletics for the first time, and the programs would be better coordinated under the direction of one central organization. This effort was a classic example of combining an effective media campaign with a skillfully executed legislative strategy.

An added goal for lobbying is the redress of grievances held against the regulatory agencies and other arms of the executive branch of the government. Especially since Watergate, Congress has become very jealous of its constitutional prerogatives. It is careful to guard its delegated authority from executive encroachment and is even more attentive when the direction of that encroachment runs counter to what it believes was the spirit of the authority it delegated to the executive agency.

The troubles of the Federal Trade Commission make an obvious case in point, for the FTC finds itself in trouble not from failing to do its job (the standard complaint offered before those responsible for congressional oversight) but from having extended its conception of what the job is. In a sense, Sen. Wendell H. Ford's consumer subcommittee of the Commerce, Science, and Transportation Committee took the FTC to task for doing its job too well.

Many in the business community would be delighted to see an easing of the FTC's investigatory and corrective powers. The constant broadening of its powers led the FTC to create an atmosphere of doubt and contempt on the part of those businesses it sought to regulate. When any constituency finds itself doubting the legitimacy of those who hold authority over it, the result is chaos and conflict. Businesses, in doubt over the legitimacy of their own actions as well as those of their federal overseers, begin to contract and wither rather than to expand and prosper. In times of international, political, and economic flux, in times which witness the subsidization of foreign industry's competition with domestic industry, in times which see the American people in an energy war of survival, such uncertainties as those raised by regulators run amok are especially crippling. At such times, public affairs efforts by businesses and trade groups should be considered.

7 LIVING WITH AGENCY ACTION

AL LANGER
Publisher, McGraw-Hill's Regulatory Impact Service

The recent outflow of publicity and political discussion focused on the negative aspects of federal regulation seems to have produced one of two reactions in the hearts and minds of American businesses: mortal fear or seething resentment at being generally "victimized" by an elusive band of conspirators known as the regulators.

But just as these reactions are not particularly comfortable human emotions, neither are they sensible business reactions to current realities. The fact is, these primal responses often emanate simply from a fear of the unknown—a lack of awareness, understanding, and informed involvement in a legislative-administrative-judicial process that, despite its intricacies and complexities, is nonetheless knowable. Knowledge itself, of course, does not guarantee accommodation: "Know thine enemy" remains legitimately operative when businesses choose to wage the good fight against specific regulations. But many a battle can be averted and more harmonious living with agency action can be structured if business will invest in some reliable long-range strategies for enhancing its basic awareness of the shifting idiosyncrasies and dynamics of the individual regulatory agencies as they address their separate missions and agendas.

At a minimum, these strategies can reduce vulnerability to the "surprise attack." Better yet, they can empower business to exert greater control over its own destiny, allowing it to work effectively with the regulators before battle lines are drawn and the situation has become hopelessly or needlessly adversarial. Best of all, such strategies can actually pay off by enhancing a business's ability to anticipate the many genuine profit opportunities which continue to flow directly from a host of regulatory activities.

STRUCTURING INTERNAL INFORMATION NEEDS

At the heart of any meaningful strategy for dealing with regulatory agencies is a business's ability to identify its own needs for reliable information on what's happening within what specific agencies. Obviously, most businesses needn't feel compelled to cover the full array of agencies or expect that all the activities within even the most "relevant" individual agencies will necessarily be of interest to them. On the other hand, the splintered activities of more than one agency may be germane to just one small operating aspect of a specific business. And, to complicate matters even further, multiagency activities centered in similar concerns may not be consciously coordinated but, instead, diffuse and confused, leading ultimately to unintended overlapping or conflict among final regulations—the "layering effect."

What any business first needs to develop is its own firm sense of which specific programs and activities within which specific regulatory agencies portend ultimate impact on that business. This may sound like an obvious and simple chore until one contemplates the fact that, even among the specialized services and publications dedicated to regulatory coverage, few approach the organization of the information they deliver from the perspective of a discrete industry or business. Most of these services were chartered and launched on the heels of the creation or expanded authority of a specific agency. Consequently, they tend to monitor a particular agency's activities across the board without special regard for the highly different information needs of the sometimes strange bedfellows who are affected by the diverse activities encompassed by a single agency. For example, the concerns of a Florida citrus grower could hardly seem more different from those of a glass manufacturer, and yet both of these entrepreneurs are vulnerable to regulations promulgated by the Consumer Product Safety Commission (CPSC). Again, by way of example, the concerns of a giant feed-grain processor and a local mom-and-pop candy-making operation would seem to have little in common until, as is now fact, both are hit by a regulation affecting the allowable concentration of polychlorinated biphenyls (PCBs) in equipment integral to both their manufacturing processes.

What may be obvious, but in our experience needs emphasis, is that each individual business or profession must organize its focus and penetration of the regulatory arena with a working inventory of what it assesses as its own regulatory "targets"—something like a perceived hit list of its own vulnerabilities. The next step might be to matrix these potential targets in two ways: according to the agency or agencies with power to regulate and according to broader generic classifications which reflect a natural clustering of individual targets into groups of issue concerns.

These two information-organizing strategies are what McGraw-Hill developed for a specific profession when it launched, in 1980, its first edition of *Regulatory Impact Service (RIS)* for building design professionals (primarily architects and engineers). A key facet of our initial research was to identify what this discrete group of professionals perceived as their own vulnerabilities in terms of federal regulation. In tandem, we independently identified what agencies actually promulgated rules, regulations, standards, and guidelines affecting building design. The "fit" (more precisely, the lack of fit) between perception and actuality was, in this case, itself revelatory. As we had anticipated, the respondents to a mail survey quickly revealed their impatience with the Occupational Safety and Health Administration (OSHA) and the Departments of Health, Education, and Welfare (HEW) and Housing and Urban Development (HUD) but showed little awareness of the potential impact of other agencies on their businesses.

Through a matrixing process, as described above, we were also able to effect a generic clustering of issues; this facilitated both our own information gathering and analyses and the delivery of information to our clients in relatively simple file-and-retrieve schemes intended to mirror clusters and make it easier to identify conflicting or overlapping regulations. For example, by using the generic file key "accessibility," we could continually update our clients on new regulations being developed independently in this area by four different federal agencies—the Department of Defense (DOD), the Department of Housing and Urban Development, the General Services Administration (GSA), and the U.S. Postal Service—each of which was, in varying degrees, coordinating its own efforts with an independent, voluntary standards-setting organization (the American National Standards Institute) and yet another federal creation, the Architectural and Transportation Barriers Compliance Board.

SATISFYING INFORMATION NEEDS

For any business seriously committed to following the rule-making procedures of any federal agency, the *Federal Register* remains the indispensable bible of the trade. Published each weekday, Monday through Friday, the *Register* is the official record of agency rules at their various stages of development. But as if the *Register*'s sheer bulk (87,012 pages in 1980) were not sufficiently intimidating, its language is often accessible only to those thoroughly conversant in legalese. (In fairness, it should be noted that the clarity of a rule's format and language is the responsibility not of the Government Printing Office, publisher of the *Register,* but of the individual agency promulgating a rule; great variations in rule structuring and basic prose style are apparent across the gamut of agencies.) Furthermore, the *Register*-recorded explanations of various issues which an agency has considered in its efforts to choose among alternatives in shaping a rule are often obscure or fail to reflect or even acknowledge the concerns of a particular industry or business which may be seriously affected by the rule. The point is, it is nearly impossible merely to read through a given rule of major significance with the expectation that its full impact can be grasped.

Any major rule generally passes through a long and complicated process of development. This, a rule's history, bears heavily on its final shape, which may be a mere remnant of that history. However, buried or strewn along the development path are substantial and substantive clues to the final scope and intent of the rule. Among these clues are, for example, records documenting policy shifts (at administrative levels within an agency and/or at the secretarial or presidential level), interagency memoranda of agreement, draft reports (accepted, modified, revised, or rejected) from outside firms contracting with an agency, written comments and additional research data submitted after a rule was first proposed, and transcripts of public hearings on a proposed rule. What of this cumulative input one does or does not see reflected or acknowledged in a final rule may be even more important to an informed sense of what rule making in the same area might be expected in the future.

Illustrative Example

In the spring of 1980, in an admirably coordinated effort, three federal regulatory powers—the Department of Agriculture (USDA), the Food and Drug Administration (FDA), and the Environmental Protection Agency (EPA)—simultaneously published proposed new rules extending their respective authorities to restrict further the potential contamination of the food chain by a class of identifiably hazardous substances known as polychlorinated biphenyls (PCBs). Together, the rules proposed to mandate the removal of PCBs in concentrations of more than 50 parts per million from virtually all equipment and machinery found in or around facilities that handle, process, package, or store the nation's food, feed, or commercial agricultural chemicals (pesticides and fertilizers). In addition, the rules proposed to ban any on-site storage of PCB liquids in a concentration exceeding 50 parts per million.

The agencies' concerted action followed less than a year after EPA's "final PCB ban rule." Since July 1979, that rule has prohibited all manufacturing, processing, and distribution in commerce of PCBs, with certain case-by-case exemptions and two broader exemptions: "totally enclosed" systems, such as those found in transformers and capacitors; and certain authorized uses of PCBs in hydraulic and heat transfer systems. The two other agencies cooperating in this new rule making have enforced PCB bans of even longer standing. By September 4, 1973, all FDA-regulated establishments were to have replaced PCB-containing fluids in all equipment that would come in direct contact with materials being processed; specifically exempted under the FDA's rules had been electrical transformers and condensers. Similarly, since July 1970 the USDA has rejected any new PCB-containing food-processing equipment and the use of any PCB-containing compound in any machinery or equipment likely to come in contact with food. Further, in February 1980, the USDA proposed a rule which would ban all new or replacement equipment containing PCBs from meat, poultry, and egg product plants and establishments inspected under its authority (or by cooperating state authorities).

The three agencies' proposed new rules essentially narrow, if not totally close, the gaps and discrepancies left by previous rule making, by:

- Setting a *common cross-agency cutoff point* for acceptable concentrates of PCBs at not more than 50 parts per million, thus bringing an additional million pounds of PCBs under regulatory control

- Applying the PCB ban (50 parts per million limit) *even* to equipment and machinery *not in direct contact with food, feed, or food-packaging materials,* thus including under the ban several formerly "exempt" items (transformers; capacitors, with one exception; heat transfer systems; electromagnets)

- Extending the PCB ban (50 parts per million limit) *beyond* new and replacement equipment *to include also existing, in-place equipment and machinery* used or stored in or around the affected facilities

- *Banning the storage,* in and around regulated facilities, of any PCB materials in concentrations exceeding the 50 parts per million limit

In October 1980, the USDA, FDA, and EPA extended the original comment periods on these proposed rules to December 4, 1980. While the shape of the final rules has not yet been determined, clearly they will supersede what EPA called its "final PCB ban rule" in January 1979.

This is a classic example of how the regulatory process takes on momentum and dynamism that demand constant tracking from the earliest possible time and betray any firm notion of "final," an appellation that can seduce the unwary into the dangerous assumption that there is no longer a need to track a specific issue. In other words, it's never too early to begin, but it's always too early to quit when solid investigation of regulatory agencies is a professional commitment. The savvy industry or facility affected by the PCB rules of any one of these three agencies would have expanded its vision to encompass the others and, with intelligent tracking, have surmised long before the fact that there would indeed be a progessive, across-the-board tightening of PCB restrictions. In 1979, several real or near-miss industrial accidents attributed to leaking transformers themselves lent impetus to this tightening up. But the most significant clue to long-range possibilities was probably the first report on hazardous substances issued by the government's Interagency Regulatory Liaison Group (IRLG). That report not only set forth a tentative schedule of proposed actions for 1978 but also clearly recommended the joint development of EPA-FDA regulations on PCBs. The EPA and FDA subsequently joined with the Food Safety and Quality Service of the USDA to determine whether any additional controls were necessary to protect public health further from the use of PCB-containing equipment in or around food and feed facilities; hence the three-party development of new rules. Any potentially affected industry or facility that had restricted its attention to only one of the agencies with the power to regulate hazardous substances had, in effect, however unwittingly, been jeopardizing its efforts to anticipate the future intelligently.

"Never Underestimate . . .": Sizing Up the Breadth and Scope of Authority

The preceding case illustrates the necessity of creating a tracking system sensitized to picking up the potential congruence and impact of the activities of a multiplicity of regulatory authorities with overlapping concerns and jurisdictions. Equally important, however, is the analytical ability to make an early assessment of the dimensions—breadth, scope, and impetus for development—of a single isolated regulation. For in many cases the regulation's ultimate size and force can assume proportions far beyond those anticipated by the public at large or even intended by the enabling authority. Conversely stated, be kindly warned: Never underestimate the potential of even a seemingly innocuous legislative mandate, because the regulatory agency charged with casting the technical program to enact it can often reveal a startling ambition and overreach never envisioned by Congress.

Illustrative Example

In November 1978, the Department of Energy (DOE) published an advance notice of proposed rule making to add to Title 10, Chapter II, of the *Code of Federal Regulations* a new part 435, "Energy Performance Standards for New Buildings" (BEPS), developed in response to a mandate issued in the Energy Conservation for New Buildings Act of 1978 (Public Law 94-385). This advance notice (ANPR), published not by requirement but at the DOE's own discretion, afforded the public its first real exposure to the preliminary format of the standards. The ANPR also set out a calendar of one-day public meetings in each of three cities, scheduled, however, to begin only 10 days later, with written comments requested by December 15. Reflecting this time compression and the limited distribution of the ANPR itself, the DOE received only 105 written and 33 oral comments: a total of 138, including the input of only seven identifiable architectural or engineering firms—without a doubt one of the professional groups that could have been expected to be most severely impacted by this sweeping and controversial new approach to energy conservation.

The DOE's target date for a final rule on BEPS at that time was August 1979, but despite the relatively small number of comments generated by the ANPR, the die was cast for a long and protracted battle between the DOE and the building industry and, indeed, within the building industry itself.

One year after the publication of the ANPR, the DOE published a heavily revised notice of proposed rule making (NPR) on BEPS and opened a comment period extended through the end of April 1980, including 19 days of public hearings in six cities. The NPR spanned 61 pages in the *Federal Register* and was ultimately supplemented by nearly 2000 pages of technical support documents. But still missing from the proposed rule were two key subjects, "Implementation" and "Administrative Review," as well as two key appendixes, all reserved for future rule making but absolutely critical to any informed judgment on the efficacy of BEPS in their totality.

The vulnerability of BEPS became so apparent in this second lively (if not absolutely bruising) round of comment that the DOE itself finally petitioned Congress for an extension of time to modify further the proposed standards. In October 1980, the President signed into law (Public Law 96-399) a new act of Congress (Housing and Development Act of 1980), which includes authorization for the DOE to delay final notice of rule making on BEPS until April 1, 1983, and implementation until April 1, 1984.

Much of the dust having now settled and a delay having been won, the architectural and engineering professions are adopting a more conciliatory attitude toward each other and toward the DOE as it enters the second phase of developing BEPS. But how much of the initial controversy could have been spared, and how many dollars saved, had additional industry groups involved themselves earlier with the DOE's plans for rule making and been poised to perform and articulate more critical analyses at an earlier stage?

Lessons about the value of early recognition of and continuing involvement in the development of a rule of this potential magnitude have apparently been well, if painfully, learned. But in the hope that they will not be forgotten, one of the organizations that credits itself with being among the first to perceive the problems associated with the early versions of BEPS exhorts:

In the course of our work, nearly all other organizations in the building, construction, and design fields came over to our side. But this should be no cause for complacency. We must keep a keen eye on BEPS as they are modified in the months ahead. We want to be sure that the amended document will serve our country well, and our industry too. To this end, we want to cooperate with DOE. We would certainly prefer to have a peaceful resolution of any differences to a confrontation.[1]

Breaking and Entering: Ferreting Out the Hidden Agendas of the Agencies

The most embarrassing revelation of cracks and leaks in any information system designed to track regulation is the publication of a rule that appears, seemingly, without warning and has apparently been developed with little or no consultation with certain businesses or professions that would logically be expected to withstand significant impact.

Illustrative Example

In 1977, after more than 2½ years of study, the CPSC quietly issued a mandatory national *Architectural Glazing Standard.* Unfortunately, few architects were even aware that the standard was in development. And more than a few were caught in the professionally embarrassing circumstance of learning at third hand (manufacturer to contractors to designer) that the materials they had specified on projects that had moved as far as the construction stage were no longer acceptable under the rule.

Then, in the fall of 1979, the CPSC proposed revocation of a certain portion of this standard, in a move that threatened to provoke as much confusion for architects and/ or engineers as the original rule making. Both actions, interestingly, were developed by committees including no representatives of these professions. In September 1980, the CPSC voted 5 to 0 to proceed with revocation of a portion of the standard, in a move applauded lavishly by the International Conference of Building Officials but accepted resignedly, at best, by the community of architects and engineers.

Obviously, there will always be winners and losers in the resolution of disputes that arise between interested and affected parties when a rule is in development. But one cannot expect to come out on the winning side if one is not in there fighting. The key to being a contender is knowing when and where a battle is shaping up. The CPSC is a good example of a particularly tough agency to know, despite its much-admired tendency to make rules in relative openness during the last few years. The difficulty stems perhaps from the breadth of its mandate; Congress authorized it to require labeling to warn consumers of potentially dangerous characteristics of an item or to prohibit the sale of a good which imposes an unreasonable risk to consumers. With such a broad mandate, CPSC can move in hundreds of different directions against a virtually limitless number of targets. Keeping tabs on its every move is well-nigh impossible and certainly is inefficient from the perspective of any one business. The only sensible alternative is planning an intelligent schedule of checkups and check-ins with key staff members at CPSC who have, through an ongoing dialogue, become familiar with a firm's specific interests and information needs. This is, ideally, a function that one should expect to be handled by specialized personnel within trade associations or professional societies or by diligent reporters and analysts on spe-

[1]Charles F. Sepsy, president, American Society of Heating, Refrigerating and Air-Conditioning Engineers, "ASH-RAE Questions BEPS Workability, Cost & Clarity," *Consulting Engineer,* January 1981.

cialized information services, the price of which is often justified many times over by their ability to plug the kind of information gaps which can result in costly errors.

PINPOINTING PROFIT OPPORTUNITIES GROWING OUT OF REGULATION

Business has grown accustomed to viewing regulation negatively, for the most part focusing its planning and analyses on avoiding the costs of complying with rules *after* they have been written. The reasons for this perspective are logical and obvious. A firm naturally wants to minimize any alteration in its operations and thereby avoid incurring the inevitable expenses associated with the disruption of business as usual. This defensive posture is what generally spurs the desire and commitment to keep abreast of regulatory development.

But excellent reasons also exist for early awareness of regulatory developments from a positive, offensive viewpoint. It is probably safe to say that for every regulation developed, a new opportunity is created. At a minimum, a firm thoroughly apprised of new and impending regulations can enhance its marketability by underscoring the value of this knowledge to clients (and potential clients) who stand to be affected by new regulation. The following lead paragraphs from two articles published last spring in McGraw-Hill's *Regulatory Impact Service (RIS)* should demonstrate this point.

Illustrative Examples

"During the next five years, at least, building design professionals could turn a little-publicized provision within the Crude Oil Windfall Profit Tax Act of 1980 (Public Law 96-223) to the distinct advantage of their clients. The Act is an amendment to the Internal Revenue Code of 1954; as such, it offers an expanded tax incentive to individuals deciding to incorporate energy-conservation measures into their homes. Amended in part by Title II of the Act (Energy Conservation and Production Incentives) is the residential energy credit incentive. By advising clients of which energy-conservation measures are eligible for deduction under the Internal Revenue Code, as amended by the windfall profit tax act, design professionals may in effect stretch a client's budget and at the same time allow themselves more room for innovative design experiments."

"Engineers and architects can anticipate an increasing number of projects involving alternative energy sources, such as solar, wind, geothermal, ocean thermal, hydro-electric, and other energy systems. The reason is that, over the next five years particularly, many businesses will be investing more than ever in the remodeling, rehabilitation, alteration, and addition of alternate energy properties. These businesses will be planning to take advantage of increased tax incentives provided by the Crude Oil Windfall Profit Tax Act of 1980. The Act increases credit percentages for certain business energy investment expenditures, expands the definitions of some of the qualifying energy properties, and adds a number of items (from hydroelectric generating facilities to solar process heating systems to alumina electrolytic cells) to the list of properties eligible for credit under the Internal Revenue Code."

Similarly, a close tracking of three other bills before the Ninety-sixth Congress allowed *RIS* to inform its clients that they could inform *their* clients (owners and developers) of special tax deductions available to them for rehabilitating certified historic structures and removing architectural barriers. Direct feedback from both design professionals and their attorneys indicated the marketing edge that this information provided them in generating new business.

Other regulations open up direct avenues to new profits. For example, the EPA's Construction Grants Management Program now requires that small communities comply with public participation regulations. To effect compliance, many communities are now engaging consulting architects and engineers to prepare applications and manage programs that assure the receipt of grant moneys and a new source of fee-paid work for design professionals. Again, a myriad of new legislation and regulations expressing national commitments to conserving energy has opened up, for the design community, the opportunity to fill a demand for services ranging from providing technical surveys and recommendations for the installation of energy conservation measures to actually designing for both retrofit and new construction of federal buildings required to meet new standards of energy consumption.

Yet other regulations provide invaluable tips on what technological or service innovations could prove profitable for a business in the future. For example, the implications of the progressive tightening of controls on PCBs cited earlier led a few aware companies to accelerate their development of retrofill techniques and services that are now in greater demand than can be met, as affected facilities hasten their efforts to comply with what they perceive will soon be final regulations in this area.

The Reagan Administration's Appeal to Business for Aiding Regulatory Reform

During the 1980 presidential campaign, candidate Ronald Reagan repeatedly pledged that, if elected, he would move swiftly to relieve industry and the private sector of the "burdens" of excessive regulation. Once in office, President Reagan wasted little time in translating that pledge into a document that assumes the force of law.

Spelled out in Executive Order 12291 of February 17, 1981, the presidential intent could hardly be clearer: "to reduce the burdens of existing and future regulations, increase agency accountability for regulatory actions, provide for presidential oversight of the regulatory process, minimize duplication and conflict of regulations, and insure well reasoned regulations." Also spelled out in the order is the creation of the Presidential Task Force on Regulatory Relief, headed by Vice President George C. Bush.

The President's order is a *major departure* from past regulatory policy. It requires, for one thing, that "regulatory action shall not be undertaken unless the potential net benefits to society outweigh the potential costs to society." Furthermore, it directs federal rule makers to choose the *least costly alternative* among regulatory approaches.

To those ends, a regulatory-impact analysis is now required for *every major rule* that an agency intends to issue. According to the executive order, a "major rule" is described as one which is *likely* to have an effect of more than $100 million on the economy annually; *likely* to cause a major increase in costs or prices for consumers, individual industries, or geographic sectors; and/or *likely* to produce "significant" adverse effects on competition, employment, investment, productivity, or the ability of United States–based enterprises to compete with foreign-based enterprises in domestic or export markets.

The required regulatory-impact analysis must:

- Describe the *potential benefits* of the rule, including benefits which cannot be measured in monetary terms, and specify *who* will receive these benefits.

- Describe the *potential costs* of the rule, including adverse effects which cannot be measured in monetary terms, and specify *who* will bear these costs.

- Determine the *potential net benefits* of the rule.

- Describe *alternative approaches* that could achieve the same regulatory goals at lower costs and show cause why, if proposed, such alternatives could not be legally adopted.

The order reasserts the power of the executive over the agencies by delegating to the director of the Office of Management and Budget (OMB) the responsibility and authority to *review any proposed or final major rule* and the regulatory-impact analysis attached to it. By virtue of this authority, OMB is now in a position to delay publication of any proposed or final rule by indicating an intent to comment. Once the OMB director has decided that a rule will be reviewed, the rule may not be published in any form until OMB's review has been completed.

Under the excutive order, the agencies are also ordered to *review existing major rules* and perform regulatory-impact analyses on them. The OMB director, under the direction of the presidential task force, is allowed to designate what rules currently in effect are ripe for review. In addition, the agencies are ordered to make their preliminary and final impact analyses available to the public. (Preliminary analyses will accompany proposed rules; final analyses will accompany final rules.)

Any business may request a review of an existing federal regulation by filing with the secretary (or titled head) of the agency enforcing the rule a document which should include a written "summary page," constructed in the following format, supported with appropriate documentation:

- Source of regulation (agency enforcing the regulation)

- Citation (precise legal reference)

- Description of problems (adverse impact/or impacts)

- Estimated cost (defensible estimate)

- Estimated benefits (defensible estimate)

- Other impacts (nonquantifiable impacts)

- Originator of request (name, address, and telephone of person to reach)

A copy of the *summary page only* should be sent to *each* of the following:

The Hon. Malcolm Baldridge
Secretary of Commerce
Washington, D.C. 20230
Attention: Regulatory Relief

C. Boyden Gray, Esq.
Office of the Vice President
Washington, D.C. 20501
Attention: Regulatory Relief

Dr. James C. Miller, III
Executive Director
Presidential Task Force on Regulatory Relief
Old Executive Office Building
Washington, D.C. 20503
Attention: Regulatory Relief

Under Executive Order 12291, the OMB is also mandated to *identify duplicative or conflicting rules*. In this effort, too, the administration is seeking business input in identifying the impacts of regulation on industry customers so that the ripple effect of various regulations can be more clearly established. Finally, the OMB is authorized to *develop methods for estimating both the benefits and costs* of agency regulations, either individually or in aggregate.

In a flurry of spring briefings for business leaders following the release of Executive Order 12291, top administration officials fleshed out the details on precisely how business could most effectively state its case to regulators (and those charged with monitoring them). Basically, their advice underscores the new cost-benefit ethic and clearly connects the item "estimated costs" (in the request-for-review document outlined above) with the administration's emphasis on the necessity to improve productivity and "reindustrialize" the American economy. For example, these officials point out that among the defensible estimated costs of a regulation are business estimates of the amount of capital drained away—say, from funds available for modernizing plant facilities—simply to cover either the technical costs of *actual compliance* or the administrative costs of *documenting or proving compliance* with a particular regulation or set of regulations. Business is also being urged to examine regulations in market terms: What market failure does a regulation address? What caused that market failure? Does the regulation proposed (or in existence) alleviate or aggravate the problem? Do any alternatives exist—particularly market-oriented alternatives such as labeling strategies, performance standards, or economic incentives?

In essence, the administration is inviting businesses and associations to perform and submit their own regulatory-impact analyses—the more specific, the better—to assure more rational rule making. The extent to which businesses can be responsive (especially to the implicit demand for cost analyses) depends, of course, on what internal mechanisms might already have been developed for tracking expenses associated with regulatory compliance or on what resources a business is willing to commit to instituting such a tracking system. This is basically a policy decision within any corporation.

In arriving at this decision, business should weigh two factors that will condition federal responsiveness to any cost-benefit input from the business community. First, Executive Order 12291 requires that review and revision work on major regulations continue to be performed by the regulatory agencies themselves. It remains to be seen whether the appointed heads of these agencies and the Presidential Task Force on Regulatory Relief can assure that staff analysts set aside any possible vested interests in previously developed regulation and conduct their reviews in full responsiveness to the intentions of the new administration. Second, the Supreme Court can be expected to wield considerable influence on the extent to which the administration can impose strict cost-benefit analyses. This caution is supported by the Supreme Court's June 17, 1981, ruling (in the cotton-dust case) that OSHA must enforce regulations that protect American workers from exposure to toxic substances to the greatest extent feasible, *without regard* to the balance between costs and benefits.

8 MANAGING AGENCY INVESTIGATIONS

McNEILL STOKES
Stokes & Shapiro
Attorneys at Law

The problem of how to deal with administrative investigations touches almost every business at one time or another. Many techniques are available for dealing effectively with administrative investigations. A business can clearly influence the outcome by taking steps to manage actively the course of the investigation. A commitment to a practice of preventive law may totally avoid or shorten an investigation, and careful preparation can influence the course and direction of the investigation itself. Knowledge of the limits and reaches of agencies can provide another means by which an individual or a business can manage an investigation. But most important is the use of common sense in all dealings with administrative agencies. With common sense as a guide and active participation and management by the business, the chance of a successful outcome to an investigation will be increased. Regardless of the source or reason for an investigation, certain principles can always be applied.

Agencies engage in investigations either as a result of complaints or as part of a scheme to ensure compliance with the law. A business which is the object of an investigation can also take the offensive and actively manage the investigation. The best strategy is a commitment to a policy of preventive management directed toward avoiding legal problems, not of dealing with them once they occur. Management should be prepared to take the offensive to prove that practices and procedures are within the law, rather than adopting a defense that they are not outside the law.

Agency investigations are not always adverse to a business; sometimes an investigation may be conducted at the business's request. Government agencies can aid a business, and it need not always be on the defensive. Certainly employers who initiate investigations should be prepared to manage the investigative process.

Illustrative Example

A union pickets to force a general contractor to make nonunion subcontractors sign collective bargaining agreements or, if they refuse, to kick them off the job. This is an

illegal union secondary boycott in violation of the National Labor Relations Act. The general contractor or the subcontractors may file with the National Labor Relations Board (NLRB) an unfair-labor-practice charge to obtain relief. The complaining contractor should also greatly aid in managing the investigation by the NLRB and have witnesses available to testify directly as to what the union agents have said and the conduct of the picketing to prove an illegal purpose. The NLRB can then initiate an investigation, which can be completed within 72 hours in accordance with its regulations, and seek an injunction against the union's illegal activity. If the complaining contractor does not take the offensive and have the witnesses immediately available, the investigation will take considerably longer, and the construction project will be affected longer by the illegal picketing.

In addition to complying with all the rules and regulations formulated by the government, a business can best assure itself of success in an investigation by careful preparation. Advance planning and preparation are the best means of assuring that plant and facilities are ready for an inspection and that company personnel are ready to manage that inspection. Careful preparation will avoid many problems during an inspection. A business which is prepared for an inspection will normally stand a much better chance of success than a similar but unprepared business. There are many practical steps a business can take to ready itself for an inspection.

Personnel ought to be advised that they should treat a government inspector politely and courteously. There is no need to be antagonistic. It is a criminal violation to use forceable resistance or to assault a federal investigative officer. Neither should the inspector be considered a friend; there is no need to volunteer information or to elaborate on questions answered. The inspector is looking for violations, and the more information given, the greater the chance of finding something.

Many different techniques can be used to manage an agency investigation. The most important is careful early preparation for an inspection or audit of any kind. For example, the best time to prepare for an Internal Revenue Service (IRS) audit is not when word is received that a return is being audited; the income tax return should have been prepared initially with the assumption that it would be audited. Everything should have been documented and substantiated at that point, when everything was at hand. Businesses generally have fairly reliable record-keeping systems, but individuals need to make a point of organizing a system that works for them.

One technique in preparing for a *routine* inspection is the formulation of a company inspection guide. This guide is imperative for companies that have branch offices so that a branch will know how to react if an inspector is present for a routine inspection. Even smaller companies need to have procedures for their field personnel. For example, construction companies should have supervisors who know how to handle on-site inspections by inspectors. The guide should, at a minimum, outline the company's policies concerning local, state, and federal inspections. Since the guide is not privileged information and so may be obtained by the government, it must be worded very carefully. A more detailed guide should contain procedures to be followed during an inspection. A guide might list which areas of the premises are confidential and which of the company's records are confidential. Since each agency has been granted different powers and different inspection authority, a comprehensive guide should contain procedures pertaining to inspections by the individual agencies. It should set out what powers each agency does or does not have. For example, Food and Drug Administration (FDA) personnel need not be permitted to take photographs during an inspection. A guide to be used during various inspections should state limitations such as the one on the FDA. Whatever the format of the guide, it should clearly direct employees who will be dealing with inspectors as to how the company wants the inspectors treated. Although a guide is helpful for dealing with routine inspections, company personnel should not try to deal with crisis-caused investigations without the benefit of legal advice.

In addition to adoption of an inspection guide, a firm ought to select particular persons who will be responsible for dealing with inspectors. The members of an inspection team might differ according to which agency is conducting the investigation or which facilities are being inspected. One person might be selected to supervise and coordinate the team. That person might also be in charge of training the personnel. The people selected ought to be well-trained company personnel. However, not only must they be knowledgeable about the company, they must also be taught about the powers and limitations of the agency with which they will be dealing. Ignorance on the part of those personnel could cost the company money; there may be penalties for refusing to disclose what the agency has the power to obtain, and costs may arise from disclosing freely what the government is not empowered to obtain. The inspection team must also be selected for good judgment because it may be required to make some judgment calls when dealing with an inspector. A great part of its job will be public relations, and members should also be selected for their diplomacy. The members of the inspection team must be familiar with the company's practices and procedures, they must know the scope of each agency's authority, and they must know how to deal effectively with inspectors.

The inspection team might also be responsible for setting up practice inspections. Such an inspection would ensure that company personnel are familiar with the areas of the plant for which they are responsible. They would learn which facilities and which records are accessible to the government and which are not, and they would thus not need to spend time in consulting a checklist upon any request. Furthermore, a practice inspection would make the team aware of violations which would be visible to inspectors conducting a similar but real inspection. The company would be able to correct the violations before a real inspection and thereby avoid liability. For example, a practice wage and hour inspection by company-hired professionals could disclose violations which could be corrected and thus enable the company to avoid liability for back pay in a future investigation.

Setting the agenda for an inspection would also assure a better outcome. An established agenda would organize the investigation so that necessary company personnel would be ready when needed but would not be kept waiting for hours. An agenda for a smooth-flowing inspection would portray to the inspector the picture of an organized, efficient company. The inspector might not follow the agenda but would accept the schedule if it followed a logical flow. The agenda would thus save the company time and money.

STONEWALLING

The first contact that a business may have with an inspector conducting a routine inspection occurs when the inspector is present at the door requesting admission. The inspector's credentials should be checked and verified with the agency's area office. A copy of the inspection notice or order should be requested and the purpose of the inspection ascertained. All this should be done before the company decides whether to admit the inspector to conduct an investigation. These steps ought to be standard company procedure.

An important decision that a company must make in managing an investigation is whether to admit an inspector without requiring a warrant. The Fourth Amendment was adopted to protect individuals from searches without warrants and without probable cause to believe that an offense has been committed. This amendment has not been limited to cases in which an individual is suspected of criminal behavior but also serves as protection from warrantless administrative searches. Of course, many regulatory statutes and ordinances authorize on-site investigations as a primary means of enforcement. However, the statutory provisions do not override the constitutional protection against warrantless entry onto private property. Despite federal tax laws which permit seizure of private assets to satisfy unpaid tax assessments, the Supreme Court has ruled that the Fourth Amendment protects even a corporation from warrantless seizure of property on private premises to which access is not otherwise available to the seizing officers.[1] The Court has also applied the Fourth Amendment even to inspections by state and local fire and public safety department officials.[2] Thus, even when an investigation is statutorily authorized, a search warrant is probably constitutionally required when permission to enter premises is denied. Some businesses have been successful with the tactic of refusing federal inspectors entry without a search warrant issued on probable cause.

Illustrative Case

The Occupational Safety and Health Act of 1970 authorizes official entry to a workplace for purposes of inspecting the place of employment. An Occupational Safety and Health Administration (OSHA) inspector entered the customer service area of Barlow's, Inc., an electrical and plumbing installation business, and demanded to make an inspection of the shop employee area. Mr. Barlow denied the inspector admission to the shop employee area of his business. Three months later the inspec-

[1]*G. M. Leasing Corp. v. United States,* 429 U.S. 338 (1977).

[2]*See v. City of Seattle,* 387 U.S. 541 (1967); *Camara v. Municipal Court of City and County of San Francisco,* 387 U.S. 523 (1967).

tor returned with an order from the United States district court compelling Barlow to admit the OSHA official. Barlow again refused to admit the inspector and instead went to court to seek injunctive relief against warrantless searches. The lower court declared that the Fourth Amendment requires a warrant for this type of search. Upon appeal, the U.S. Supreme Court upheld the lower court's decision, declaring unconstitutional that part of the Occupational Safety and Health Act which authorized inspections without warrant.[3]

The Court in *Barlow* indicated that the reasonableness of a warrantless search will depend upon the balance of enforcement needs and the guarantees of privacy found within each statute. The Court pointed out that some statutes, such as the Mine Safety and Health Act and the Air Pollution Control Act, specifically allow for resort to the courts for injunctive relief when permission to inspect or investigate is denied, a provision which the Court impliedly regarded to be sufficiently protective of the rights of the business involved. For inspection pursuant to statutes not specifically providing procedural guarantees for privacy, the *Barlow* decision seems to require at least that the agency prove probable cause for issuance of a warrant. The requirement of a warrant when entry is denied will probably be applied to inspections under other regulatory statutes. In a case decided immediately after *Barlow,* the U.S. Supreme Court vacated a lower court order which had compelled a company doing business with the federal government to comply with Executive Order 11246, which requires, as a condition for a government contract, government access to the company's premises and books.[4] The regulated party who objects to entry is protected from unreasonable searches by the requirement that the agency prove to a neutral judge the necessity and reasonableness of its action.

However, the Supreme Court concluded in *Barlow* that a regulation setting out a procedure for ex parte warrants (warrants obtained without the employer being heard in opposition) would be within the authority of OSHA and would be constitutional. OSHA subsequently issued a final rule confirming the authority of the secretary of labor to obtain ex parte inspection warrants. In a new twist on the subject of the secretary's authority to conduct investigations, the Labor Department contended that the warrant which was sought *must* be issued ex parte.

Illustrative Case

An application for a warrant was filed by OSHA as a result of complaints by some employees of Colorado Fuel and Iron Co. (CF&I). The application assured that the inspection was part of an "inspection program designed to assure compliance with the Act and that there were reasonable legislative and administrative standards for conducting the inspection." However, it didn't describe what the program was or what the reasonable standards were. The application then listed the complaints and the "urgency" with which the follow-ups were conducted. The application, which was filed 15 months after the dates of three of the five complaints, requested that the court

---

[3]*Marshall v. Barlow's, Inc.,* 436 U.S. 307 (1978).

[4]*United States v. Mississippi Power & Light Co.,* 436 U.S. 942 (1978).

issue ex parte a twenty-man, 60-day inspection warrant. In responding to the application, Judge Fred M. Winner first asked to hear from an OSHA witness who was sitting in the courtroom in camera testimony regarding the need for the issuance of a warrant ex parte, but the secretary refused. Admitting that to meet an emergency or to avoid surreptitious removal of a dangerous situation warrants should be issued ex parte, the judge was perplexed at the argument that ex parte action was essential to a twenty-man, 60-day operation. But the secretary refused to substantiate his contention that the warrant had to be issued ex parte with any reasons for that contention. Without a showing of cause by OSHA or without granting CF&I a right to be heard, the judge refused to issue the warrant ex parte without a hearing on the issue.[5]

Even when a warrant is necessary for an on-site administrative investigation, issuance does not generally require probable cause, in the criminal law sense, to believe that conditions on the premises are in violation of agency standards. By contrast, in a state decision, an agency was required to meet criminal probable-cause requirements to obtain an inspection warrant. The California Supreme Court denied Cal/OSHA's petition for a hearing on the requirement of criminal probable cause, stating that the "neutral criteria" administrative probable-cause standards enunciated in *Barlow* were inapplicable in California because the state had broad criminal penalties for health and safety violations.[6]

The purpose of administrative probable cause is to ensure neutral application of inspection procedures to a particular establishment. In other words, probable cause for issuance of a warrant may be based upon a showing that reasonable standards for conducting an inspection are satisfied with respect to a particular establishment. When applying to a court or a magistrate for a warrant to inspect, the agency has the burden of proving that the specific place of business which is the subject of the investigation has been chosen on the basis of a general administrative plan for enforcement derived from neutral sources. Therefore, the agency's application for a search warrant should probably include a description of the enforcement plan in order to show that there is a reasonable legislative or administrative inspection program and that the desired inspection fits within that program.[7] Recently, different courts have applied various standards for approval of administrative warrants. For example, in upholding a criminal prosecution based upon evidence gathered during a Drug Enforcement Administration inspection, the Court of Appeals for the Third Circuit ruled that the fact that a pharmacy had never before been inspected to ensure compliance with compulsory record keeping was in itself a circumstance sufficient to justify an administrative warrant.[8] On the other hand, a federal court in Wisconsin ruled that receipt of an employee complaint, without indication of probable cause to believe that a violation exists, is insufficient evidence of probable cause for issuance of a search warrant and therefore quashed an OSHA citation which

---

[5]*In re C.F.&I. Steel Corp.,* _____ F. Supp. _____ (D. Colo. Docket No. 79-W-1581 1980).

[6]*Salwasser Mfg. Co.* (1979 OSHD ¶ 23,659).

[7]*In re Northwest Airlines, Inc.,* 587 F.2d 12 (7th Cir. 1978).

[8]*United States v. Prendergast,* 585 F.2d 69 (3d Cir. 1978).

was based upon evidence gathered from an inspection pursuant to a warrant.[9] Certainly probable cause for the issuance of a search warrant at least requires proof that the inspection is based upon a neutral application of agency procedures.

Illustrative Case

A compliance officer for OSHA attempted to enter a Weyerhaeuser corrugated-box plant in New Jersey but was refused admission by company officials. Afterward, the secretary of labor applied to the federal court for a search warrant, and the court sought to determine whether probable cause existed for the inspection. In denying the secretary's application for a warrant, the court ruled that (1) mere passage of time since a previous inspection does not establish probable cause where there is no information either within the warrant or otherwise in the record to support the assertion that mere passage of time has been used as a standard for conducting inspections; (2) probable cause has not been established under the inspection planning guide, or "worst first" scheme, if there are many establishments with higher hazard ratings that have never been inspected (an indication that the worst-first program has not been followed); and (3) probable cause has not been established by information concerning an establishment's previous violations when the plant has already been reinspected shortly afterward, at which time no further violations have been found and the plant's safety program has been pronounced effective.[10]

Although a business definitely has a right to demand a warrant in most cases, there are some practical considerations. In some cases the inspector may just go away and not bother with attempting to get a search warrant. In other cases an agency will obtain a warrant. Then it is conceivable that an inspector will conduct a much more thorough, picky examination (although that's not official agency policy). Also a desire to maintain a good working relationship with government agency inspectors may be an important consideration. Some companies have found that making inspectors respect their rights gains the agencies' respect. A demand for a warrant may be used defensively by a firm to buy time for some reason. Because of potential dangers a refusal should be used in this way very carefully.

In addition, a business should be aware that there are some limited exceptions to the warrant requirement. Warrantless inspections have been upheld in the enforcement of regulatory statutes aimed at traditionally highly regulated industries. In industries with such an extensive history of government regulation, the Supreme Court has found that no reasonable expectation of privacy can exist.[11] A dealer who chooses to engage in such a business impliedly consents to be subject to government regulation and inspections. Which industries are so pervasively regulated as to escape the warrant requirement hasn't yet been clearly delineated. However, they clearly include such highly regulated industries as liquor and firearms production. In addition to allowing warrantless searches, some statutes provide for penalties if permission to inspect is refused.

[9]*Weyerhaeuser Co. v. Marshall,* 452 F. Supp. 1375 (E.D. Wis. 1978).

[10]*Marshall v. Weyerhaeuser Co.,* 456 F. Supp. 474 (D.N.J. 1978).

[11]*United States v. Biswell,* 406 U.S. 311 (1972); *Colonnade Catering Corp. v. United States,* 397 U.S. 72 (1970).

Illustrative Example

> The federal Food, Drug, and Cosmetic Act provides that "refusal to permit entry or inspection as authorized by [the act] results in a one year imprisonment, a $1,000 fine, or both." Thus the statute authorizing administrative inspections for those businesses falling within the jurisdiction of the FDA includes a specific sanction for refusal to permit an inspection without a warrant. However, as a practical matter FDA inspectors who have been denied access to inspect in the past generally have obtained search warrants. The FDA's *Inspection Operations Manual* instructs inspectors to obtain a warrant when permission to inspect is refused even though the statute doesn't mandate it.

Neither does Fourth Amendment protection extend to "open fields."[12] No search warrant is necessary for an agency inspector to enter those areas of a business which are open to the public and to take note of what anyone on the premises can see. For example, the Supreme Court upheld an air pollution citation which was issued after an outdoor observation of smoke.[13] Exceptions to the warrant requirement ought to be kept in mind when a business makes its initial decision whether to cooperate voluntarily with an agency inspector or to demand a warrant from the inspector.

PROPER INVESTIGATIVE PURPOSE

An important consideration in determining whether to allow an inspector in without a warrant hinges on the purpose of the investigation. If the inspection is not being carried out for a "proper investigative purpose," a company may be justified in refusing admittance.

Even when a statute gives an agency access to all records, the agency may be required to show a proper investigative purpose for any demand for records or information. No agency has been awarded a general warrant power. An agency's request for information is invalid if the purpose for that request is not clear enough to permit a court to determine whether the agency is acting within the bounds of its regulatory authority.

Illustrative Case

> Agents of the Civil Aeronautics Board (CAB) presented themselves at the executive offices of United Air Lines and requested immediate access to all records and documents located on the premises. United offered to make available any records specifically identified and pertinent to the Board's investigation, but the agents refused to disclose the subject of their investigation. The Board sought an injunction to force the airline to comply. Although the Federal Aviation Act grants the Board access to all lands, buildings, and records kept or required to be kept by air carriers, the court held that no statute confers a general warrant power on any agency. Since a proper investigative purpose is an essential predicate to any investigative demand, the demand must be reasonably definite and reasonably relevant to some proper investigative purpose. Therefore, the court ruled that the Board was not entitled to an injunction to force the airline to comply with its overbroad demand.[14]

[12] *Hester v. United States*, 265 U.S. 57, 59 (1924).

[13] *Air Pollution Variance Bd. of Colo. v. Weskin Alfalfa Corp.*, 416 U.S. 861 (1974).

[14] *CAB v. United Air Lines, Inc.*, 542 F.2d 394 (7th Cir. 1976).

If the inspection is, in fact, being carried out for a proper investigative purpose, the company might still choose to take steps to ensure that the scope of the investigation is limited to what is reasonably necessary to accomplish the investigation's purposes. Very often, investigators are required by agency directives to limit the scope of an investigation.

Illustrative Example

OSHA issued a directive instructing its field personnel in the proper scope of a variance investigation. The directive provides that OSHA variance representatives are to inspect only areas concerned with the variance request. The representative must inform the employer that the inspection is not for enforcement purposes but only to evaluate the employer's variance request. If a violation is uncovered, the representative must notify the employer immediately but may not issue a citation. The representative will inform the OSHA area director of the violation and any employer actions to remedy it. Follow-up actions will be left to the area director. If an employee approaches a representative with a complaint, it must also be referred to the area director. The investigation is limited to the variance request.[15]

The investigatory powers of an agency are not boundless. Although with the growth of administrative powers the traditional prohibition against fishing expeditions has been limited, the agency has not been given unlimited power. A demand for information may be invalid if the request is overly broad or irrelevant to the purposes of the investigation. What information is necessary is a matter for agency discretion, though the agency must demonstrate the relevance to the investigation of any particular records requested.

Illustrative Case

Coopers & Lybrand, a firm of certified public accountants, had designed an audit program specifically tailored for its corporate client Johns-Manville Corp. but did not participate in the actual preparation and filing of the company's federal tax returns. In conjunction with its annual audit of Johns-Manville, the IRS issued a summons directing Coopers & Lybrand to produce all books and records relative to the federal audit. While Coopers & Lybrand responded by producing voluminous working papers and documents, it declined to disclose its audit program or the tax pool analysis file prepared by the client for the accountants' use. The IRS filed a petition for judicial enforcement of its summons. According to the IRS, the right to examine the accountants' files came within its statutory power to examine data which might be relevant to a tax audit because they might show tax fraud, because they might show substantial tax liability, and because they would be relevant to establish the state of mind of employees of Johns-Manville at the time when the tax returns were filed. However, the court ruled that although the IRS need not establish probable cause prior to the issuance of a summons, it must establish that the investigation was pursuant to and relevant to a legitimate purpose and that, other administrative steps having been followed, the information was not otherwise available. The court refused to enforce the summons, holding that mere convenience did not make an item producible under IRS summons.[16]

---

[15]OSHA Directive STD-6.2.

[16]*United States v. Coopers & Lybrand,* 550 F.2d 615 (10th Cir. 1977).

An agency's powers are very broad, but there are still limitations to the breadth of an investigation:

> Of course a governmental investigation into corporate matters may be of such a sweeping nature and so unrelated to the matter properly under inquiry as to exceed the investigatory power. . . . But it is sufficient if the inquiry is within the authority of the agency, the demand is not too indefinite and the information sought is reasonably relevant.[17]

RECORDS

There are other ways by which the scope of an investigation may be limited. The individual agencies are limited by what their enabling acts and regulations empower them to do. For example, under OSHA inspectors are limited to examining records which are required under the act. More sensitive internal reports, even if they bear on the subject of the investigation, may be withheld from an OSHA inspector if they aren't required under the act. In addition, certain records simply need not be made available to an agency. For example, sales and personnel data need not be made available to an OSHA inspector.

In addition, an inspector might request records which contain confidential information or trade secrets. Some of the documents may contain information which the agency has no authority to obtain. Then disclosure may rightly be refused. When there is doubt about the authority of an agency to obtain certain records, a business might choose to clarify the matter with the agency before disclosure to the inspector. This process could take a long time. If the documents are not essential to the investigation, the inspector may withdraw the request and finish the investigation without those particular records. Even when an agency is clearly authorized by regulation to obtain certain information from a business, there may still be a challenge to its right to that information.

Because records held by an agency are subject to disclosure under the Freedom of Information Act (FOIA) and the protections of the act are not well defined, it is possible that an agency will make public almost any information furnished to it. It is imperative that a business take measures to ensure the protection of trade secrets and confidential information. Some agencies have procedures for preserving the confidentiality of business information. It should be ascertained before disclosure whether such a procedure is available. In any event, if confidential documents are furnished to the agency, they should be clearly marked "confidential." Valuable property rights of the company are involved.

By statute, administrative agencies are authorized to examine some records of individuals or businesses subject to their authority. Furnishing the information requested often requires a substantial expenditure of time, effort, and resources. There is a general duty to respond to governmental

---

[17]*United States v. Morton Salt Co.*, 338 U.S. 632 (1950).

process, yet subpoenaed parties may shift some of their burden to the government. For example, it is common for a district court to require an administrative agency to inspect documents where they are stored. It appears that there is not generally a duty placed on the subpoenaed party to copy and transport records for the government. It then becomes the responsibility of the government to copy and transport any records which it considers important. When faced with the burden of going to the business, copying records, and taking them away, an agency may choose to forgo inspection of those records.

INTERVIEWS

An inspector is attempting to learn as much as possible during an inspection. The inspector knows that the fastest way to learn anything is to ask questions. Members of an inspection team should be advised to take great care when speaking with an inspector, for what they say can be used against the company. The team should cooperate as much as possible and answer frankly any reasonable questions. Yet members should not answer any unasked questions or go beyond the scope of the questions actually asked. They should also know the limits of the agency's authority and that they need not answer questions which the inspector has no right to ask.

Illustrative Example

At the beginning of an antitrust investigation the Antitrust Division may turn to the Federal Bureau of Investigation (FBI) for help. The FBI will locate and interview people. When the FBI is acting under these conditions, it is not armed with process to permit search or arrest. Compliance with the FBI at the beginning of an antitrust investigation is voluntary. Because limited immunity is awarded to someone who testifies before a grand jury, a person who talks to the FBI might lose any immunity that might otherwise have been awarded. As a general rule, there are few advantages to be gained from granting an interview to the FBI. However, if there is a possibility that an interview will uncover facts which will clear someone and prevent further investigation, then an interview should be granted. Although the FBI doesn't generally like to conduct interviews with attorneys present, a person may demand as a condition of the interview that counsel be present. Copies of notes that are made of the interview should be requested. If the request is refused, a memorandum should be drawn up. It may be a long time before the investigation is concluded, and a witness may forget what was said. A memorandum will help a witness remember what was said in the interview.

When an inspection is being made of a facility where employees are working, the employees should be instructed not to speak with federal inspectors. However, for OSHA inspectors that instruction is not appropriate since OSHA involves statutory worker rights to talk with an inspector. Most other statutes are silent on the subject and can be construed to best advantage by a consistent policy that inspectors should not direct questions to any working employee. For example, wage and hour inspectors may be refused interviews with employees during working time. A list of employees may be handed to the inspectors with a request that they get in touch with the employees while they are not working. The *Wage and Hour Field Operation Handbook* recognizes that interviews do not necessarily have to take place on the employer's premises.[18] However, it may be to an employer's advantage to allow inspectors to conduct employee interviews during working hours in order to be able to monitor who is interviewed. Employees should be advised that they do not have to give statements. It is their choice. Employees should also be advised that if they do give statements, they ought to get copies of their statements at that time. Subsequent requests for statements will go through channels and may be delayed.

FACILITIES

To ensure that the scope of an investigation will be confined to its proper parameters, an inspector should always be accompanied by company personnel. The employer has the right to accompany an inspector during an inspection. In this way the employer can ensure that the inspector will not gain access to facilities which are not within the authority of the act. For example, the Flammable Fabrics Act permits inspection of products but not of fabrics. Accordingly, a court may refuse to allow the Consumer Product Safety Commission (CPSC) to inspect a company's testing laboratory.

OSHA also specifically requires employers to permit an employee representative to accompany an OSHA inspector during a workplace safety inspection. The employee is to be selected by an employee organization. However the act neither prohibits nor compels pay for walk-around time. An attempt by OSHA to promulgate a regulation requiring an employer to pay an employee for time spent in accompanying an OSHA inspector during walk-around inspections was struck down.[19] If the employee representative is not authorized to enter any particular areas, the employer should advise the inspector. The inspector must then limit employee contacts to those who work in that area. In addition, it appears that striking workers are not entitled to accompany OSHA inspectors on an inspection.

Illustrative Example

Striking members of the Oil, Chemical and Atomic Workers International Union attempted to gain entry to a refinery to accompany OSHA inspectors on an inspection. The District Court for the Southern District of Texas granted a motion by Amoco Oil Co. to quash the warrant seeking entry by a union representative. The court held that the provisions permitting an employee representative to accompany an OSHA inspector on a walk-around inspection were intended to give employees a chance to provide information and air complaints about the workplace. Since this inspection followed a refinery explosion, the court held that striking workers would not have knowledge of conditions leading to the explosion and had no right to accompany the inspector.[20]

[18]Wage and Hour Division, *Field Operation Handbook,* § 52(c)01.

[19]*Chamber of Commerce of the United States v. OSHA,* 636 F.2d 464 (D.C. Cir. 1980).

[20]*Amoco Oil Co.* (1980 OSHD ¶ 24,789).

Inspectors are further limited by directions contained in inspection manuals. "Administrative staff manuals and instructions to staff that affect a member of the public" are available under the FOIA. An employer might examine various staff manuals to determine the limitations placed on inspectors by their own agency's rules. (See Chapter 4, subsection "Staff Manuals and Guides.")

Illustrative Example

The CPSC *Inspection Guide* contains rules which limit an inspector's actions during an inspection. For example, it specifically provides that no recording devices are to be used during any inspection or investigation. It also directs inspectors to proceed on the assumption that photographs can be taken. However, it adds that if management insistently objects to the taking of photographs, the inspector should stop taking photographs. The authority of federal inspectors to take photographs is a gray area at this point, and most agencies will not pursue the matter if management strongly objects.

SAMPLING

Agency inspectors may generally request sample products, labeling materials, or effluents. Management should recognize the importance of sampling, which may be the best evidence of wrongdoing. The company should isolate and preserve a duplicate of any sample given an inspector. It should also get a receipt for any sample so given. Samples should be clearly marked. In some cases, for example, under the Solid Waste Disposal Act, if a sample is subsequently analyzed, the results must be sent promptly to the company. It may pay the company to include a knowledgeable employee to observe the sampling by an inspector in case a challenge later is made to the sampling results. The government may be charged for samples, although most firms do not do so.

Often several methods can be utilized in sampling, and a business should object if an inspector uses a sampling technique that might be less favorable to the company. If the inspector insists on using such a sampling technique, the company should consider taking duplicate samples by a more favorable sampling method. The company representative should take notes of what occurs throughout the inspection. Management can be informed of everything that happens, and the company will have a permanent record to be consulted in any future proceedings by the agency.

FOLLOWING UP AN INSPECTION

At the end of an inspection representatives of a company will generally meet with the inspector to discuss the inspection. The meeting might be limited to the personnel who conducted the inspection or be extended to the upper levels of management. At that point the investigator should be encouraged to inform the company of any findings and recommendations. Individual agencies deal differently with discovered violations.

Illustrative Example

During OSHA inspections apparent violations that can be corrected immediately may be found. Even though corrected, the condition can still form the basis for a citation or a penalty. After the walk-around the inspector must discuss with the employer any probable violations which have been discovered. There may be penalties for OSHA's failure to do so. In one case a backup-alarm charge was vacated along with a $300 penalty because the employer was prejudiced by not being offered the opportunity of an opening or closing conference.[21] An inspector does not have authority to impose a penalty or close down a business on the spot. After the inspector returns to the office and turns in a report to the area director, the director will determine whether any citations will be issued and any penalties be proposed. The results will then be sent to the company.

At the closing conference the company may wish to furnish the investigator with other information. The investigator is the initial trier of facts. If faced with only one side, the investigator has no choice but to recommend enforcement action. However, if the company has marshaled facts and evidence to show that there was no violation, the investigator may be persuaded not to proceed against the company.

Many agencies also provide for informal conferences with agency personnel during which settlements are encouraged. To avoid lengthy and costly review procedures, agency personnel are encouraged to amend citations and adjust penalties during such conferences. This is a great chance for a company to marshal all the evidence on its side and present it to the agency. For example, once an employer determines what issues the investigator has focused on, affidavits or sworn testimony which disprove the investigator's contentions can be taken from employees. This is very effective in wage and hour and equal employment opportunity investigations. It is important that the employer present another side to the controversy. When the decision makers are presented with only one side, that is, the evidence and testimony presented by the government investigator, they will naturally file charges against the employer. However, if the employer presents the other side, the decision makers will have something against which to weigh the investigator's evidence. The agency may be particularly receptive to the company at this stage in the interest in avoiding appeal procedures. Area directors are often empowered to reduce charges or penalties or to amend or altogether withdraw a citation. The company should pursue negotiations with an agency with an eye to limiting liability and containing costs.

---

[21]*Henkles & McCoy, Inc.* (1979 OSHD ¶ 23,687).

9 FIGHTING AGENCY ENFORCEMENT

McNEILL STOKES
Stokes & Shapiro
Attorneys at Law

Can you fight the government? You bet you can! The problem is that businesses, when they are faced with enforcement actions by governmental agencies, surrender cheaply rather than fight dearly. They think that the overwhelming power of the government and their inadequate knowledge will certainly cause them to lose. Nothing could be further from the truth. In fact, statistics show that businesses win against agencies the majority of times. For example, statistics show that appeals from an Internal Revenue Service (IRS) auditor's determination to the next administrative level result in a substantially reduced tax deficiency. Appeals to the next level in IRS administrative appeals result in even less tax deficiency. On the average, each year the businesses that contest Occupational Safety and Health Administration (OSHA) decisions win some favorable relief approximately 2 out of 3 times.

Some governmental actions are nuisances but will not have a substantial adverse impact on a business. A business might weigh the cost of surrendering to an agency's position against the advantages to be gained from fighting, and often it is much easier and cheaper to comply. However, as a result of the passage of the Equal Access to Justice Act, it is now cheaper for a small business to challenge agency actions than ever before. The act requires reimbursement to small businesses of costs and expenses spent in successfully defending against unreasonable government actions. Fees and other expenses will be awarded as a result of costs incurred in connection with agency proceedings or legal actions. Furthermore, the new law places the burden on the government to prove that it was "substantially justified" in bringing the action or that "special circumstances make an award unjust." No longer does fighting the government cost more than it's worth. Of course, if the business is wrong, it should comply with the government regulation, but if the agency is wrong, then the company may wish to fight.

Governmental action may disrupt the strategic driving force of a business. When agency action might adversely affect a company's source of supply, energy requirements, production techniques, advertising, distribution system, or supply system, it may be imperative that the company fight the agency to preserve its way of doing business.

Businesses presently have the tools to take on agency enforcement and often to win. They can insist upon fair and unbiased agency adjudications which provide adequate notice and a fair hearing without biased administrative judges. Tactics which can be employed include ambush and delay, challenging regulations that an agency seeks to enforce, challenging the authority of an agency, requiring the government to prove its case, challenging the application of a regulation to the business, and making the government follow its own procedures and precedents. If a business is not satisfied with the result of an agency determination or adjudication, it can take the agency to court to review the action. In some cases, it may even sue the government for damages.

State and federal regulations touch in some manner almost every enterprise and business activity. The ultimate purpose of any given regulation is to protect the public welfare. Thus, in the spirit of public interest and respect for the law, most regulated parties comply with regulations even though compliance may be achieved only at considerable private expense and effort. Unfortunately, the impositions of government agencies sometimes become so burdensome that an otherwise compliant party must, in realistic self-interest, choose to ignore or resist regulatory rules. This chapter contains suggestions and examples of lawful ways to resist adverse administrative action and to challenge administrative rules.

DEALING WITH AGENCY ADJUDICATION

Administrative agencies not only investigate facts; they also issue final decisions on matters of fact or policy. When rules are applied to particular fact situations, agencies must adjudicate disputed facts and issue findings or decisions in much the same manner as do courts of law. Since the rulings of administrative agencies carry the force of law, parties subject to administrative action should be thoroughly cognizant of their rights in administrative proceedings. Each agency formulates its own system of procedure, which is duly published in the *Federal Register* and the *Code of Federal Regulations*. Since each agency deals with different subject matter and has different administrative goals, the particular form of adjudicatory procedure will vary between agencies. However, each system must meet the constitutional guarantees of due process and fairness. The following subsections outline the basic procedural rights due to respondents of agency adjudicatory proceedings.

Notice

Inherent in the due-process guarantee is a right to notice. If notice of proposed action which may adversely affect an individual is not given to that individual prior to the action, most of the other due-process rights granted to the individual will have little meaning. A person has little protection against an action of which the party is unaware. Therefore, before an agency may take action which may have an adverse impact on an individual, it must give notice.

The right to notice in this respect actually consists of two aspects. There must, first of all, be notice to the affected party of any procedural rights which are guaranteed in that situation. For example, there must be notice to an individual of any proposed agency action adversely affecting that individual and of any right to a hearing in the matter. When the agency proposes to take action adverse to regulated parties, the facts upon which such action is based must be available so that the regulated parties have an opportunity to respond with a rebuttal of the evidence.

Illustrative Case

Hess & Clark had been manufacturing and selling diethylstilbesterol (DES), a synthetic estrogen used since the 1950s to promote rapid growth of cattle. Though DES had long been recognized as a carcinogen, the Food and Drug Administration (FDA) had continued its approval of production of DES pellets for animals, since tests of slaughtered animals had revealed no chemical residues in edible tissue. However, in 1971, under a new testing technique, traces of DES were found in carcasses. Although the commissioner issued a statement that there was no reason to believe that use of DES on cattle presented a public health hazard, the FDA in 1972 issued a notice of intent to withdraw approval of manufacturers' applications for DES in order to hold a public hearing to collect information necessary for making a decision in the matter. Almost a year later an order withdrawing approval for DES pellets for cattle and denying a hearing to drug manufacturers was issued. The order claimed that responses to the notice of intention to withdraw approval had not raised issues requiring a hearing and that the results of the latest study, which had become available since the date on which notice of withdrawal had been given, called for the withdrawal of approval.

The drug company challenged the determination on the ground that the commissioner had erred in failing to grant a prewithdrawal hearing. The court noted that, absent in a health hazard emergency, the commissioner may withdraw approval of an application without a hearing, through summary judgment proceedings, only if the requesting party fails to raise a material issue of fact. However, adequate notice of opportunity for a hearing must contain enough information to provide the party with a genuine opportunity to identify material issues of fact. Notice must include references to the facts which, according to the commissioner, establish the need for withdrawal so that the responding party is given a meaningful opportunity to controvert the alleged facts. The court invalidated the order withdrawing approval of DES pellets, since the determination that no hearing was required was based upon test results which had not been made public and to which the adversely affected parties had not been given an opportunity to respond.[1]

In cases in which there is a right to a trial-type hearing, the administrative proceeding generally commences with the issuance of the notice of the hearing. The notice actually serves as the administrative equivalent of a complaint. Since an essential requisite of the right to be heard is that the person involved have notice of the hearing, an agency must make sure that notice is received by the respondent. Service by mail is usually considered suffi-

[1] *Hess & Clark, Div. of Rhodia, Inc. v. FDA*, 495 F.2d 975 (D.C. Cir. 1974).

cient; most agency regulations require service by registered mail. Generally, service is considered adequate when it is conducted by a method which ensures that notice will be received by the party involved. Generally, personal service is not required, although particular statutes may require that notice be served on the parties personally.

Not only must the notice be received by the parties for whom it is intended, but it must also be timely. For the notice to be considered timely, it must be received early enough to give the parties sufficient time to prepare for the hearing, considering the facts of the case involved. The standard is one of reasonableness that depends to an extent on the facts and issues of the particular case. Usually no rigid time limits are set, although some statutes do fix minimum time limits. The standards which are set are based on the aim of providing parties with an adequate opportunity to prepare a defense.

The second aspect of notice in an administrative proceeding, in addition to giving notice of procedural rights, is that the individual must be apprised of the issues involved in the proposed agency action. The real function of notice in such a proceeding is to ensure the individual's right to be heard. If the responding party were not aware of the issues in time to defend against the charges, the right to be heard would almost be rendered a nullity. However, technical formalities are almost entirely dispensed with as long as the individual is provided with fair notice of the "matters of fact and law asserted."[2] The requirements of notice for administrative proceedings are not rigid and formal. Procedural standards for administrative adjudication are based upon the notion of fundamental fairness. The test is really whether the individual is given notice that is sufficient to enable preparation of a defense which is intended to rebut the charges made.

Notice must also alert the party to the matters of law to be asserted in an administrative hearing. Fairness requires that the finding be based on the same theory as the complaint so that the party has an adequate opportunity to respond in defense. The complaint, the hearing, and the decisions must be based on the same theory of law.

Illustrative Cases

Rodale Press, a family-owned business, is the publisher of books and pamphlets on health and preventive medicine. The Federal Trade Commission (FTC) issued a complaint against the company alleging false advertising, in that the advertising and the publications themselves allegedly represented that the suggestions in the books were cure-alls for various ailments. After a hearing at which the company's advertising was reviewed, the hearing examiner sustained certain of the specific allegations but dismissed the complaint as to the other counts. Upon appeal, the commission, after oral argument, vacated the trial examiner's decision and issued its own findings of fact, concluding that each of the alleged cure-all representations had been made and was false. A cease and desist order was issued. The court noted that the theory under which the complaint had been issued and under which the hearing before the exam-

---

[2]5 U.S.C. § 554(b)(3).

iner had been held differed from the theory upon which the commission ultimately sustained the complaint. The original complaint was based on the charge that the advertising was false because the materials in the books it promoted were false. Thus at trial expert testimony was directed at establishing the truth or falsity of the claims regarding the remedies contained in the books. However, the commission's decision was based on the theory that the advertising inaccurately represented the contents of the books. The court ruled that the publisher was improperly deprived of notice and hearing since this change in theory hampered the company's defense. The cease and desist order was vacated and the case remanded to the FTC.[3]

Bendix is a large industrial corporation involved in the manufacture of component parts for aerospace and automotive uses. Bendix acquired the Fram Corporation, a manufacturer ranking third in the market for replacement-part automotive filters. Though Bendix manufactured automotive filters for new cars, previous to acquiring Fram it had been only marginally involved in the replacement-part market. The FTC found Bendix to be in violation of the Clayton Act, which prohibits acquisitions when the effect may be substantially to lessen competition in a market. In the hearing, the FTC counsel limited the case to the theory that the merger of the two companies eliminated potential competition by virtue of the fact that Bendix was a potential entrant into the replacement-part market for automotive filters by internal expansion of its own operations. Therefore, the issue of the case at trial was whether Bendix would have entered the passenger-car filter replacement market by internal expansion had it not acquired Fram. However, the commission decided the case on the basis of the "toehold" theory that, as an alternative to merging with Fram, Bendix could have acquired a smaller firm so as to develop it into a major competitor. On appeal, the court noted that the case would have been tried differently had Bendix known that the toehold theory would be used against it. In the trial, Bendix sought only to prove that it would not otherwise have entered the market through internal expansion. Under the toehold theory it would also have sought to prove the acquisition of a smaller firm was not feasible. The court ruled that Bendix was deprived of notice and hearing on the substituted issue. The case was remanded to permit parties to offer additional evidence.[4]

The standard for administrative complaints is not as strict as that for courtroom pleading. The real concern is the actuality of notice, not the technicality of it.[5] Even if notice of some issues is not provided until the hearing, most courts will not declare an order void merely because notice of that issue was not contained in the complaint. Inquiry will be made into whether, although not contained in the complaint, the issue nevertheless was one of which the respondent had actual notice. Therefore, even when there is a technical defect in the notice, it can be overcome if the proceeding itself provides notice to the participant.

Illustrative Case

A pasta-manufacturing company was charged with monopolization of the market under the Sherman Antitrust Act after it had purchased three other such companies. Instead, the FTC found that the company had violated the Clayton Act, which prohibits

---

[3] *Rodale Press, Inc. v. FTC,* 407 F.2d 1252 (D.C. Cir. 1968).

[4] *Bendix Corp. v. FTC,* 450 F.2d 534 (6th Cir. 1971).

[5] *Kuhn v. CAB,* 183 F.2d 839, 842 (D.C. Cir. 1950).

acquisitions when the effect may be substantially to lessen competition or to create a monopoly. Though no mention of the Clayton Act had been made in the complaint, on appeal the court ruled that the issues concerning violation of the Sherman Act and violation of the Clayton Act were identical and were fully litigated. It was evident from the proceedings that all facts relevant to the alleged unlawful acts were litigated. Thus, the company was given adequate notice and opportunity to defend against either charge.[6]

At a minimum, the individual must be granted actual notice of an issue at some point when there is still time to prepare an adequate defense. In an administrative hearing, which is generally conducted with breaks in the proceedings, the individual almost always has time to prepare a defense. However, if there is any surprise to the responding party as a result of the failure to give notice of a particular issue before the hearing, the party is entitled to a continuance in order to cure any prejudice. If prejudice does result, the order may be set aside. For example, in an action by a former civil service employee to examine his removal, the court found that the notice of charges provided to him was totally inadequate and thus found that his removal was unsupportable. It was stressed that while the technical rules of criminal proceedings were not applicable, the charges must inform the plaintiff with sufficient particularity to enable him to refute the allegations. In this case the notice was found to be much too general to give him a fair opportunity to oppose his removal.[7] The crux is whether the individual has actual notice and an opportunity to defend. However, if the individual does not object at the hearing to the introduction of an issue which wasn't contained in the complaint, the individual may not be able subsequently to challenge it.

Pleadings in administrative hearings are very liberally construed and easily amended. The aim, once again, is to assure fundamental fairness to the responding party, and the test of fairness in administrative proceedings is whether the party was given an adequate opportunity to prepare a defense.

Hearing

When agency action is based upon disputed issues of fact, adversely affected parties are entitled to a trial-type hearing. In a trial-type hearing, the defending party is allowed to offer factual evidence and is given the opportunity to cross-examine witnesses and rebut evidence presented by the agency. The final determination is made on the record, based upon the proven facts. Trial-type hearings do not necessarily include an opportunity for oral argument since oral argument typically is suited to resolving nonfactual issues of law and policy. Depending upon the agency's discretion, interested third parties may intervene in an administrative proceeding. Some agencies are statutorily authorized to issue subpoenas for witnesses or evidence. The party requesting the subpoena must show the general rele-

---

[6]*Golden Grain Macaroni v. FTC,* 472 F.2d 882 (9th Cir. 1972).

[7]*Burkett v. United States,* 402 F.2d 1002 (Ct. Cl. 1968).

vance and reasonableness of the evidence sought. The right to a jury trial does not apply to administrative hearings. The *Federal Rules of Evidence* do not specifically apply to administrative proceedings, though they may be used as guides for the agency's own evidentiary rules. The Administrative Procedure Act (APA) permits any oral or documentary evidence, merely requiring that the agency exclude "irrelevant, immaterial, or unduly repetitious evidence."[8] In an administrative hearing, even hearsay is admissible and may constitute substantial evidence if it is sufficiently convincing. In contrast to court trials, since no procedure for pretrial discovery is generally available in administrative proceedings, the defending party may be unable to acquire evidence that the agency plans to use in the proceedings. However, just as courts may take judicial notice of facts not presented by the litigating parties, agencies also may take "official notice" of facts not appearing in the evidence in the record. To guard against unfairness the APA gives the defending party an opportunity to controvert extrarecord facts assumed by the agency. For purposes of a hearing, the case is assigned to a presiding officer, who makes a record of the proceedings. After the hearing, the records are studied by an administrative law judge (ALJ), who prepares a decision containing findings and conclusions. Therefore, the most important aspect of the administrative hearing is the record. Generally, the ALJ's decision becomes the decision of the agency unless it is appealed to the agency for review. The agency may also review the decision of its own accord. However, the agency must explain its rejection if the ALJ's decision is overturned.

According to the APA, the proponent of a rule or an order has the burden of proof in an administrative proceeding. However, the burden of proof may be shifted to the defending party by provision of the particular statute. For example, when the Environmental Protection Agency (EPA) moves to cancel registration of a poisonous substance under the federal Insecticide, Fungicide, and Rodenticide Act, the registrant has the burden of proving that the product is in compliance with the statute. The FDA may summarily deny a new drug application if the producer fails to meet the burden of presenting sufficient evidence of the drug's efficacy to call for a trial. However, other statutes require that the agency investigate controverted facts before issuing summary judgment in a case.

Illustrative Case

When employees of an electronics company voted to be represented by a union, the employer filed with the National Labor Relations Board (NLRB) objections to the union's preelection activities and refused to bargain with the union after the election. The union then filed an unfair-labor-practice charge against the employer, and the Board granted summary judgment against the company, declaring it to be in violation of law for refusing to bargain. The company challenged this finding on the ground that the Board had failed to investigate the company's allegations of union misconduct. The court noted that under the Board's rules and regulations it was obligated to investigate the facts when objections were made concerning the conduct of a union elec-

---

[8] 5 U.S.C. § 556 (d).

tion. Here, the Board did not follow its own rules when the employer offered evidence that the union had used threats and violence to influence the election. Therefore, the court denied enforcement of the Board's judgment against the company.[9]

The APA stipulates that an agency employee involved in the investigation of a case may not then participate in the agency review and final decision on the matter. In actuality, however, the same members of an administrative agency may investigate facts, institute proceedings, and then make the necessary findings in a case. This combination of investigative and adjudicative functions is not in itself a denial of due process. Agency proceedings meet the requirements of due process when all material facts and evidence are fairly considered.

Grounds for the agency's action must be clearly disclosed in the statement of findings since the findings serve as a basis for judicial review. By requiring that the final decision be based upon a reasoned consideration of the evidence, findings help to keep agencies within their jurisdiction by protecting against arbitrary action. Order resulting from an administrative hearing must be reasonably related to the findings. They must not be overly broad and must state specifically the acts which the respondent is to do or to refrain from doing.

Unreasonable Delay

Unreasonable delay in holding a hearing and making a finding may prejudice the party against whom agency action is brought. In that case, agency action may be set aside.

Illustrative Case

After the Equal Employment Opportunity Commission (EEOC) had filed charges against a company alleging wrongful discharge of an employee, 3½ years passed before the commission officially determined that conciliation efforts had failed, and another 1½ years lapsed before suit was filed against the company. At the trial the company argued that it had been prejudiced by the delay in filing suit since potential witnesses for the company, including former coworkers of the discharged employee and her supervisor, had left the company employ and that all time cards for the period in question had been destroyed during the normal course of business. The court ruled that the company had reasonably concluded that the case was closed after the charging party's right to sue had lapsed and a considerable amount of time had passed with no word from the commission. Therefore, the company was justified in disposing of its personnel records within the normal course of business. The court dismissed the action since the employer would have been prejudiced in its defense.[10]

However, before agency action can be set aside for delay, there must be a showing of prejudice to the defending party. In a case similar to *Moore Group,* owing to a backlog of cases the EEOC did not serve notice of a charge

---

[9]*Electronic Components Corp. of N.C. v. NLRB,* 546 F.2d 1088 (4th Cir. 1976).

[10]*EEOC v. Moore Group, Inc.,* 416 F. Supp. 1002 (N.D. Ga. 1976).

of racial discrimination against a company until an officer was available for the investigation. The company filed suit to set aside the formal demand for information, which EEOC had issued when it finally began to investigate the case. The court ruled that, because of the backlog of cases to be reviewed by the commission, the delay was not unreasonable. Since there was no showing that the delay would prejudice the company in its defense, the agency action was not set aside.[11]

Bias

Just as a party in court is entitled to an impartial judge, a party subject to agency action is entitled to a neutral and detached review of the evidence in an administrative hearing. One whose opinions or statements indicate prejudgment of a case or one whose personal interest in a matter to be decided would interfere with fair judgment is disqualified from serving as judge. Preconceived opinions on matters of law and policy do not disqualify an officer. To prove bias it must be shown that the judge is unlikely to consider fairly the full range of evidence.

Illustrative Case

Cinderella Career and Finishing Schools was charged by the FTC with false, misleading, and deceptive advertising. After a 16-day hearing, the hearing examiner ruled that the complaint should be dismissed. However, when the agency appealed the decision to the full commission, the commission reversed the examiner's decision and entered cease and desist orders against the school. Upon appeal, the court declared that the commission could not completely disregard the evidence presented at the hearing. If the agency chose to modify or set aside the conclusions of the hearing examiner, it must give reasons for doing so. Furthermore, while the appeal from the examiner's decision was pending before him, the chairman of the FTC made a public speech referring to questionable advertising practices, which gave the appearance that the case had been prejudged. Therefore, the court found that the chairman was biased. The commission's order was vacated and the case remanded to the commission for further consideration of the hearing record of evidence without the participation of the chairman.[12]

CHALLENGING THE WAY THE RULE WAS MADE

Practically speaking, Congress could not possibly decide all problems of public policy. Consequently, power to administer acts of Congress must be delegated to federal agencies and executive departments. Since it is impossible for legislators to draft the code explicitly enough to cover every conceivable future problem, in most instances the actual statute outlines congressional policy only in the most general terms. Congress then delegates to the agency the power to establish rules and regulations for carrying out the intent and purpose of the law. The presumption is that the specialized agency, with expertise in the field, can deal better with the detailed facts and circum-

[11] *Chromcraft Corp. v. EEOC,* 465 F.2d 725 (5th Cir. 1972).
[12] *Cinderella Career & Finishing Schools, Inc. v. FTC,* 425 F.2d 583 (D.C. Cir. 1970).

stances to which the statute must apply. Even so, the agency is not given unlimited authority to formulate and enforce rules. Through the APA[13] Congress has established a uniform procedure for rule making to assure that agency regulations having the force of law are promulgated fairly after an opportunity for input from interested parties. The APA allows three types of rule making: (1) rule making for interpretative and procedural rules, which requires no more party participation than the agency chooses; (2) informal rule making for substantive and legislative rules, which requires public notice and opportunity for written comments from interested parties, as provided by Section 553 of the act; and (3) formal rule making on the record, which, when specifically required by statute, calls for a trial procedure according to Sections 556 and 557 of the act. Interpretative rules or general statements of policy do not require rule-making procedures since they merely announce the agency's intentions and policies and do not carry the force of the law. The following discussion will focus on rule making for substantive rules which impose legally binding standards upon regulated parties.

Requirement of Notice and Opportunity for Comment

Administering the law necessarily requires the formulation of policy and the making of rules to fill in gaps left by Congress. The agency charged with carrying into effect the will of Congress as expressed in a particular law usually is given quasi-legislative authority to promulgate rules within the scope of the statute. While the substance of each set of regulations naturally depends upon the issue addressed by the statute, the process of rule making must in all cases satisfy the APA. The purpose of rule-making procedure is to educate the agency and to assure that rules are based upon a fair and reasonable consideration of the facts. If regulations have not been formulated according to rule-making procedure, they may be challenged and may be found unenforceable. The "informal" system of rule making described by Section 553 of the APA requires notice, opportunity for comment, and a statement of basis or purpose for the rule. When the agency intends to promulgate a rule, general notice of proposed rule making must be published in the *Federal Register*. The agency must allow those with an interest in the area to be regulated an opportunity to submit written data, comments, or arguments. The agency should consider all relevant matter presented when formulating its final rule. Opportunity for oral presentation is left to the discretion of the agency under Section 553 but generally is not required for notice-and-comment rule making. Particular statutes, however, may provide opportunity for oral presentation or cross-examination in the rule-making proceedings. Finally, the adopted rule must be accompanied by a general statement of basis and purpose sufficient to show that the rule was not framed in an arbitrary or capricious manner.

[13]5 U.S.C. §§ 553, 556, 557.

Before a rule may be promulgated or amended, interested parties must be given notice of what the agency proposes to do. Notice is sufficient if it describes subjects and issues involved so that interested parties may offer informed criticism and comment. A rule promulgated without notice and opportunity to comment may be unenforceable.

Illustrative Case

Under the applicable statute, the secretary of agriculture is allowed to make adjustments in the announced price supports for any commodity by using informal rule-making procedures. After opportunity for comment, price differentials for peanuts were announced. One group of growers was displeased and protested the decision, requesting a reconsideration of the facts. After repeatedly assuring that the announced differentials would remain in force, the Department of Agriculture completed an internal review of the data and then announced that the previous decision was revoked and a new differential was in effect. Arlington Oil Mills and other southeastern growers and shellers challenged the announcement since, contrary to the APA, no public participation had been allowed in the reconsideration. The court ruled that the secretary was required to give notice that reconsideration of the rule was under way and to allow opportunity for comment before a new price differential was enforced. The rule was remanded to the secretary so that proper price differentials could be fixed in a manner in compliance with rule-making procedures.[14]

Not every bit of background information used by an administrative agency in formulating a proposed rule need be published for public comment. However, since the purpose of rule-making procedure is to assure that the agency hears and considers all aspects of an issue, notice of rule making must include references to the facts or information upon which the rule is based so that affected parties have a meaningful opportunity to challenge the alleged facts. If the proposed rule is based on evidence of test results or data, the parties must have access to the data in order to respond to it.

Illustrative Case

The EPA promulgated standards for the emission of particulate matter for new or modified portland cement plants pursuant to the Clean Air Act. At the time when notice of the proposed rule was given and again at the time when the adopted rule was announced, the EPA noted that the standard was based upon testing of existing cement plants and upon data from the technical literature. Yet the methodology and location of the tests were not made available for comment until well after the rule was adopted, and specific citation of technical data was never offered. Electrostatic precipitators or glass-fabric filters are employed by the industry to remove particulate matter from the exhaust gases of the kilns used to combine limestone and clay. Petitioners, an association of cement manufacturers, challenged the rule on the basis that the ability of current control devices to achieve the promulgated standard of emissions had not been adequately demonstrated. In the opinion of petitioners, the testing methods, which were not disclosed until after the standard had been adopted, raised problems on which they had not had the opportunity to comment. Upon analyzing the testing data, one company concluded that the test results were "grossly erroneous" owing to inaccurate sampling techniques used to measure particulate matter. The

---

[14]*Arlington Oil Mills, Inc. v. Knebel,* 543 F.2d 1092 (5th Cir. 1976).

manufacturers argued that accurate testing would demonstrate the need for less strenuous standards. The court declared: "It is not consonant with the purpose of a rule-making proceeding to promulgate rules on the basis of inadequate data or on data that to a critical degree, is known only to the agency." The court decided that the decision had not been based upon a reasoned consideration of relevant facts and remanded the rule to the EPA for further proceeding.[15]

Since the purpose of rule-making procedure is to assure that the agency considers relevant facts and arguments presented by interested parties concerning a proposed rule, the agency may certainly respond by altering the proposed rule. Therefore, the rule adopted may differ from the rule proposed. The fact that it differs does not generate a new opportunity for comment. However, the resulting rule should not be of a different scope from that of the rule of which the public had notice. Notice of a proposed rule must include a description of the subject or issue under consideration sufficient to alert interested parties to the scope of the final rule.

Illustrative Case

Federal highway safety standards for automobile signal flashers were based upon the industry-established standards of the Society of Automotive Engineers. Notice of proposed rule making was given for amending the federal standards by incorporating recently updated industry standards. The amendments subsequently published by the National Highway Traffic Safety Administration (NHTSA) retained industry performance criteria but omitted the industry's testing failure allowances, requiring instead 100 percent compliance with the standards. In response to objections that notice was insufficient, the agency withdrew the amendment and published a new notice proposing that the federal standards be amended by incorporating the updated industry standards but omitting the industry's failure rate allowances. The new notice made no reference to other proposed changes. In response to comments, the agency concluded that eliminating the industry failure rates while retaining its rigorous performance criteria was not reasonable and practicable. Therefore, the agency published new standards which required perfect compliance with the standards but which also downgraded the performance criteria. In response to a challenge to those regulations, the agency contended that notice of intention to amend the standards was sufficient to give interested parties the opportunity to comment on the entire subject matter of the standards. The agency pointed to the fact that some manufacturers responding to the notice did in fact discuss the desirability of downgrading the performance criteria. However, the court ruled that notice was insufficient since it did not advise all parties who would have considerable interest in a change in the general standards that revision was under way.[16]

However, in a case similar to the automobile signal case, the court found that sufficient notice had been given. In 1973 a regulation was proposed to classify as banned hazardous substances "all bicycles intended for use by children of less than 16 years of age," except those complying with the safety requirements of the regulation. After opportunity for comments, the Consumer Product Safety Commission (CPSC) published regulations which

---

[15]*Portland Cement Ass'n v. Ruckelshaus,* 486 F.2d 375 (D.C. Cir. 1973), *cert. denied,* 417 U.S. 921 (1974).

[16]*Wagner Electric Corp. v. Volpe,* 466 F.2d 1013 (3d Cir. 1972).

applied to all bicycles, not just to those intended for use by children. Upon receiving further comments and complaints, the commission announced that it would reopen discussion, and further comments were solicited on two subsequent occasions. When the resulting set of final regulations applying to all bicycles was challenged on the basis of improper notice, the court found sufficient notice that the commission intended to regulate substantially all bicycles in the fact that opportunity for comment had been reopened after announcement of a rule applying to all bicycles.[17]

Unless the specific statute otherwise requires a hearing, opportunity for written comments satisfies informal rule-making requirements. Whether to permit oral presentation is left to agency discretion. There is no constitutional right to a hearing in informal rule-making procedures and no right to cross-examine agency witnesses. To challenge an agency's decision not to grant an oral hearing the party must show that the refusal to grant a hearing is arbitrary and capricious, in that had testimony been offered, different information would have been available to the agency. Trial-type hearings are granted only to resolve specific issues of fact and not to debate general issues of policy. Requests for cross-examination in hearings may also be denied. However, courts have held that cross-examination should be allowed on specific technical issues which are critical to the decision when general procedure is inadequate to probe the subject matter. The party demanding cross-examination must prove that critical questions cannot be satisfactorily pursued by general notice-and-comment procedures.

Exception for Interpretative Rules

Generally, rule-making procedure is not required for rules relating to internal management of the agency or for statements of agency policy and interpretation of rules or statutes. Only those rules which have the force of law, thereby creating rights and obligations for regulated parties, must be promulgated after an opportunity for public input. The difference between substantive rules and general statements of policy is the different practical effect that the two types of pronouncements have on subsequent administrative proceedings. Substantive or legislative rules create law or implement existing statutes, whereas interpretative rules are statements as to what the administrative officer thinks a statute or regulation means. Clearly, how an agency chooses to enforce a rule may affect the rights of regulated parties. Thus, courts have recognized that fairness may require notice-and-comment procedure even for interpretative rules if they have a "substantial impact" upon private rights and obligations. To require rule-making procedure for agency instructions to staff would be impractical. However, notice-and-comment procedure should be employed whenever there are genuine grounds for differences of opinion concerning the policy of a rule so as to make the rule-making process a meaningful and important requirement. Moreover, even

---

[17] *Forester v. CPSC*, 559 F.2d 774 (D.C. Cir. 1977).

though the agency may consider a rule to be interpretative or a general statement of policy, courts are not bound by a label given a rule by the agency.

Illustrative Case

Under the federal Food, Drug, and Cosmetic Act, a new drug can be marketed only if a new-drug application approved by the FDA is in effect. Pursuant to 1962 amendments to the act, the FDA determined to review the effectiveness of drugs that had been approved for marketing between 1938 and 1962. As part of this review, manufacturers were invited to submit data to support claims of effectiveness for those drugs. A new set of regulations which accompanied this review, prescribing in detail the kinds of clinical investigations deemed necessary to establish the effectiveness of existing and future drug products, materially changed the previous basis upon which a drug's efficacy had been evaluated. These new standards of evidence necessary to demonstrate the effectiveness of a product applied retroactively and were necessary to avoid the summary removal of a drug from the market. A drug industry association challenged the evidentiary rule on the basis that inadequate rule-making procedures had been used. The commissioner of the FDA characterized the rule as "procedural and interpretative" and therefore exempt from notice-and-comment rule making since it merely described the procedure by which the agency would review drug applications. However, the court noted that the particular label placed upon an action is not necessarily conclusive. Since the proposed regulation was of general applicability and had a substantial impact upon the regulated industry, notice and opportunity for comment should have been provided. The rule was held invalid.[18]

Beyond Notice-and-Comment Rule Making

Notice-and-comment rule making does not require that a rule be supported by substantial evidence on the record. The general statement of basis and purpose required by notice-and-comment procedure need not include an explanation of specific findings. When the statute requires rule making to be made "on the record" in accordance with Sections 556 and 557 of the APA, a trial procedure must be used and the rule must be based upon findings of fact noted in the record. Laws requiring rule making on the record are becoming less prevalent since trial procedure has been found to be cumbersome and ill-suited for determining rules of general applicability. For example, an FDA trial proceeding to determine whether peanut butter should contain 87 percent or 90 percent peanuts lasted 9 years and was recorded in a 7736-page transcript. Instead, Congress and the courts have been adding requirements to the APA minimum of notice-and-comment rule making. Some statutes require more than a general statement in support of rules. For example, the Clean Air Act requires that findings be published at the time when the final regulations are promulgated. The federal Mine Safety and Health Act requires the secretary of the interior to consult with advisory committees before issuing a regulation. When the secretary revised a rule without consulting advisers, the court held the revision invalid.[19] The Occupational Safety and Health Act provides that during the comment period

---

[18] *Pharmaceutical Mfrs. Ass'n v. Finch*, 307 F. Supp. 858 (D. Del. 1970).

[19] *United States v. Finley Coal Co.*, 493 F.2d 285 (6th Cir. 1974).

any interested person may file written objections to the proposed rule and may request a public hearing based upon those objections. Some statutes make a particular finding prerequisite to the issuance of a rule. In that case, the rule must have the requisite factual support. For example, for a rule controlling toxic substances the Toxic Substances Control Act requires factual support in the rule-making record of the harmful effects of the substance on health. Before a product may be banned, the CPSC requires facts showing that the product presents an unreasonable risk of injury. A regulation may be challenged on the basis that the agency did not follow procedural requirements specifically contained in the statute.

Illustrative Case

The CPSC issued a regulation classifying all aerosol products containing vinyl chloride as "banned hazardous substances" and requiring repurchase by the manufacturer of all existing quantities of those items. The statute authorizing the commission to take such action allows for notice-and-comment rule making for issuing a proposed ban but requires a public hearing for receiving evidence on the matter if within 30 days of publication of the proposed rule any person adversely affected by the order files a specific objection to the order and requests a public hearing based upon those objections. Pactra Industries, which manufactures and sells aerosol spray cans, had at one time used vinyl chloride as a propellant in cans of hobby paint. Though it had previously stopped using that propellant, many cans containing vinyl chloride still remained in the chain of distribution. Pactra submitted timely objection to the order, contending that the commission had considered information dealing solely with the high-intensity and long-term industrial use of the ingredient. Pactra argued that there was no evidence that exposure resulting from home use of aerosol products was harmful to humans. The commission denied the petition for a hearing, claiming that a hearing was warranted only when an objection established reasonable grounds for concluding that evidence presented at the hearing would defeat the proposed rule. The court examined the legislative intent of the Food, Drug, and Cosmetic Act and concluded that Congress fully intended to require a formal hearing when the drastic action of banning a product was opposed by persons adversely affected by the agency's action. Since the objections were made in good faith, the commission might not deny a hearing. Therefore, the court set aside the determination to ban aerosol sprays.[20]

CHALLENGING THE SUBSTANCE OF THE RULE

The most logical time to challenge the substance of an agency regulation is by immediate appeal upon adoption of the rule. Parties with an interest in the matter covered by the proposed regulation will have actively participated in the rule-making proceedings and will be able to object immediately if the promulgated rule does not reflect the evidence and recommendations offered through public comment. However, the validity of the rule may also be challenged in an enforcement proceeding. When charged with a violation of an administrative regulation, one defense may be to take the offensive: to argue that the rule itself is invalid and therefore cannot be enforced against you.

[20]*Pactra Indus. v. CPSC*, 555 F.2d 677 (9th Cir. 1977).

Lack of Authority

A legislative rule is valid and is as binding as a statute if it is within the granted power of an agency, is issued pursuant to proper procedure, and is reasonable. When an agency has no delegated power to make law through rule making, the rules it issues are necessarily interpretative and not legislative rules. Judicial review of interpretative rules is not limited to a determination of whether the rules are arbitrary or capricious since interpretative rules are not binding upon courts. The court may weigh the rationality of the agency's interpretation and consistency with other rules, but it is free to substitute its own judgment in the matter. Even if the agency has been delegated the power to make legislative rules, its authority is limited by the scope of the statute. The agency has no authority to regulate activity not addressed by the statute.

Illustrative Case

The FTC authorized an investigation of Morgan Drive Away, Inc., a common carrier engaged in the business of transporting mobile homes, to determine if Morgan had violated the FTC Act through false and misleading advertising. The act gives the commission power to investigate businesses affecting commerce "excepting banks and common carriers subject to the Act to regulate commerce [the Interstate Commerce Act]." Subpoenas were served on the president and vice president of the company. Morgan challenged the subpoenas on the ground that as a common carrier it was exempt from FTC regulations and investigation. The court ruled that when the subject of a subpoena was clearly exempted from investigation by statute, the agency had no authority to enforce a subpoena.[21]

An agency's power to take remedial action is limited by the actions which have been authorized by the statute. If the statute does not vest a particular remedial power in an agency, it cannot be assumed to have that power.

Illustrative Case

The CPSC found that a certain make of carpet was flammable. It ordered the manufacturer to cease and desist from manufacturing or selling that carpet. The CPSC also ordered the manufacturer to notify purchasers of the defective carpet and to recall and repurchase all the defective carpeting. The carpet manufacturer challenged the findings of the CPSC. The court held that the CPSC has only the power to issue cease and desist orders. The commission was not granted the authority to require notification, recall, and repurchase of flammable fabrics by the Flammable Fabrics Act or the FTC Act, nor is that authority inherent in either act.[22]

Statement of Findings

The APA does not require findings or factual support for informal rule making. However, courts have recently called for more than the minimal statement of basis and purpose required by the act.[23] The rationale for a rule

[21]*FTC v. Miller*, 594 F.2d 452 (7th Cir. 1977).

[22]*Congoleum Indus., Inc. v. CPSC* (9th Cir. Aug. 14, 1975).

[23]*Kennecott Copper Corp. v. EPA*, 462 F.2d 846 (D.C. Cir. 1972).

should provide a meaningful basis for judicial review. It should be sufficiently detailed to permit a court to ascertain how and why the regulation was adopted. The statement of basis and purpose should indicate the major policy issues which were raised during the informal proceedings and explain the agency's rationale for resolving those issues. Generally, the statement of basis and purpose should provide sufficient factual support to permit a reviewing court to determine that the regulation was not framed in an arbitrary or capricious manner. Statutes have always carried a presumption of validity so that the challenger bears the burden of proving the statute to be unacceptable. Previously, administrative regulations were likewise presumed valid in the absence of clear evidence to the contrary. However, the Supreme Court has rejected the presumption of validity if no statement of factual findings is offered[24] or if the offered statement of findings is not sustained by the record.[25] Essentially, the agency bears the burden of a reasoned presentation of support for a rule.

Illustrative Case

Under OSHA, the Department of Labor issued an emergency temporary standard banning exposure to fourteen chemicals said to be carcinogens. In regard to two of the substances covered by the temporary order, chemical industry representatives objected to the standard on the grounds that there was insufficient evidence in the record and that the findings of fact and statement of reasons for the standard were inadequate to justify the promulgation of an emergency standard. Under the OSHA statute, before a substance can be banned under a temporary standard, it must be determined to be toxic or harmful. The court found that in this case, since there were no reliable data on the carcinogenicity of the two chemicals in humans, only a potential danger to humans had been shown. Furthermore, the act provides that any standard must be accompanied by a statement of the reasons for the action. Here, the court found the statement of reasons to be inadequate. A concluding statement that the substances were carcinogens did not allow interested persons to determine and challenge the basis for the standard, failed to explain why the standard was necessary to protect employees from dangerous exposure, and did not present the reasoning of the agency for judicial review. To satisfy the statutory requirement of a statement of reasons, the agency should indicate which data in the record are principally relied on and why those data suffice to show the substances to be harmful. Because the statement of basis and purpose was inadequate, the standard was vacated and remanded to the agency.[26]

Substantial Evidence to Support a Rational Rule

Officially, the APA prescribes the substantial-evidence test of judicial review only for rules which, by statute, must be promulgated according to formal rule-making procedures. This means that rules made on the record are valid only if supported by substantial evidence contained in the record. By contrast, rules promulgated according to informal rule-making procedures are

[24] *Citizens to Preserve Overton Park v. Volpe*, 402 U.S. 402 (1971).

[25] *Camp v. Pitts*, 411 U.S. 138 (1973).

[26] *Dry Color Mfrs. Ass'n v. Dep't of Labor*, 486 F.2d 98 (3d Cir. 1973).

valid unless they are shown to be arbitrary, capricious, or abusive of agency discretion. The arbitrary-and-capricious standard of review is considered to be less rigorous. However, in certain statutes Congress has stipulated that ensuing rules, even though promulgated through informal procedures, must be supported by substantial evidence. For example, rules promulgated under the Occupational Safety and Health Act[27] and the Clean Air Act amendments[28] must be supported by information gathered in the notice-and-comment rule-making record. Furthermore, courts have begun to require more than a mere statement of basis and purpose. When the validity of a regulation is challenged, the court's job, under the arbitrary-and-capricious standard of review, is to determine whether there exists a rational basis for the rule. Therefore, even when a rule is not required by statute to be supported by substantial evidence, the arbitrary-and-capricious standard of review necessarily also calls for factual support. Courts have often required a rule to be accompanied by supporting facts and by a summary of facts constituting a statement of findings. The agency may also be required to articulate its response to important factual comments which have been rejected.

The burden of proving a rule to be arbitrary is said to be on the challenging party. However, particularly for rules required by statute to be supported by evidence, the agency is responsible for offering support for its determination. When the rule is not based on substantial evidence, it may fall from its own lack of support.

Illustrative Case

To protect farm workers from the harmful effects of pesticides, the Department of Labor, under OSHA, issued a temporary emergency standard fixing the period during which an employee might not enter a sprayed area. When farmers challenged the rule, the court ruled that the proper standard for review of an OSHA regulation was the substantial-evidence test, not merely the arbitrary-and-capricious standard. Under OSHA, emergency standards may be issued without regard to the usual requirements of notice and opportunity for a hearing when the order is necessary to protect employees from grave danger. In this case the court found no substantial evidence on the record to support the secretary's determination that emergency temporary standards were necessary. In fact, all the findings by the secretary's own investigative teams indicated that no emergency existed. The court noted that although the secretary was not bound by these findings, they indicated the strength of the evidence contrary to his determination. Since substantial evidence of grave danger from pesticides which would justify the issuance of emergency orders was not shown, the court declared the order to be invalid.[29]

The challenging party may offer evidence to disprove the factual assumption of a rule. When evidence inconsistent with the regulation exists, the rule-making record must show that such evidence was considered and must indicate a rational basis for discounting contrary evidence. If, in light of con-

[27]29 U.S.C. § 651.

[28]42 U.S.C. § 7401.

[29]*Florida Peach Growers Ass'n v. Dep't of Labor,* 489 F.2d 120 (5th Cir. 1974).

trary evidence, agency action cannot be justified, the rule is arbitrary and unreasonable.

Illustrative Cases

The FDA, after notice-and-comment procedure, issued a regulation requiring a controlled-heat process for designated periods for hot-smoked fish as a protection against botulism. Nova Scotia, a food-processing company, argued that the history of botulism in whitefish did not support the application of the general regulation to the whitefish-processing industry. It offered evidence that between 1899 and 1964 there were only eight cases of botulism known to have resulted from whitefish. All eight instances occurred between 1960 and 1963 and involved vacuum packing, which the industry abandoned in 1963. Despite the great volume of whitefish processed annually, there had not been a single case of botulism associated with commercially prepared whitefish since 1963, and despite the fact that Nova Scotia had been in business for 56 years, there had never been a case of botulism reported from the whitefish it processed. Furthermore, since scientific data upon which the regulation was based were not offered for comment, public criticism of the methodology used or the agency's interpretation of the data was impossible. The court ruled that application of the regulation to the whitefish industry was invalid.[30]

The National Traffic and Motor Vehicle Safety Act of 1966 mandated that new and retreaded tires be permanently labeled with the actual number of plies in the tires and the maximum permissible load of the tires. The act also granted the secretary of transportation authority to order other standards appropriate for motor vehicle safety. Pursuant to the act, the Department of Transportation issued a safety standard requiring that all retreaded tires have permanently molded onto one sidewall information concerning the size, the maximum inflation pressure and load, the actual number of plies, the words "tubeless" or "tube-type" as applicable, and the words "bias/belted" or "radial" as applicable. Since this information was currently affixed to tires in a nonpermanent label, the court failed to find a relation between the standards and the statutory goal of vehicle safety. Furthermore, the record indicated that permanent labeling would not be economically feasible. The secretary ignored the considerable number of comments in the record that compliance with the standard would be unreasonably costly and unfeasible owing to the nature of the retreading process. Since the secretary did not offer adequate support for the determination that despite evidence to the contrary the standards were reasonable, the court concluded that that part of the standard not already specifically mandated by Congress through the National Traffic and Motor Vehicle Safety Act was arbitrary and capricious. The order was set aside.[31]

An agency's decision is not arbitrary and capricious merely because the evidence can be interpreted to support a different conclusion. Even when the facts are scientifically inconclusive, a rule may be sustained if it is based upon a reasonable interpretation of the known facts. Only if the regulation is clearly erroneous in light of the factual evidence of the matter or is not based upon a reasoned consideration of the evidence is the rule invalid. For example, the secretary of labor rejected the advice of an advisory board that medical examinations for workers should be required when airborne asbestos concentrations exceeded one fiber per cubic centimeter of air. Instead, the

[30] *United States v. Nova Scotia Food Products Corp.*, 568 F.2d 240 (2d Cir. 1977).

[31] *Nat'l Tire Dealers & Retreaders Ass'n v. Brinegar*, 491 F.2d 31 (D.C. Cir. 1974).

secretary interpreted the Occupational Safety and Health Act to require medical examinations for those exposed to any concentration of airborne asbestos. Upon judicial review the court noted that the secretary was not bound by the recommendations of the board. Although the effects of asbestos are not fully known, exposure to relatively low levels of asbestos is known to cause serious disease. Therefore, the court ruled that the standard was reasonable and based upon substantial evidence.[32]

Available Technology

Most statutes which authorize the promulgation of industry standards stipulate that those standards be fixed at reasonably and practicably achievable levels. If a standard effectively prescribes a new technology, the agency must explain its conclusion that the necessary technology is available and how the technology can be applied. If the standard is technologically impossible or economically burdensome to achieve, the standard may be held to be arbitrary and capricious.

Illustrative Cases

Truck and automobile manufacturers sought review of the decision by the administrator of the EPA to deny application for a 1-year suspension of 1975 emission standards prescribed by the Clean Air Act. Congress had intended the statute to serve as "shock treatment" to force the industry to strive for cleaner emissions on automobiles, but the statute also allowed for petition for a 1-year reprieve as an escape hatch to relieve manufacturers should the standards be shown to be technologically impossible or overly burdensome to achieve. On petition, the administrator refused to suspend the standard for 1 year even though the National Academy of Sciences, which had been directed by Congress to study the feasibility of compliance with the standards, reported that the technology necessary to meet the requirements of the act for the 1975 model year was not yet available. The court ruled that while the EPA was not bound by the report of the National Academy of Sciences, it must have a reasonable basis for altering the conclusion of the report, such as reliance upon more current research and experience. In this case, the EPA used the academy's test data but unreasonably altered the mathematical formulas for predicting whether each manufacturer could meet the 1975 standards. Although reluctant to overturn the agency's determination on such a technical matter, the court rejected the agency's decision to deny the 1-year suspension and remanded the issue back to the agency for further consideration.[33]

Several chemical companies sought review of EPA regulations establishing different limitation guidelines for the phosphate-manufacturing industry. The guidelines were issued pursuant to the federal Water Pollution Control Act amendment, which mandated that standards to be achieved by 1977 "shall require the application of the best practicable control technology currently available" and that standards to be achieved by 1983 "shall require application of the best available technology economically achievable." The court found that the 1977 standards, which restricted the allowable discharge of wastewater, were properly based upon data of actual discharge rates of three exemplary plants, yet remanded the regulation for further proceedings since the

---

[32] *GAF Corp. v. OSHRC,* 561 F.2d 913 (D.C. Cir. 1977).

[33] *Int'l Harvester Co. v. Ruckelshaus,* 478 F.2d 615 (D.C. Cir. 1973).

concededly would increase the discharge flow. The 1983 standards, which altogether prohibited the discharge of wastewater, were based upon the settling-pond treatment of wastewater employed at one plant which had already achieved zero discharge except in times of heavy rainfall. However, the agency failed to consider whether such a system would be feasible in cold climates where ponds would freeze. The EPA claim that alternative technology which was not affected by subfreezing temperatures existed was not included in the administrative record but was offered for the first time in the EPA's argument before the court. The court noted that it was reluctant to set aside a regulation merely because it was based upon technology which was still in a developmental stage. Even though no plant in a given industry had adopted a pollution control device which could be installed, this did not mean that the device was not "available." However, the court ruled that since the administrative record failed to disclose a reasonable basis for belief that a new technology would be available and economically achievable, the 1983 regulation was deficient.[34]

CHALLENGING THE APPLICATION OF THE REGULATION

Even if the regulation is not challenged on its face, the most fundamental defense, of course, is to claim, "But the rule doesn't apply to me." A careful examination of the published regulation and its history may reveal grounds for distinguishing the facts of the case from the subject matter to which the regulation was intended to apply. Just as an agency may not promulgate rules outside the scope of the authorizing statute, it may not bring enforcement proceedings against a party whose activities are not covered by the rule. In the interest of due process, rules must be enforced reasonably and fairly.

Language of the Regulation

Upon being charged with a violation of an agency regulation, the party's first step should be simply to reread the regulation. Any rule which may be applied as law must be published in the *Federal Register* to give notice to those subject to it. The agency must give notice of what is required, and those subject to the rule should not be held to standards not expressed in the regulation. In fact, in the interest of notice, courts have refused to enforce a regulation beyond the scope of its explicit language. In an effort to encourage agencies to issue regulations in clear and concise language, the courts have construed the language of rules literally and "according to the natural meaning of the words."[35] The regulation should not be construed to mean what the agency allegedly intended but did not adequately express. Thus, if the regulation does not clearly refer to the situation at hand in the charged violation, the rule does not apply. As one court complained of an OSHA regulation, "To strain the plain and natural meaning of words for the purposes of alleviating a perceived safety hazard is to delay the day when the occupational safety and health regulations will be written in clear and

---

[34] *Hooker Chemicals & Plastics Corp. v. Train*, 537 F.2d 620 (2d Cir. 1976).

[35] *Diamond Roofing Co. v. OSHRC*, 528 F.2d 645 (5th Cir. 1976).

concise language so that employers will be better able to understand and observe them."[36]

Illustrative Cases

Defendant roofing companies were installing a flat roof 25 feet above ground at a construction site when a government inspection was made. Since no guards were found on the open-sided edges of the roof, the secretary of labor issued a citation for violation of an OSHA regulation requiring that a standard railing be placed around an open-sided floor. Other subsections of the regulation distinguished between a floor and a roof and specifically stipulated that those subsections applied to both. The roofing companies argued that since the subsection requiring a railing around open edges of floors did not indicate that the rule should also apply to roofs, it must apply to floors only. The court held that the language of the regulation must be construed literally and did not apply to roofs.[37]

A roofing materials plant which used asphalt in its manufacturing process was inspected by an agent of a state occupational safety and health bureau. The agent conducted a sampling of asphalt fumes which reportedly showed readings in excess of maximum permissible limits according to the standard for coal-tar-pitch volatiles established by federal regulations and adopted by the state. The plant was issued a citation for violation of the coal-tar-pitch standard. The citation was contested on the basis that asphalt, and not coal tar pitch, was used in the plant. Expert testimony was offered to prove that coal tar and petroleum asphalt were entirely different materials having different chemical compositions and different documented effects upon the health of workers. Whereas coal tar had long been considered highly biologically active and carcinogenic, asphalt fumes were not considered by experts to be carcinogenic. The citation alleging a violation of the standard for coal-tar-pitch volatiles was rescinded on the ground that it was irrational to include petroleum residues in the definition of coal-tar-pitch volatiles.[38]

History of the Regulation

Even the explicit language of a regulation must be interpreted in light of its legislative history. As already mentioned, courts are reluctant to broaden the scope of a rule by inferring an agency's unexpressed intention. In the name of fairness, it may be necessary for a court to construe narrowly the intended meaning of a rule. The record of how and why a rule was framed as it was is indicative of the rule's intended scope. One source for discovering the intended scope of a rule is the statement of basis and purpose which is required to help guide agencies and reviewing courts in properly applying the rule. A charged party may be able to prove by reference to the agency's own statement that the rule was not intended to apply to the case at hand. Another source for discovering the intent of the rule is the history of the industry's self-regulation. Many government regulations were originally developed by the industry as voluntary standards. An inquiry into the development of these standards may reveal a rationale not clearly stated in the

---

[36] *Id.* at 650.

[37] *Diamond Roofing Co. v. OSHRC,* 528 F.2d 645 (5th Cir. 1976).

[38] *GAF Corp.,* No. W6259-003-77, Maryland Dep't of Licensing & Regulation, Hearing Examiner Decision (Oct. 26, 1977).

language of the agency regulation. Data on which the industry standard was based become part of the legislative history of the rule which may be used to prove intent. If the original standards had a narrow intent, the regulations should be construed accordingly. If the regulation was developed by the agency, the legislative intent of the rules may be inferred from the record of comment or testimony gathered during rule making. From the data which were relied upon in promulgating the rule one may be able to prove that the facts at hand do not contribute to the hazard against which the regulation is aimed.

Illustrative Case

Buckeye Cellulose Corporation is in the business of processing cottonseed and cotton linters into bulk and sheet cellulose. The company was issued a citation by a state official who testified that there were "clouds" of cotton dust in the dock areas of the plant and who claimed that tests revealed particles in the air far in excess of OSHA standards for milligrams of "cotton dust (raw)" per cubic meter. Buckeye presented expert testimony to prove that by industry definition cottonseed linters are not cotton. Linter fiber is distinctly different from cotton fiber chemically and structurally. Furthermore, the cotton dust standards were developed by the textile industry to protect against byssinosis, a disease due to the inhalation of dust. Evidence from the industrial hygienist Dr. R. F. Shilling of England, who had composed the standards, was introduced in which Dr. Shilling stated that the standards were not intended to be applied to industries handling cottonseed or lint. The company presented evidence that it was not the cellulose fibers of raw cotton which caused the disease; rather, the disease was most probably caused by trash carried with the raw cotton. If trash were the harmful ingredient, most of it would have been removed by the time it reached the cottonseed processor. Therefore, the protective standards need not extend and were not intended to extend to cotton linter fibers. The administrative law judge therefore found that according to the intent of the regulation Buckeye was not in violation of the rule.[39]

Reasonableness

Just as the substance of the rule must be reasonable, the agency must apply the rule in a reasonable manner. Most regulations are aimed at achieving a standard of performance in a given area. It would not necessarily be unreasonable for a regulation to prescribe a particular method of control. If the regulation does not prescribe a particular method for implementing the standard, the agency may not impose an impractical or unfeasible manner of achieving the required result when the regulated party is achieving the desired result by practicing a reasonable method of control.

Illustrative Case

Continental Can operates eighty metal-can-manufacturing plants throughout the United States. All plants have similar machinery which produces sound levels in excess of OSHA standards. The applicable regulation stipulates that "feasible administrative or engineering controls shall be utilized" to reduce sound levels if employees

[39] *Secretary v. Buckeye Cellulose Corp.,* (1971–1973 OSHD ¶ 16, 313).

are subjected to sound exceeding the allowable standard. It further provides that if such controls fail to reduce sound levels, personal protective equipment shall be used. Over a period of several years, nineteen of Continental's plants received OSHA citations for noise-level violations, each charging that feasible engineering and administrative controls were not utilized to reduce sound levels. In all its plants, Continental was providing ear-protective equipment for employees which attenuated the noise level to an even lower range than that which would have been achieved by use of the engineering controls advocated by the secretary of labor. Yet the noise abatement method insisted upon by the secretary would cost $33.5 million to implement plus $175,000 per year to maintain, as compared with about $100,000 per year for the companywide earplug program already in existence. Eight of the cases were consolidated for a hearing before an administrative law judge, who held the standard invalid as interpreted by the secretary and dismissed the citations. The OSHA Review Commission found the regulation valid as properly interpreted but decided that economic feasibility was a factor to be considered and that Continental had shown engineering controls to be economically unfeasible. The commission dismissed the citations in these eight cases.

Continental then moved for summary judgment to dismiss the citations in the cases still pending. However, the Review Commission denied the motion, holding that the requirements for collateral estoppel (the theory that once an issue has been determined by a final judgment, it cannot be litigated again) had not been met. Upon review the court ruled that the secretary's noise abatement plan was not feasible when it was considerably more costly than the existing program and was not as effective for protection against noise. Furthermore, since the company's noise problem was national in scope, a plant-by-plant approach to OSHA enforcement was unreasonable. To force the company to litigate numerous similar cases was governmental abuse and harassment which violated the Fifth Amendment guarantee of due process of law. Since the issue of economic feasibility had already been decided in favor of the company, collateral estoppel applied. The court ordered that the pending noise citations against the company be dismissed and enjoined the secretary from issuing future similar citations.[40]

OSHA standards are often stated in terms of general requirements for protection and safety in hazardous situations. Such rules are not considered to be unenforceably vague. Instead, courts have held that such standards are enforceable to the extent that a reasonable employer would recognize the situation in question to be hazardous and therefore call for protective measures. In an enforcement proceeding, the agency has the burden of proving that a reasonable employer would have recognized the conditions to be hazardous and would have taken the particular precaution allegedly necessary for guarding against the danger. Industry custom does not absolutely define what is reasonable, but it may be used as evidence of reasonable behavior under the circumstances. Thus the fact that safety measures are typically thought to be unnecessary in a particular situation may be offered as a defense to safety citations.

Illustrative Case

An insulation company employing workers at a construction site was issued a citation for violating the general OSHA requirement that "protective equipment" be worn when there was "exposure to hazardous conditions." Two of its employees were

[40] *Continental Can Co. v. Marshall,* 455 F. Supp. 1015 (S.D. Ill. 1978).

walking down a rack of parallel pipes 20 feet off the ground while wrapping insulation around a steam pipe. When the trail of wiring used to fasten the insulating material accidently touched a live electric wire strung beneath the pipes, one employee was electrocuted and the other lost consciousness from the electrical shock and fell to the ground, breaking his skull. The company was charged with failure to require the use of safety belts or lifelines. On review, the court concluded that enforcement of such a standard required application of the test of whether a reasonable person would have recognized the hazard. The customary conduct of those in the industry provided evidence of reasonable behavior under the circumstances. To establish a higher standard of safety performance than that generally practiced by the industry, a rule-making procedure whereby the input of industry experts and the costs of such practices to the industry can be considered must be used. The employer produced witnesses representing labor and management to demonstrate that a reasonable employer would not have acted differently. Since the agency failed to meet its burden of proving that a reasonable insulation industry employer would have provided safety belts when the company in question did not, the agency's decision was overruled.[41]

Stare Decisis: The Requirement of Following Precedents

Courts generally follow their own precedents. This is the doctrine of stare decisis. In a given case, parties may expect a court to adhere to previous decisions issued in identical cases. The requirement of consistency with precedents also applies to administrative decisions. The trend of decisions on a given rule creates a body of "common law" and a record of how the rule is interpreted and applied upon which parties should fairly be able to rely. However, when a court decides that previous law is unsound and changes it, stare decisis does not prevent the court from applying the new decisions retroactively to a case currently before it. Agencies are also free to change rulings if a change will better effectuate the purposes of the authorizing statute. Administrative agencies are allowed discretionary authority in enforcing rules, though rules may not be enforced in an arbitrary or unreasonable manner. Thus a previous decision may be overruled if the agency is not acting arbitrarily. For the protection of parties acting in good-faith reliance upon previous decisions, the agency must explain departures from its own precedents. An agency may deviate from previous rulings or interpretations of a statute because of changes in understanding or shifts in official policy or political climate. When similar cases are decided in dissimilar ways, more than an enumeration of factual differences between cases is required. As a rationale for its decision the agency must explain the relevance of those differences to the purposes of the regulation. The agency bears the burden of proving that its new decision is a conscious and reasonable departure from precedent. Otherwise the ruling may be appealed on the ground that it is unjustifiably inconsistent with previous rulings.

Illustrative Case

An employer was charged with unfair labor practices, according to the National Labor Relations Act, in allegedly discharging employee Burinskas for union activities. The Board originally dismissed the complaint for lack of evidence that the employer had

---

[41]*B&B Insulation, Inc., v. OSHRC*, 583 F.2d 1364 (5th Cir. 1978).

violated the act. However, when Burinskas appealed to the court, the case was remanded to the Board for reconsideration. The Board then reversed its decision, found that the employer had violated the act, and ordered the employer to reinstate Burinskas with back pay from the date of discharge. The employer appealed the order, claiming, among other objections, that the remedy of the Board as to back pay was inappropriate. In similar cases in which an original decision in favor of the employer had been reversed to find a violation, the Board, as a general rule, had not tolled back pay between the period of the original dismissal and the subsequent finding of violation. The court agreed that the Board must not be allowed to act arbitrarily by treating similar situations in dissimilar ways. Therefore, the question of whether back pay should be awarded was remanded to the Board.[42]

Some agencies issue private rulings in answer to questions posed by individual parties. The IRS has continually claimed that its private rulings are not binding upon the agency and that taxpayers may not rely on private rulings as precedents. However, the Freedom of Information Act (FOIA) would seem to invalidate this policy. The court has held that under the FOIA letter rulings of the IRS must be open to the public.[43] The court has also held that the NLRB must disclose certain memoranda since advise memoranda are "instructions to staff that affect a member of the public" and appeals memoranda are "final opinion," both of which are required to be disclosed under the FOIA. Since previous rulings must be disclosed, it seems likely that courts will now rule that they may be relied upon as precedents.

Equitable Estoppel

The doctrine of equitable estoppel is applied in the name of fairness to protect a party who relies upon the representations of another. A party may not take a position inconsistent with previous representations when another has relied to his or her detriment on those representations. Previously, equitable estoppel was not applied to government, since "the king could do no wrong to his subjects." Now estoppel is applied to the actions of government bodies in instances in which it would be inequitable to allow inconsistencies. It is only fair that regulated parties be able to rely in good faith upon the official interpretation and previous rulings of administrative regulations. Otherwise, no business could ever be assured that it is acting in compliance with law. If the regulated party has in fact acted in reliance upon previous agency actions the agency may be estopped from applying a different rule against the party. The charged party bears the burden of proving that it has, in fact, relied upon previous policy.

Illustrative Case

A chemical company was charged with a violation of Section 13 of the Rivers and Harbors Act. The company allegedly had discharged industrial refuse matter into the Monongahela River. By its terms the act prohibits the discharge into navigable waters of "any refuse matter of any kind or description." The act provides, however, that the

[42]*Burinskas v. NLRB,* 357 F.2d 822 (D.C. Cir. 1966).

[43]*Freuhauf Corp. v. IRS,* 522 F.2d 284 (6th Cir. 1975).

secretary of the army permit the deposit of refuse matter deemed by the Army Corps of Engineers not to be injurious to navigation, provided application is made prior to depositing such material. The company argued, for various reasons, that Section 13 of the act did not apply to the circumstances and that failure to obtain a permit for the discharge of liquid sewage was excusable since the corps had not established a formal program for issuing permits and because the corps had consistently construed Section 13 to be limited to deposits that would impede or obstruct navigation. Therefore, the company argued that it had been misled into believing that a permit was not required in this case. The district court rejected the company's arguments, and a jury convicted the company of a violation.

Upon appeal, the Supreme Court noted that previously the corps consistently had construed Section 13 to be limited to refuse deposits that affected navigation and that in fact the published regulation read to that effect. The Court ruled that the company had a right to look to corps regulations for guidelines. Rulings and interpretations of administrative agencies, while not binding upon courts, do constitute a body of judgment to which litigants may resort for guidance. Whether there was reliance by the company was an issue of fact for the trial court. Therefore the case was remanded to the lower court to allow the company to present evidence in support of its claim that it had been misled into believing it was not in violation of the law.[44]

Res Judicata and Collateral Estoppel

When a judgment has been made on a matter, the judgment is binding and further judicial action on the same claim or cause of action is barred. This is the doctrine of res judicata, which literally means "thing adjudicated." In the same manner, collateral estoppel prevents a second litigation of identical issues between the same parties even though the issues may pertain to a different claim or cause of action than that involved in the previous litigation. The purpose of res judicata and collateral estoppel is to avoid constant relitigation of issues already resolved. The doctrines apply to administrative adjudication of facts as well as to judicial action. Factual decisions of administrative agencies are conclusive. Thus a determination of whether specific actions of a regulated party constitute a violation of a rule is final and cannot be retried. Other administrative determinations do not have res judicata effect. Agencies are allowed broad discretion in administering and interpreting statutory law. Thus rule making, interpretations, and decisions concerning law or policy may be reconsidered and changed.

Res judicata prevents harassment of the regulated party by repeated prosecution for the same practices. Once an agency has determined that the facts of a case do not constitute a violation of the law, a retrial of the matter is barred. The determination of an issue by one federal agency bars relitigation of the same issue between the regulated party and another agency. The party asserting res judicata or collateral estoppel has the burden of showing that the issues in the two actions are identical and that the previous decision was adjudicative in nature, in that the decision was made on the factual merits of the case. In *Continental Can Co. v. Marshall*,[45] the OSHA Review Commission had considered the facts of a noise-level citation in a hearing con-

---

[44]*United States v. Pennsylvania Indus. Chemical Corp.*, 411 U.S. 655 (1973).

[45]455 F. Supp. 1015 (S.D. Ill. 1978).

cerning eight of the company's plants and found no noise-level violation. The court ruled that collateral estoppel then barred further litigation against the company for alleged violations in other essentially identical plants.

Most agencies allow parties to apply for the reopening of a case within a limited time for purposes of considering new evidence. Of course, agency determination may be appealed through proper channels to review commissions and to the courts. Res judicata and collateral estoppel merely bar the retrial of factual issues on which a final determination has already been made. A judicial decision on an issue which has first been litigated in court is not res judicata to bar subsequent consideration of the issue in an administrative proceeding if the issue is one over which the agency has specifically mandated authority and special expertise. An administrative decision may be res judicata for purposes of an issue which is subsequently litigated in court. The court may defer to the agency's determination on the matter.

Illustrative Case

Traders Oil Mill Co. was served a citation for an alleged violation of an OSHA regulation which required an employer to implement controls whenever employees were exposed to excessive concentrations of raw-cotton dust. The company filed a motion for summary judgment with an affidavit attached which stated that the plant where the alleged infraction had occurred was engaged solely in the processing of cottonseed and was not involved in the processing of raw cotton. An earlier decision, *Secretary v. Buckeye Cellulose Corp.,*[46] had held that the cited safety standard was not intended to apply to the processing of cottonseed because this processing did not produce the contaminants of raw-cotton dust. Relying on this previous decision, the judge granted the summary judgment because no triable issue was involved. The judge held that on the basis of the doctrines of collateral estoppel and res judicata a prior decision on the same issue served to answer the question.[47]

Ambush Tactics

There is very little discovery in most administrative law cases. This lack of discovery can be used advantageously by a business in bringing up for the first time at the hearing aspects of the case which the government failed to discover. Typically, much of a business's case will be unknown to the government when the dispute reaches the hearing stage. Because the government generally is not adequately prepared to deal with aspects of a case which become known for the first time at trial, this is a tremendous advantage in administrative proceedings. Ambush tactics in which a party withholds evidence until trial are perfectly legal and proper in most administrative proceedings.

The same philosophy applies to preliminary motions by a business. Revealing the business arguments in a preliminary motion allows the agency attorney better to prepare arguments and evidence if the administrative law judge denies the motion or defers decision on it (which is most often the

[46] 4 OSAHRC 356.
[47] *Traders Oil Mill Co.,* (1974–1975 OSHD ¶ 19, 216).

ruling). Even if a motion is granted on some defect in the charges or notice of the charges, the agency will usually be allowed to cure the defect. Therefore, any motion which is not a "lead pipe cinch" should probably not be made until just before or just after the government has presented its case, when it is usually too late to cure any procedural defect or restructure the government's case.

However, the company attorney must raise all affirmative defenses at the earliest possible time and make all objections and raise all defenses no later than the time of the evidentiary hearing; otherwise an appeals court may find that the defenses have been waived. For instance, in defending an OSHA case, an employer must raise in the answer to the charges such defenses as impossibility of compliance with the regulation, inapplicability of the regulation, greater hazard that would be created by compliance, and invalidity of the regulation. Otherwise, the employer may be barred from raising these defenses on appeal of an adverse administrative decision.

Similarly, a company should consider not making an opening statement, when the defense has the option, in order to hold back its evidence and arguments until after the government's evidence is in. Also, if the practice of the agency is to accept simultaneous briefs from the parties after the hearing is closed, a company should not make a closing statement giving away arguments which the government would then have the opportunity to research and attempt to rebut in its brief. If the government attorney does not have this opportunity, the defense is in an excellent posture to "outgun" the government on the closing brief, given the heavy case load and inexperience of most agency attorneys.

Attorneys for agencies are generally very busy in handling a number of cases and generally do not seek discovery in routine cases. Of course, any agency action is not routine to the business involved. Therefore, the business may want to keep its main gun below the table until the trial and then blow the government away with both barrels at trial. Of course, this tactic must be balanced against the advantages of trying to convince the agency early that the business's case is meritorious and perhaps reaching a good settlement. It is a matter of judgment whether a business wants to cooperate fully on the front end in trying to convince the agency not to take action because of the evidence it has or to hold the evidence for an ambush tactic at the trial. For example, a business may want to withhold any notice that it is going to bring in an expert of renowned reputation as a part of its case in order to prevent the government from lining up an expert on its side.

Making the Government Prove Its Case

The burden of proof in almost all administrative actions is on the government. Government attorneys usually are not experienced in trial matters and certainly are not very well experienced in the rules of evidence, even though a party can often defend merely by insisting upon proper evidentiary procedures before the administrative law judge and putting the government to its proof. Although formal rules of evidence may not be followed in some agencies, in matters of hearsay secondary evidentiary sources should certainly be objected to because such objections also go to the weight to be accorded to the evidence. A proper objection or the lack of one may be persuasive to the administrative law judge or to a court of appeals in deciding the overall case. The government may even omit vital evidence for the case, and after it has completed its case, the lack of a key element may knock out its case on proper motion by the party. If the government's evidence is lacking on some vital element or if the defense is based on a pure question of law, such as the inapplicability of a regulation, a motion to dismiss should always be made at the conclusion of the government's case. In making such a motion, the business attorney should be extremely persistent and even include a previously prepared memorandum. Without such persistence, the administrative law judge will take the easy way out and defer ruling until the defense evidence has been presented. However, if the business puts on its evidence, the government has a chance to cross-examine defense witnesses and attempt to patch up its case. The government should not be given this chance if the business attorney can prevail on a motion to dismiss.

In cross-examining government witnesses, the key word is brevity. The inspector or compliance officer or auditor will usually be prepared to "attack" an ill-advised question (such as "How could you use that safety device and still perform the work?"), and he or she will be well coached to evade tough questions. If there is one consistent trait in OSHA compliance officers, it is that they become good witnesses very quickly, albeit not as polished as most "professional" expert witnesses. It is most often fruitless to fish for concessions from one of these witnesses. However, if approached in a positive, rather than an abusive or hostile, manner, an inspector will occasionally make a concession about a questionable violation because he or she is under the impression that this relates only to the amount of the penalty. Defense counsel should also explore all notes, memoranda, or reports prepared by the inspector, since counsel is entitled to discover these types of documents.

In cross-examining a government agency's expert witness in a compliance proceeding, questioning the witness's background and experience can often be a valuable approach, since the agency will usually try to use an in-house "expert," i.e., a senior compliance officer, rather than an outside consultant who is truly experienced and qualified in the industry or activity in question. The agency will attempt to qualify its witness as an expert on the basis of the inspections the witness has made even though the inspector has no experience in the industry or activity in question. On most questions on which expert opinion is necessary, this type of witness is not qualified as an expert.

By comparison, businesses should most often call as industry experts employees of the business or of its competitors on the basis of their long years of experience in the industry and the liberal federal rule on opinion testimony by lay witnesses. Most administrative law judges will tend to weight very heavily such witnesses' opinions on gut issues such as feasibility, as compared with opinion testimony of either professional consultants or inspectors.

Demonstrative evidence is often important to the defense, because the agency will almost always introduce photographs of the violative conditions and sales materials on equipment available for abatement, and neither will usually be sufficient for demonstrating the defenses of a business. Thus, the defense should have its own photographs to demonstrate the site of alleged violations, reasons for infeasibility or impossibility of compliance, safe methods which employees use in the activity in question, and any other matters on which a vivid understanding of industry practices and problems is necessary.

Delay

Delay has been used at times as a tactic to postpone the effect of an agency decision. There are circumstances in which extra time is needed by a party before an agency decision becomes operative; otherwise that decision would have devastating effects. Many challenges can properly be made both in agency proceedings and later in court actions. As long as the challenges have some basis, the aggrieved party is justified in making them. However, a challenge which clearly has no basis should not be made.

Illustrative Case

The FTC issued a complaint in December 1962 relating to J. B. Williams's advertising for Geritol. The gist of the complaint was that the advertising gave the impression that Geritol was an effective remedy for tiredness or a rundown feeling, where it really was effective in only a small minority of cases in which these conditions were caused by a deficiency in iron or the vitamins found in Geritol. After a number of different proceedings, the FTC issued a cease and desist order in September 1965. The defendants petitioned for review of the order, and the FTC entered a modified order in November 1967. The defendants submitted a compliance report, but they were found not be in compliance and were directed to issue another compliance report by January 1969. Appellants submitted that report and were then informed what steps needed to be taken to achieve compliance with that order. Defendants submitted a third compliance report in accordance with the FTC's request.

Counsel for Williams then advised the FTC that the company was marketing a new product called Fem Iron. The company didn't consider Fem Iron to be within the provisions of the cease and desist order because it was substantially different from Geritol.

The FTC concluded that the third compliance report did not comply with its requirements, that several Geritol commercials violated the cease and desist order, that Fem Iron and Geritol had substantially similar properties, and that Fem Iron was subject to that order. The FTC stated that it was going to begin an investigation looking toward a possible enforcement proceeding.

In an action by the government for civil penalties for violations of the FTC's cease and desist order, the court granted summary judgment to the government. Defendants appealed and demanded a jury trial. The court decided that the question of whether the commercials violated the FTC order and whether the new product was within the reach of that order was a task for the court.

In the civil penalty action, respondents moved for an order compelling discovery of documents. The motion was referred to the magistrate, and the magistrate's report was received in September 1975. Counsel for the defendants then objected to the magistrate's report, and the district court made its findings in September 1975.[48]

The dispute between J. B. Williams Co. and the FTC took years in the court systems before it was resolved. In compliance cases it is not unusual for a case to spend years in discovery and pretrial stages before coming to trial. In many agencies, several appeals can be taken within an agency, and there are also appeals from the final agency order to the court of appeals. Moreover, frequently there are available to the affected business collateral attacks such as attacking the validity of the rule or regulation in a separate court action. As in the *J. B. Williams* case, there may be reasonable disputes about the agency order which can be raised in the courts even after the initial appeals have been completely exhausted.

---

[48] *United States v. J. B. Williams,* 498 F.2d 414 (2d Cir. 1974); *United States v. J. B. Williams,* 402 F. Supp. 796 (S.D.N.Y. 1975).

10 TAKING THE AGENCY TO COURT

McNEILL STOKES
Stokes & Shapiro
Attorneys at Law

Once an agency has taken action which adversely affects an individual or a business and every available appeal on the administrative level has been pursued without success, what is the next step? An individual aggrieved by agency action is not foreclosed from further appeals by a final agency determination. At that point the focus of the battle may shift to the courts in an action for review of the agency's decision.

Judicial review is important because it provides a check on the wide discretion generally afforded administrative agencies and ensures that there is an appeal available above the agency level. The primary function of this review is to ensure the integrity of the decision-making process. Agency personnel are aware that their decisions may be reviewed by a court and that any which are made arbitrarily may be overturned. Thus the courts incorporate a measure of checks and balances in the administrative system.

Judicial review is made even more attractive by the passage of the Equal Access to Justice Act. In recognition that some individuals and businesses may be deterred from seeking review because of the cost, the act provides for reimbursement to individuals and businesses of costs and expenses spent in successfully fighting the government when the government's action is not substantially justified. The act is an attempt to ensure that review of agency actions will be available to all individuals and businesses regardless of cost. It implicitly recognizes the importance of judicial review to the protection of individual rights.

SCOPE OF REVIEW

In determining when to review an agency's actions, courts have commonly attempted to balance two important considerations: that the administrative process must be protected as a separate system and that individuals must be protected against agency abuses of power. In considering the scope of review, the reviewing court bears the responsibility of exercising restraint to ensure that there is no unwarranted intrusion into the administrative area, while at the same time making certain that there are no arbitrary exercises of power by an agency. If a court can be convinced that fundamental interests are being affected by arbitrary exercises of power by the agency, its review of the administrative action will be much more active. In fact, it is probably true that "a judge will do what he thinks he should, no matter how we try to corral him."[1] No matter how theories limit a court's scope of review, if a judge can be persuaded that justice demands it, the agency action may be overturned.

The judiciary is still the final supervisor of the agencies. The courts must ensure that the agencies don't exceed their powers and follow proper procedures in their rule-making, investigative, and enforcement activities.

Illustrative Case

The publisher of an airline guide that listed only connecting flights for certified airlines was ordered by the Federal Trade Commission (FTC) to publish the connecting-flight listings for commuter airlines and to refrain from discriminating arbitrarily against any carrier in publishing its listings. The U.S. Court of Appeals for the Second Circuit declined to enforce the order, holding that enforcement would give the FTC too much power to substitute its own business judgment for that of the publisher. Section 5 of the Federal Trade Commission Act does not give the FTC the power to stop a monopolist in one business from arbitrarily discriminating among customers in another business. The court held that the FTC could not restrain a business from choosing the parties with which it would deal as long as that business was not attempting to restrain its competition or enhance its own monopoly.[2]

Although normally the courts will defer to an agency's power to promulgate its own rules and regulations, there are times when the courts will oversee the agency's exercise of its rule-making authority. A court will step in when the agency exceeds its authority.

Illustrative Case

The Occupational Safety and Health Administration (OSHA) promulgated an industry standard reducing drastically the permissible exposure limit on airborne concentrations of benzene. OSHA's rationale for lowering the permissible exposure limit from 10 parts per million to 1 part per million was based, not on any finding that leukemia had ever been caused by exposure to 10 parts per million of benzene and that it would *not* be caused by exposure to 1 part per million, but rather on a series of assumptions indicating that some leukemia might result from exposure to 10 parts per million but that the number of cases might be reduced by lowering the exposure level to 1 part per million. Accordingly, OSHA set the exposure limit at the lowest technologically feasible level that would not impair the viability of industries regulated. The Supreme Court concluded that the standard was invalid, holding that, as a threshold matter, the secretary must find that the toxic substance in question posed a significant health risk in the workplace and that a new, lower standard was therefore "reasonably necessary or appropriate to provide safe or healthful employment and places of employment." The Court then held that the burden was on OSHA to show, on the basis of substantial

---

[1]*Russo v. United States Trucking Corp.*, 140 A.2d 206, 214 (N.J. 1958).

[2]*Official Airline Guides, Inc. v. FTC*, 630 F.2d 920 (2d Cir. 1980).

evidence, that it was at least more likely than not that long-term exposure to 10 parts per million of benzene presented a significant risk of material health impairment. In relying on a special policy for carcinogens that imposed the burden of proving the existence of a safe level of exposure on industry, the secretary had exceeded his power.[3]

It is stressed that courts should not interfere with discretionary agency decisions but that at the same time they must oversee the reasonableness of those decisions. It is not the responsibility of a court to examine the alternatives available to an agency to determine which alternative is more reasonable, for that is the exercise of discretion which has been granted to the agency. However, the court has power to review when this discretionary authority has been exercised unreasonably.

Illustrative Case

The Gonzalez Corporation was temporarily debarred from doing business with the Commodity Credit Corporation (CCC) pending investigation of possible misuse of official inspection certificates relating to commodities exported by the Gonzalez Corporation. Gonzalez sought review by the secretary of agriculture, who declined to reconsider unless it presented new evidence. Gonzalez then brought an action for declaratory and injunctive relief against the secretary. The government defended on the ground that the blacklisting was action committed to agency discretion and was thus unreviewable. The court held that the fact that there was no "right" to a government contract did not mean that the government could act arbitrarily against a person or that that person was not entitled to challenge the processes before being officially declared ineligible for government contracts. The court stated that debarment from participation in government contracts could not be left to administrative improvisation on a case-by-case basis but must be handled in accordance with regulations which established standards for debarment. The court held that, absent procedural regulations and absent notice, hearing, and findings, the debarment was invalid.[4]

A reviewing court's consideration of the dispute is limited to what is contained in an agency's record. As one example, a reviewing court is not supposed to accept new evidence. The court's examination of the agency's decision is to be based on the evidence before the agency when that decision was reached. It would be unfair to allow a party to withhold evidence from the administrative board only to present it to the court on appeal if the decision were unfavorable. The administrative process is not to be used as a stepping-stone to the courts. The party is not generally entitled to a completely new trial, which is called a trial de novo, but is restricted to the confines of the case as presented to the agency.

Illustrative Case

Carlo Bianchi and Co. entered into a contract with the Army Corps of Engineers to construct a flood control dam and also to construct a tunnel for the diversion of water. The tunnel was to be lined with concrete and to have permanent steel supports at

---

[3] *Industrial Union Dep't, AFT-CIO v. American Petroleum Inst.*, 100 S. Ct. 2844 (1980).

[4] *Gonzalez v. Freeman*, 334 F.2d 570 (D.C. Cir. 1964).

either end. Supports required for the rest of the tunnel were only those necessary for temporary tunnel protection for the safety of the workers. After the tunnel had been drilled, Bianchi determined that unforeseen conditions created extreme hazards for the workers and thought it necessary to construct permanent protection throughout the tunnel. Bianchi sought compensation for the unanticipated expense. The contracting officer denied the claim, but while the appeal was pending before the Board of Claims and Appeals, Bianchi installed the supports and completed the tunnel. A hearing was held before the Board, to which each side offered its evidence, and a record was made. The Board issued a decision against the contractor. Bianchi then brought an action against the government for breach of contract, alleging that the decisions rendered previously were "capricious or arbitrary or so grossly erroneous as necessarily to imply bad faith, or were not supported by substantial evidence." At a completely new hearing, the court received evidence that had not been before the Board and concluded that Bianchi was entitled to recover. On appeal the Supreme Court held that in the absence of fraud the court's consideration should have been confined to the administrative record. The Court concluded that "determination of the finality to be attached to a departmental decision on a question arising under the disputes clause must rest solely on consideration of the record." No de novo proceeding might be held.[5]

Even though the formal rule is that the reviewing court should not grant de novo review, a broader review than that which is required is very common. Federal courts often review tax determinations by the Internal Revenue Service (IRS) de novo. The court will often take its own evidence and make its own findings on facts, policy, and legal issues when it considers this to be warranted.

The failure to raise an issue in an agency proceeding, when there has been an opportunity to present it, usually precludes the raising of the issue before the court. Objections to agency proceedings must also be raised while the dispute is still before the agency. In addition, a reviewing court will normally consider only the grounds on which the agency has relied in making its decision. When an agency is required to set out the grounds upon which it has based its decision, the reviewing court must examine those grounds to ascertain whether they support the decision. If the decision is not supported by the grounds which are specified, it may be vacated. This is so even if the decision can be supported by grounds other than those relied on by the agency. The court is limited to an examination of whether the decision is supported by the grounds identified as the basis for the agency's decision.[6]

There are limited exceptions to the rule that a reviewing court may not consider anything that has not been presented at the agency proceeding. When unusual circumstances exist or when justice for some reason demands it, a court on review may consider something that has not been brought up before the agency. In addition, the Supreme Court has said that an objection to the jurisdiction of an agency need not be presented to the agency first but

[5] *United States v. Carlo Bianchi & Co., Inc., 373 U.S. 709 (1963).*

[6] *SEC v. Chenery Corp., 318 U.S. 80 (1943).*

may be made for the first time before the court.[7] Lack of jurisdiction can generally be raised at that later stage, but it is always advantageous to raise any objections at the earliest stage possible.

The scope of review of the judiciary is also shaped by the requirement that findings of fact are to be made by an agency and questions of law are to be determined by a court. The courts are specially equipped to deal with legal issues. When a question of law is involved, a court must examine an agency's legal decision but may substitute its own judgment for that of the agency. Its determination of a legal issue is to be made independently of the agency findings. Whenever possible, an issue should be framed as a legal issue in order to assure complete review by the judiciary. A court's review of legal issues is in much greater depth than its review of a factual determination.

An administrative agency is presumed to have special expertise to answer technical factual questions. However, a court must still be able to examine those findings. Judicial review of the agency's factual findings is limited to an examination of the entire record to determine whether those findings are supported by substantial evidence. The court will not weigh the alternatives and substitute its own judgment for that of the agency. The court has power to overturn an agency decision, but the test is relatively strict. The court may not reach its own conclusion even if that conclusion would differ from the agency's. Only if the agency finding is unreasonable may the court overturn it.

However, there is an elusive line between what is an application of the reasonableness test and what is actually a substitution of the court's judgment. A broader review than that which is required is very common. Courts do not commonly sit back and accept an administrative finding which is not warranted. Administrative findings of fact are often set aside because a court believes that the evidence justifies a different finding. Whether that is a determination of the reasonableness or the rightness of a finding is not clear. But courts do not depend on the label to justify setting aside an administrative finding.

One problem in determining whether to appeal a particular agency finding is that there is no clear distinction between law and fact. Some findings are definitely factual and some are definitely legal, but many questions seem to fall in between. Most agency findings consist of the application of legal principles to findings of fact. The question arises whether these are factual findings for which great weight will be accorded the agency determination or legal findings subject to an independent determination by the court. When considering the extent of review, the determination can be reviewed as either (1) findings of law or (2) findings of fact or (3) be separated into legal and factual elements. That determination would outline the scope of review. The judiciary determines whether the findings are legal or factual or composed

---

[7] *United States v. L.A. Tucker Trucklines,* 344 U.S. 33 (1952).

of both elements. If the legal aspects of an issue are stressed, the court will take a more active role in reviewing agency action.

AVAILABILITY OF REVIEW

Generally, judicial review of a particular agency action is provided for by statute. A statute which authorizes a particular agency action or the regulations which structure the action to be taken usually contain specific review provisions. For example, jurisdiction to review proceedings conducted by the FTC pursuant to Section 7 of the Clayton Act is vested in the court of appeals by virtue of another provision of the act. That jurisdiction is made exclusive because all jurisdictional, constitutional, procedural, and substantive issues may be raised in that appeal. This method of direct review of agency action is the method most commonly used in the federal statutory framework. Review is conducted almost as if there were an appeal from a lower court. Review is initiated by the aggrieved party's filing a petition for review in the appropriate court. The statute outlines the method of review, the form of action to be used, and the procedure to be followed. Many statutes require that the review provisions be followed to the letter; otherwise the aggrieved party will be precluded from review by the courts.

In addition to direct review, review of some actions can be obtained indirectly by failure to comply with an agency order. Many agencies are not granted the power to enforce their own orders. Thus an agency must bring an action in court for enforcement of any orders with which a party does not voluntarily comply. This is not the same kind of direct review discussed above, yet it still has the effect of providing a court as a forum for the aggrieved party's objections. For instance, the National Labor Relations Board (NLRB) does not have the power to enforce its own orders. It must issue its orders and wait for voluntary compliance. If compliance is not forthcoming, the Board must petition a court for enforcement. At this point an aggrieved party may obtain judicial review of an NLRB order.

There is a strong presumption that administrative actions are subject to judicial review. Even when a statute is silent as to judicial review and an order is self-operative, the presumption of reviewability remains. That the presumption does remain has been reflected in both statutes and court decisions. The absence of a statutory grant of review is not an indication that the judiciary lacks the power to review an agency determination. Statutory review provisions often supplement the common-law procedures for review. The courts seldom restrict access to judicial review for those who have been injured by agency action. Courts have consistently stressed that judicial review of a final agency action will not be precluded unless Congress has shown an intention to cut off review. Legislative silence does not by itself evidence an intent to deny review.

Some courts have held that when Congress provides an adequate procedure for review, that procedure must be followed unless there is an extraordinary reason to deviate from it. Other courts have held that, given the liberal standard of availability of judicial review, the fact that a statute includes a specific procedure for review does not always lead to a presumption that other types of review have been excluded. Traditional avenues of appeal which would normally be available to an individual may still be available despite the inclusion in a statute of a specific remedy.

Illustrative Case

The Food, Drug, and Cosmetic Act contains a saving clause in Section 701(f), which provides some special review procedures and then directs that the remedies shall be in addition to and not in substitution for any other remedies provided by law. The legislative history evidences the intention that this provision was designed as a general saving clause and not intended to apply merely to Section 701(f) remedies. The House report stated that this clause "saved as a method to review a regulation. . . . whatever rights exist to initiate a historical proceeding in equity to enjoin the enforcement of the regulation and whatever rights exist to initiate a declaratory judgment proceeding."[8] In interpreting the Food, Drug, and Cosmetic Act, the Supreme Court considered the congressional purpose in enacting the particular review provisions to determine whether they were intended to eliminate other avenues of judicial review. The Court stated that it was clear that the special review provisions were intended merely to assure adequate judicial review and not to cut off other kinds of judicial review of agency action.[9]

However, the presumption of reviewability may be cut off. Although it will generally be presumed that agency action is reviewable, preclusion of judicial review may be provided by different means. The statute itself may expressly cut off any appeal above the agency level. This evidence not only may be drawn from a statute's explicit language but also may be garnered from the purpose and design of a particular statute. Although the inference that Congress did not intend that an individual be able to appeal to the judiciary may be gathered elsewhere than in the explicit language of a statute, it will not be lightly made. A clear showing of legislative intent must be made to do so. Nonreviewability of an administrative action is the exception and not the rule. A federal agency seeking to preclude review of an action bears the heavy burden of overcoming the strong presumption that judicial review of agency actions is always available.[10]

There may also be no jurisdiction in the courts to entertain an appeal when "agency action is committed to agency discretion by law."[11] This exception applies when statutes are drawn in such broad terms that in a given case there is really no standard for the court to apply. Courts have formulated criteria to be used in determining when agency action is so committed to the discretion of the agency as to cut off the availability of an appeal to the courts. The exception will apply when statutory standards are expressed in

[8]H.R. Rep. No. 2139, 75th Cong. 3d Sess. 2.

[9]*Abbott Laboratories v. Gardner,* 387 U.S. 136 (1967).

[10]*City of Camden v. Plotkin,* 466 F. Supp. 44 (D.N.J. 1978).

[11]5 U.S.C. § 701.

broad, general concepts rather than in specific guidelines, when the statutory language is permissive rather than mandatory, and when the decision contemplated by the statute requires the exercise of expert judgment within the special competence of the agency rather than requesting a legal determination. The congressional intention to commit the decision to the discretion of the agency can be drawn from the plain language of the statute or gathered from the purpose and history of the act at issue. However, the exception is a very narrow one, and even agency actions which have traditionally been viewed as matters to be left to the discretion of the agency have been reviewed by the courts.

Illustrative Case

In 1962 the Southwestern Power Administration (SPA) entered into contracts with the Associated Electric Cooperative for the sale of federal hydroelectric power at rates set by the secretary of the interior and approved by the Federal Power Commission (FPC). The contracts provided for the allowance of credits for services to be performed by Associated in connection with the transmission of power for SPA's account. In 1970 the secretary revised the rate schedule by adding a "transmission service charge" to recover costs incurred by SPA. Associated Electric then brought an action to have the modification of the rate schedule declared illegal on the ground that the cancellation of credits allegedly due under the 1962 contract was in violation of the secretary's statutory authority and in violation of the contract. The government contended, among other things, that the secretary's exercise of his rate-making authority was not subject to judicial review because it was "agency action . . . committed to agency discretion by law." The court held that that exception was a very narrow one, applicable only in those rare instances in which statutes were drawn in such broad terms that there was really no law to apply. Even though this case involved rate making, the court held that it was still subject to judicial review.[12]

Although the Administrative Procedure Act (APA) provides that judicial review is available "except to the extent that . . . agency action is committed to agency discretion by law,"[13] this hasn't been interpreted as completely forbidding review of discretionary agency action. Discretionary actions are expressly made reviewable in another section of the APA, which provides for review of agency action "found to be . . . an abuse of discretion."[14] The interpretation given these provisions when read together is that when discretion is exercised reasonably by the agency, it will not be subject to review by the courts. However, arbitrary exercises of discretion must always be reviewable by the judiciary. The courts must have the power to reverse actions which are abuses of discretion; otherwise administrative decisions would be placed beyond the reach of the law. Therefore, the exception for action "committed to agency discretion" has been very narrowly construed. It remains that

---

[12]*Associated Electric Coop., Inc. v. Morton*, 507 F.2d 1167 (D.C. Cir. 1974), *cert. denied*, 423 U.S. 830 (1975).
[13]5 U.S.C. § 701.
[14]5 U.S.C. § 706.

"judicial review of such administrative action is the rule, and nonreviewability an exception which must be demonstrated."[15]

Illustrative Case

Hughes Air Corporation became the successor in interest to three other airlines. The Civil Aeronautics Board (CAB) attempted to require Hughes Air to refund to the government over $1 million of the subsidies that its predecessors had received. Hughes sought review of those orders of the CAB. The court held that it did have jurisdiction to review administrative actions which were alleged to be arbitrary or an abuse of discretion. It found the CAB's actions to be arbitrary and unenforceable because the carry-back requirement applied only if tax loss had been reported before final subsidy determination, so that airlines whose determinations had been made earlier escaped the requirement. The court held that its scope of review was narrow but that it could set aside agency action which was arbitrary and an abuse of discretion if the court was convinced the agency was wrong. The court set aside the CAB's orders.[16]

FORMS OF ACTION

In addition to providing for judicial review, a statute will also provide the form of action to be used to obtain review. This form of action may be exclusive unless the statute provides that other forms may be used. The form of action provided for by the statute must be followed completely. Adherence to these statutory requirements may be a prerequisite to judicial review.

The APA provides specifically for nonstatutory judicial review. First, it grants a right of review to all those "suffering legal wrong because of agency action or adversely affected or aggrieved by agency action." It follows that grant of review by providing that "the form of proceeding for judicial review is the special statutory review proceeding . . . or in the absence or inadequacy thereof, any applicable form of legal action, including actions for declaratory judgments or writs of prohibitory or mandatory injunction or habeas corpus in a court of competent jurisdiction."[17]

A commonly followed form of action used to obtain review of an administrative act is an injunction. An action may be brought in district court to enjoin an agency from acting in a particular way. In granting an injunction, courts generally have proceeded as if it were a private tort action against an individual. The theory is that the agency must be restrained from taking whatever action is contemplated; otherwise the plaintiff will be injured. The courts have frequently granted injunctions against an administrative agency as the remedy for its actions which have injured a party.

Actions are often brought for a declaratory judgment to have a particular ruling declared illegal and, at the same time, to have the agency enjoined from enforcing that ruling. A declaratory judgment also can be used alone to have an administrative ruling declared illegal. The declaratory judgment

[15]*Barlow v. Collins*, 397 U.S. 159, 166 (1970).

[16]*Hughes Air Corp. v. CAB*, 482 F.2d 143 (9th Cir. 1973).

[17]5 U.S.C. § 703.

involves no coercive measures as a part of that judgment, but it is assumed that an agency will refrain from taking action that has been declared illegal.

An action for judicial review would not by itself stay the operation of the challenged administrative determination. When justice requires, an agency may postpone the effective date of action taken, pending judicial review. In addition, the reviewing court may issue a stay to postpone the effective date of agency action or to preserve the rights of an individual pending the conclusion of review proceedings.

There have traditionally been certain requirements before a stay will issue. Most important, irreparable injury must be threatened before a stay will issue. If there were no threat of irreparable damage, there would really be no reason for such an intrusive action as postponing an agency decision. Courts have held that mere economic loss may not constitute irreparable injury. A stay will be granted only upon a showing that plaintiff is likely to prevail on the merits. If a party cannot demonstrate a likelihood of prevailing on the petition for review after a full hearing thereon, a stay will generally be denied. Also in determining whether to grant a stay, a court must examine the possibility of harm to opposing parties or to the public if a stay is granted. A party moving for a stay must establish the absence of substantial harm to others if an administrative action is to be stayed pending judicial review. The court must balance the needs of the party against the possibility of harm to others.

Illustrative Case

An association of lead industries petitioned the Supreme Court to stay implementation of a new OSHA lead standard pending judicial review of the standard. The stay was sought to enable the industry to seek judicial review without having to make substantial expenditures to begin compliance before the standard was reviewed. The petition alleged that there would be no harm to the public from the stay because the industry would continue to meet OSHA's permissible exposure limits through other engineering, administrative, and respiratory controls. In addition, the petition contended that there was a great likelihood that the Supreme Court would grant review of the standard because it presented issues strikingly similar to those in a case which had recently been granted review. Accordingly, the Supreme Court granted a partial stay of the lead standard to allow the industry to postpone major construction of new facilities needed to comply with the standard until it could be reviewed.[18]

In addition to the requirement that review of a particular administrative action must be generally available, there are other specific requirements which must be fulfilled before judicial review will be granted to a party. If review is generally available, the next requirement is that the party seeking review must be a proper party to bring that action. In other words the party must have standing to challenge an administrative action. If the party is the proper one to seek review, the question becomes whether the action has been brought at the proper time. Several elements of this requirement which must

[18]*Lead Indus. Ass'n. v. Marshall*, 101 S. Ct. 603 (1980).

be individually satisfied are finality, exhaustion of administrative remedies, primary jurisdiction, and ripeness. All these elements will be examined individually, for they stand as requirements which must be satisfied before a party can gain judicial review of an administrative action.

STANDING

For a party to obtain judicial review it must have standing to seek that review. In its basic meaning, "standing" refers to the capacity of a party to obtain judicial relief. A particular statute may confer standing on an individual or an entity to seek review of an administrative action taken pursuant to that statute.

Besides statutory standing, a party may have standing because of injury caused by agency action. This is the classic concept of standing. Standing is conferred on a person who suffers harm from administrative decisions. The APA employs a classic standing concept by awarding judicial review to "a person suffering legal wrong because of agency action, or adversely affected or aggrieved by agency action within the meaning of a relevant statute."[19] That provision actually grants review in two distinct situations: when the party suffers legal wrong and when the party is adversely affected by agency action. At one point these were cumulative requirements. Courts required that a party suffer a legal wrong before examining a particular action.

The Supreme Court has enunciated a two-pronged standing test that the party seeking review must be injured by an agency action and that the interest sought to be protected must fall within the zone of interests which were intended to be protected by that particular statute or regulation, or by some constitutional guarantee.[20]

Illustrative Case

Several professional physical therapy corporations were awarded standing when they filed a complaint alleging that a Medicare regulation which required nonprofit home health agencies to contract only with nonprofit therapy organizations deprived them of property without due process of law. The court held that the test was not whether the plaintiffs themselves were regulated by the statute but rather whether the interests asserted by the plaintiffs arguably fell within the zone of interests which were regulated. Although the court didn't require an injury to a legally protected right, it required that the injury be to an interest which was arguably within the zone of interests protected by the statute. Thus, even as a government agency regulates contractual relationships between a regulated and an unregulated party, the unregulated party also has interests which are affected by that regulation. Those interests are sufficient for the unregulated party to have standing to challenge that particular regulation.[21]

The party being regulated by an administrative order is very often not the only one affected by the order. An agency's actions may impact on another

---

[19] 5 U.S.C. § 702.

[20] *Association of Data Processing Serv. Organizations v. Camp*, 397 U.S. 150, 153 (1970).

[21] *Cotovsky-Kaplan Physical Therapy Ass'n, Ltd. v. United States*, 507 F.2d 1363 (7th Cir. 1975).

party besides the regulated party. Standing has been granted to other parties who are not directly regulated to seek review of agency decisions. In addition to granting standing to parties who have contractual relationships with regulated parties, courts have granted standing to competitors of regulated parties. The economic interest of a competitor has been deemed sufficient to give that party standing to challenge an order which is not directed at the competitor if it has an impact on the unregulated party's position with respect to the regulated party.

Illustrative Cases

The Association of Data Processing Service Organizations brought suit against the comptroller of the currency to challenge a ruling that national banks could make data processing services available to other banks and to bank customers incident to their banking services. The Court held that a competitor might be within the zone of interests protected by the Bank Service Corporation Act. The Court, in so holding, looked to the legislative history of the act, in which it was stressed that the original prohibition against banks engaging in services other than performance of bank services had arisen as a result of fear that banks would engage in nonbanking activities. The Court thus found petitioners, as competitors of the banks engaging in data processing services, within the class of aggrieved persons to be afforded standing. It went on to say that whether anything in the Bank Service Corporation Act gave petitioners a "legal interest" which would protect them against violations of the act went to the merits.[22]

Hayes Corp. was an unsuccessful bidder for a government contract and brought suit to have the contract that was awarded set aside. It alleged that the contract was awarded in violation of Department of Defense regulations governing federal procurement. The court granted Hayes standing to challenge the award of the contract to a competitor. It stated that the trend of recent Supreme Court cases had been toward finding standing whenever "the plaintiff alleges that the challenged action caused him injury in fact, economic or otherwise" and "the interest sought to be protected by the plaintiff is arguably within the zone of interests to be regulated or protected by the statute or constitutional guarantee in question." The court held that there was little doubt that Hayes had suffered economic loss by the award of the contract to another bidder. Furthermore, the interests of Hayes were at least arguably within the zone of interests to be protected by the regulations despite the fact that Hayes could not claim a legal right to the contract. The regulations were designed at least in part to protect a competitor by preventing one contractor from obtaining an unfair competitive advantage over another one.[23]

Standing is not confined to those who show economic harm. Injuries of a noneconomic nature may be direct enough to permit challenge of administrative actions. Noneconomic injuries which may be sufficient to satisfy the standing test include aesthetic, conservational, recreational, and environmental ones.

Illustrative Case

In an action brought pursuant to the National Environmental Policy Act (NEPA) of 1969 several oil companies challenged the FTC's institution of an enforcement pro-

---

[22] *Association of Data Processing Serv. Organizations v. Camp,* 397 U.S. 150 (1970).

[23] *Hayes Int'l Corp. v. McLucas,* 509 F.2d 247 (5th Cir. 1975), *cert. denied,* 423 U.S. 864 (1975).

ceeding without having first filed an environmental-impact statement. The court determined that to have standing under NEPA the plaintiffs must allege environmental injury. The oil companies demonstrated that the relief requested by the FTC would have a detrimental effect on the environment. By virtue of their status as oil companies, the plaintiffs were found to have a stake in the environment and were awarded standing.[24]

The trend has clearly been toward an enlargement of the class of plaintiffs who have been allowed to challenge an administrative order. Recently, courts have even allowed suits by individuals whose only interest in a ruling is that of a consumer. The recent cases recognize the interest of a consumer in an order which increases the price that an individual has to pay. For instance, consumer standing has been awarded to challenge minimum-price orders.[25] In addition, consumer standing has been recognized in cases in which an order affects the quality of a product. The standing requirement is continuously being expanded to include all those who have a genuine interest of any kind in an administrative action.

FINALITY

An agency action must be final before review of that action can be obtained. For the administrative system to work effectively, an agency must be allowed to pursue a particular action to its conclusion. A court should not consider subject matter that is particularly within an agency's specialized field until that agency has had a chance to reach a conclusion by use of its processes. The proceedings would then be at a stage in which judicial review would not disrupt the administrative system.

The test for finality is simply its suitability for judicial review. It depends ultimately on the need for a review to protect from irreparable injury threatened by an administrative decision. An agency order need not be the last administrative ruling possible in a situation to be a final decision. It may be considered final when legal consequences will follow from the particular determination. Administrative orders are reviewable when they impose an obligation, deny a right, or fix a legal relationship.

Illustrative Case

Several organizations engaged in environmental protection activities submitted a petition to the secretary of agriculture requesting that he cancel the registrations of all pesticides containing DDT and also that he suspend those registrations pending the conclusion of the administrative hearings. The secretary issued notices of cancellation for some uses of DDT and published a notice of his intention to cancel other DDT uses. The environmental organizations then sought review of the secretary's silence on the request that he suspend registration pending the hearings. The court concluded that that silence was equivalent to a denial and was reviewable as a final order. The denial was considered final because it subjected the public to an imminent hazard (the continued use of DDT) and any injury was irreparable.[26]

[24] *Mobil Oil Corp. v. FTC,* 430 F. Supp. 855 (S.D.N.Y. 1977).

[25] *Associated Indus. v. Ickes,* 134 F.2d 694 (2d Cir. 1943), *dismissed as moot,* 320 U.S. 707 (1943).

[26] *Environmental Defense Fund, Inc. v. Ruckelshaus,* 439 F.2d 584 (D.C. Cir. 1971).

A delay of an agency in taking a particular action may, in the proper circumstances, be reviewable as a final order. In *Environmental Defense Fund* the delay had the same result as a denial of the relief requested. When a delay threatens to cause irreparable harm or to have other legal consequences, a court may review an agency's failure to act. An agency cannot prevent judicial review merely by delaying a decision.

Generally, intermediate orders are not subject to review by the courts. However, in exceptional cases review may be necessary to protect from irreparable injury. When a decision which is not final may have immediate consequences, the aggrieved party may seek review by a court. The ultimate question is whether the nature and extent of the threatened injury are sufficient to justify an interruption of the administrative process prior to its conclusion. When there is judicial intervention in a preliminary stage, there must not be an alternative avenue of relief for the injured party. The court must also be convinced that review of a final agency decision in the matter would be insufficient to protect threatened rights.

EXHAUSTION OF ADMINISTRATIVE REMEDIES

The requirement that there not be an alternative avenue of relief open to an aggrieved party seeking judicial review touches on another doctrine which influences the timing of review. The doctrine of exhaustion of administrative remedies refers to the policy of withholding judicial review until an administrative procedure has been completed. The judiciary normally won't interfere in an action until the injured party has sought all available relief from the agency itself.

The basic purpose of the exhaustion doctrine is to allow the administrative agency to perform the functions within its special competence by applying its expertise to make factual determinations, to record the proceedings, and to allow the agency an opportunity to correct its own errors so as to make judicial interference unnecessary.[27] Frequent intrusion of the judiciary into the administrative procedure could weaken the effectiveness of the agency by encouraging people to ignore the procedures set up by the agency and instead go directly to the courts. The exhaustion requirement is very well established in administrative law.

However, the doctrine is subject to numerous exceptions. First, the doctrine of exhaustion assumes that there is an alternative administrative remedy available to the aggrieved party. It presupposes that the remedy is entirely adequate to provide the relief requested by the party. If the available administrative remedy is inadequate to protect the party, exhaustion will not be required.

Illustrative Case

The Virginia Chapter, Associated General Contractors of America, Inc., sought a preliminary injunction to restrain officials from enforcing certain portions of the Public Works Employment Act of 1976. In particular, the plaintiffs alleged that the 10 percent

[27] *Jackson v. Colorado*, 294 F. Supp. 1065 (D. Colo. 1968).

minority business enterprise requirement for local contracts awarded under the act created an impermissible racial classification that violated equal protection. The government contended that a waiver of the disputed requirement was available as an effective administrative agency remedy which plaintiffs should be required to exhaust before seeking judicial review. It claimed that the suit should be dismissed for plaintiffs' failure to exhaust administrative remedies. The court stated that even if it were to find the doctrine of exhaustion of administrative remedies applicable, it would be hesitant to force the plaintiffs to seek a waiver of the requirement. Since under applicable regulations only local grantees might request a waiver, plaintiffs could not seek relief from the requirement. The court held that the alleged remedy provided by the waiver clause was therefore not available to the plaintiffs and that exhaustion was not required.[28]

An agency remedy might also be inadequate if it would be futile to pursue it. This exception has been applied mainly in two circumstances. It is most generally applied when an agency has acted in bad faith. Yet parties have been allowed to bypass the administrative process when it would be futile to pursue it because all the agency decisions are adverse to the party. This exception recognizes a right to judicial review when an agency will almost certainly decide a case in a particular way and it would therefore be futile for the party to pursue the matter with the agency.

Illustrative Example

Prisoners in a federal penitentiary challenged the policy of transferring prisoners to more secure penal institutions without procedural safeguards as violative of due process. The penitentiary asserted that there was an administrative review which the prisoners must seek before they could maintain the action. The court stated that the exhaustion doctrine was inapplicable when such administrative action would be to demand a futile act. The penitentiary had continuously asserted that prisoners had no right to any kind of notice or hearing prior to transfer and that no grievous loss could possibly be shown because of a transfer to a more secure institution. The court held that when a person with the power to act had already been informed of the facts, it would be futile to require an aggrieved person first to appeal to such person before the aggrieved person could resort to the courts.[29]

In addition, agency delay may create an exception to the exhaustion requirement. When a plaintiff has sought relief from an agency but the agency hasn't responded within a reasonable time, courts will not dismiss an action for failure to exhaust administrative remedies. In such a case the agency's delay renders that particular remedy inadequate.

The most widely recognized exception to the exhaustion requirement, however, arises when an agency has actually lacked jurisdiction to consider a subject or has exceeded its powers when considering the issue.

Illustrative Case

The CAB conducted an investigation to determine whether any of the certificates authorizing operations of four air carriers between Seattle, Washington, and Fair-

---

[28] *Virginia Chap., Associated Gen. Contractors, Inc., et al. v. Krops,* 444 F. Supp. 1167 (W.D. Va. 1978).

[29] *Robbins v. Kleindienst,* 383 F. Supp. 239 (D.D.C. 1974).

banks, Alaska, should be amended, modified, or terminated. It tentatively concluded that Pan American's Alaska air service should be terminated. The Board then set up hearings to give the affected parties an opportunity to show cause why the decision should not be carried out. Pan American instituted an action for declaratory judgment and injunctive relief, claiming that the Board lacked the power to terminate the certificate. The defendant moved to dismiss the action, contending that it was premature, in that Pan American had failed to exhaust its administrative remedies. The court found that the CAB had the power to alter, amend, or suspend certificates if public convenience and necessity required it but had the power to revoke certificates only for failure of a carrier to comply with rules or regulations. The court concluded that the Board was exceeding its statutory authority when it took steps to terminate the carrier's certificate. While recognizing the general rule that administrative remedies must be exhausted before review by a court, the court rejected the doctrine of exhaustion in this case. It stated that the requirement of exhaustion of administrative remedies would not be invoked when a "claim is advanced on substantial grounds that the administrative agency is transcending its legal authority."[30]

Although some courts will intervene, others still hold that administrative remedies cannot be circumvented by an allegation that an agency lacks power or jurisdiction over a subject. On review of the final agency decision, the court can reverse the agency's jurisdictional determination.

An essential part of each exception is the requirement that if the administrative remedies were pursued irreparable injury would result. There would be no reason to allow an aggrieved person to bypass the administrative system unless there was a threat of irreparable injury. Time and expense spent on unnecessary litigation before an agency do not qualify as irreparable injury. The harm that is threatened must be of a different kind than expenditures that are incurred when exhausting administrative remedies.[31]

PRIMARY JURISDICTION

Another doctrine that governs the timing of the court's intervention in an administrative dispute is that of primary jurisdiction. The doctrine of primary jurisdiction requires a court to refrain from interference in the administrative process in deference to the administrative agency which has been statutorily authorized to regulate the field. It is assumed that the agency has special expertise in a particular area. The assumed administrative "expertise" is being challenged as fallacious in litigation and in legislative bills which have not yet been enacted.

The doctrine of primary jurisdiction is generally applied to ensure uniformity of treatment and regulation. It is invoked in cases which raise issues of fact not within the special expertise of the judiciary or in cases when the exercise of agency discretion is required. There is no formula for deference to the agency action, but its invocation depends on the discretion of the court. The question is whether the reasons for the existence of the doctrine

---

[30]*Pan American World Airways, Inc. v. Boyd*, 207 F. Supp. 152 (D.D.C. 1962).

[31]*Renegotiation Bd. v. Bannercraft Clothing Co.*, 415 U.S. 1 (1974).

are present and whether the purposes it serves will be aided by its application in the particular litigation.[32]

Illustrative Case

A livestock dealer brought an action in the district court for damages and injunctive relief against the Blue Grass Stockyards Co. for denying him the use of the stockyards. He alleged that defendant stockyards were subject to the provisions of the Packers and Stockyards Act of 1921, which required stockyards to observe and enforce just and reasonable regulations and practices in regard to the furnishing of stockyard services. The dealer contended that he was excluded from defendant's stockyards without just cause. The stockyards admitted the exclusion but defended that it was justified because the dealer had violated the rules and regulations adopted by the stockyards. The court examined the doctrine of primary jurisdiction and concluded that there were cases in which factual questions were appropriate for decision by the courts. For example, courts will decide factual questions when they don't raise issues of fact not within the conventional expertise of the judges. The court held that there must be an examination of the rules and regulations adopted by the stockyards to determine whether questions are presented which require referral to the Secretary of Agriculture.[33]

RIPENESS

When an individual wants to obtain judicial review of agency action, there are actually two options available. The individual may choose not to comply with the agency's ruling and thereby obtain review when the agency brings an enforcement action. However, if this course is chosen, the individual may be subject to fines and penalties for noncompliance. To challenge agency action only as a defense to an enforcement action brought by the government could be costly. This is especially so if the defendant is engaged in a sensitive business in which public confidence in the product is a necessity. For example, a government action brought against a business in the drug industry could seriously undermine the public's confidence in its products. If an individual pursues that option, it could cause unnecessary harm. Furthermore, there are legal limitations on the availability of review by this method. For these reasons, judicial review which can be obtained prior to the government's bringing an enforcement action has definite advantages.

The other option available to the respondent is to bring an action seeking preenforcement review of the agency action. Another timing question involved when an action is brought for preenforcement judicial review concerns whether the challenged action is "ripe" for review. The ripeness doctrine considers the question of whether the controversy has matured to a point at which judicial review is appropriate. The Supreme Court explained that "its basic rationale is to prevent the courts through avoidance of premature adjudication, from entangling themselves in abstract disagreements over administrative policies, and also to protect the agencies from judicial

---

[32]*Carter v. American Tel. & Tel. Co.,* 365 F.2d 486 (5th Cir. 1966), *cert. denied,* 385 U.S. 1008 (1967).

[33]*Crain v. Blue Grass Stockyards Co.,* 399 F.2d 868 (6th Cir. 1968).

interference until an administrative decision has been formalized and its effects felt in a concrete way by the challenging parties."[34] The policy of preserving the administrative system as a way of reaching decisions without disruption by the judiciary again is balanced against individual rights. Preenforcement review will be allowed under certain circumstances, but the courts are careful to protect the administrative system as a complete, separate process.

In *Abbott Laboratories* the Supreme Court enunciated a test for ripeness. The Court stated that "the problem is best seen in a twofold aspect, requiring us to evaluate both the fitness of the issues for judicial decision and the hardship to the parties of withholding court consideration." It went on to explain the factors which were considerations for whether the dispute was appropriate for judicial resolution. When the issue at dispute was a purely legal one not involving agency expertise, the issue might be ripe for judicial resolution.

Illustrative Case

Prior to 1966, the Fair Labor Standards Act exempted conventional retail or service establishments and further specifically exempted "any employee employed by any establishment engaged in laundering, cleaning, or repairing clothing or fabrics." Employees of ordinary laundries or dry-cleaning businesses were thus not subject to the act's provisions. The administrator ruled that coin-operated laundries were engaged in renting the service of the laundry machines, rather than in laundering or dry cleaning. However, they could still qualify for exemption under the retail or service establishment exemption if they fitted the criteria. In 1966 the specific laundry exemption of the act was repealed, and a provision was added specifying that establishments "engaged in laundering, cleaning or repairing clothing or fabrics" no longer qualified for the retail exemption. The National Automatic Laundry and Cleaning Council (NALCC), the trade association for the coin-operated laundry industry, reasoned that it was unaffected by the 1966 amendments because of the ruling that it was engaged in renting the service rather than in laundering or cleaning. The administrator contended that the coin-operated laundries were subject to the act. The NALCC brought an action for a judgment declaring invalid the ruling of the administrator that the launderettes were subject to the act. The court of appeals held that direct judicial review prior to an enforcement action was appropriate in this case. The issue tendered for judicial review was a purely legal one involving the validity of a final administrative interpretation of a statute. The court also held that agency action "need not have independent coercive effect in order to possess sufficient quality of expected conformity to constitute final agency action requisite for pre-enforcement judicial review."[35]

There is an additional problem with the ripeness question that is commonly confronted by the courts. That problem arises when an agency takes action which has no independent effect on a person but does form the basis for another action by the agency. That future action will most probably harm the party. Courts have decided this issue in both ways. When they have

---

[34]*Abbott Laboratories v. Gardner*, 387 U.S. 136, 149 (1967).

[35]*National Automatic Laundry & Cleaning Council v. Schultz*, 443 F.2d 689 (D.C. Cir. 1971).

decided that the dispute is not ripe for review at the point at which the agency takes its initial step, it is usually a case in which judicial review will be available at a later stage without too much injury to the petitioner. The decision not to grant review at the initial stage of the process has seldom had the effect of precluding review altogether.

Other courts have taken a more relaxed view of ripeness and allowed review of the initial agency action. These courts have examined the practical effect of the action and have concluded that even though the adverse effect is contingent on the agency taking further action, the party should be able to challenge an order before suffering adverse consequences. These courts would allow review of a general action taken by an agency if it formulated conclusions that in the absence of change would determine future agency action and if the proceedings were not overly contingent on future actions.

Illustrative Case

The Federal Communications Commission (FCC) issued a notice of proposed rule making on August 14, 1948. It proposed to amend the rules governing multiple ownership of broadcasting stations. The new rule would place a limitation on the number of broadcasting stations in which a party could have an interest. Its purpose would be to avoid overconcentration of broadcasting stations. Storer Broadcasting filed a statement objecting to the proposed changes. The FCC entered an order amending the rules. Storer then sought review in court. The Court held that the order was reviewable against the contention that the adoption of the regulations didn't command Storer to do or refrain from doing anything. The rules did operate to control the business affairs of Storer. Even though Storer did not control more stations than were allowed by the new rules, it could not enlarge the number of stations it held without being in violation of the rules. The purchase of Storer's voting stock by some member of the public presently holding a large interest in other stations could also endanger its existing structure. Clearly the rules presently restricted Storer's operations. The process of rule making was complete, and Storer was aggrieved by the promulgation of the new rule even though the rule didn't operate to deny or cancel an existing license.[36]

The other requirement that must be fulfilled before an agency action will be considered ripe for review is hardship to the parties if review is withheld. The Supreme Court in *Abbott* examined the harm to the petitioners if they were not granted judicial review. This is the point at which a court will examine alternative courses of action available to the parties. If petitioners are required to go to great expense and effort to comply with a ruling which must go unchallenged at that point because review is withheld, then the courts must consider the effect on the parties of withholding judicial review until an enforcement action is brought. This is when the focus is placed on the adverse effect on the petitioners caused by the particular agency action. When an agency action requires parties to make a significant change in their actions or suffer adverse consequences, it would be unjust to deny access to the courts. On the other hand, when there would be no harm to a party until a rule was enforced in an enforcement action, courts may deny judicial

---

[36] *United States v. Storer Broadcasting Co.*, 351 U.S. 192 (1956).

review in a preenforcement action. The real test of ripeness is that of adverse effect. If a regulation has no immediate effect on a party, preenforcement judicial review *may* be premature.

The form of a particular agency action is irrelevant to the question of ripeness. If adverse consequences stem from an agency action, it doesn't matter what type of action it is. Clearly, formal agency actions which meet the test of adverse effect may be ripe for review. But review may extend to other, less formal agency actions. An agency action may be ripe for review if a party suffers injury from that action regardless of its form. The courts will look to the practical effect of the action rather than to its form. Agency delay or inaction has been found reviewable when that delay or inaction would inflict irreparable injury. Policy statements, news releases, informal internal letters, opinions, notices, and interpretations have all been found reviewable.

11 SUING THE GOVERNMENT

McNEILL STOKES

Stokes & Shapiro
Attorneys at Law

Judicial review alone is not always adequate to remedy an injury to a private citizen resulting from governmental action. A review action, under most statutes and under the Administrative Procedure Act (APA), merely allows an individual to have an administrative order declared improper or compels an administrative official to take action. In most cases a review action provides no other relief. Judicial review of an administrative action is adequate only when a declaration of the impropriety of an agency action will itself prevent any harm to an individual. When the individual has already been damaged, setting aside the order which caused that damage might not also correct the damage. A further action might be necessary to compensate an individual for damages already inflicted.

An adequate remedy must encompass the possibility of payment of damages in cases when compensation is necessary to make an individual or a business whole again. An examination of the possibility of other courses of action against the government is important not only to indicate how an injured individual or business can be made whole again but also to indicate whether judicial review will be available.

An important consideration in bringing suit is the fact that individuals or organizations that are successful in a civil action brought by or against the United States or any agency and any official may be able to obtain costs and fees expended by them. As a reaction to the finding that certain individuals, corporations, and other organizations may be deterred from seeking review of or defending against unreasonable government action because of the expense involved, Congress passed the Equal Access to Justice Act.

The Equal Access to Justice Act provides for costs and fees for small businesses that prevail in litigation with the government unless the position of the agency is substantially justified or special circumstances make an award unjust. In agency actions, a party seeking an award of costs and fees must file within 30 days of a final decision an application alleging that the position of the agency was not substantially justified and that the party prevailed in the action and including an itemization of costs. An award of fees and other expenses is also available to a prevailing party under similar circumstances in judicial proceedings.

At common law it was the rule that the government was not generally liable for acts done by it as a sovereign. The doctrine of sovereign immunity stemmed from the theory that the king could do no wrong. At the time when the doctrine was developed, it was absurd to imagine a private citizen filing a suit against the king. It is even harder to justify the transplantation of the doctrine into a society in which the king no longer constituted the government. The doctrine continued, however, even where there was no king.

The government began enacting various statutes which subjected it to suit on almost all legal and equitable claims against it. The purpose of these statutes was to provide compensation to the victims of governmental action without leaving compensation to the enactment of individual private laws. The statutes were designed to remove the doctrine of sovereign immunity as a barrier to suits and to render the United States liable as a private individual would be under similar circumstances. The doctrine of sovereign immunity remains, and the government can't be sued unless it consents. The statutes provide the consent. Permission to sue must be found in the wording or construction of a particular statute. Consent will not be implied; there must be clear words to that effect.

There are a variety of statutory sources of permission to sue the government, depending partially on the type of dispute involved. When Congress creates rights in individuals against the government, the statute may provide only an administrative remedy, may grant claimants only a judicial remedy, or may give an individual the option of pursuing either course. A particular statute may provide its own route to obtain a remedy. If a statute provides a remedy for improper governmental action, that route should be followed.

The restrictions set out by statute are generally jurisdictional prerequisites to a suit against the United States. The procedures must be closely followed; otherwise the suit can be thrown out of court. The conditions which have been set out by most of the statutes include designation of a particular forum in which suit must be brought, procedural prerequisites which must be followed, statutes of limitations governing the time within which a suit must be initiated, and the particular cause of action upon which the suit must be based. The prerequisites must be strictly observed.

The most common way in which a particular statute is construed as waiving sovereign immunity is by virtue of a "sue or be sued" clause. For example, the National Housing Act provides that the secretary of housing and urban development may sue and be sued in any court of competent jurisdiction; this provision has been construed as a waiver of sovereign immunity. Not only may a statute provide for liability when the government might otherwise not be liable, it may also create changes in the liability of the government which have been provided for by other general-liability statutes.

Illustrative Case

The Tennessee Valley Authority (TVA) was made susceptible to suit by virtue of its enabling act, which contained the clause "sue or be sued."[1] Because it was liable under its own act, Congress specifically exempted it from liability under the Federal Tort Claims Act (FTCA).[2] The TVA is subject to common-law liability except for claims which are contrary to public policy. In a suit brought against the TVA for damage to property caused by its blasting and excavating activities in the construction of a new power substation, the court held that the TVA was subject to common-law liability. Under Kentucky law an individual is absolutely liable for harm from blasting operations. Although the Tort Claims Act expressly excludes the government from strict liability, those provisions do not apply to the TVA. There is nothing in the TVA's act which precludes strict liability, so the TVA can be held strictly liable.[3]

A party injured by government action often has the option of pursuing the claim in a district court or in the Court of Claims. There are very definite advantages to pursuing a claim in the Court of Claims. This court sits exclusively for the purpose of allowing citizens to sue the United States. Chiseled into the wall of the building is the court's "motto": "The Government must pay its just debt the same as must its citizens." That motto is certainly applicable to the Court of Claims because it is notoriously a plaintiff's court. Just as with all courts, its decisions discuss fine legal niceties, but the decisions are result-oriented. It appears that the court merely tries to find out whether in fact the government has injured someone; if such injury is found, the court is very flexible in trying to fit legal theories to the facts to support a recovery for the injured citizen. Claims against the government should be presented in the Court of Claims when the option is available.

The United States has also waived its sovereign immunity by more general statutory consents to suit. The Federal Tort Claims Act and the Tucker Act create jurisdiction in the courts to hear many kinds of complaints against the federal government. Congress can consent to liability in a specific situation with a congressional reference case.

CONGRESSIONAL REFERENCE CASES

Historically, a party injured by governmental actions was afforded no remedy. Congress first began to circumvent the harsh results of sovereign immunity by establishing private acts which were designed to remedy a wrong done by the government to a specific individual. This is accomplished by an individual petitioning a congressional representative to sponsor a bill which will provide monetary damages to that individual for an injury caused by the government. Businesses can take advantage of congressional reference cases for injuries caused by the government.

Before the enactment of statutes waiving sovereign immunity, private

[1] U.S.C. § 831c(b).
[2] U.S.C. § 2680(i).
[3] *Brewer v. Sheco Constr. Co.*, 327 F. Supp. 1017 (W.D. Ky. 1971).

congressional bills were the only mechanism providing a remedy for an injury caused by the actions of federal agencies and their employees. With the enactment of statutes allowing legal and equitable claims against the government, the emphasis of private acts has shifted to use when there is only a claim of moral obligation. However, a private bill can still provide a remedy in many ways. It may remove an existing statutory bar to a claim, refer the claim to the Court of Claims for judicial investigation, create jurisdiction in a federal court where no such jurisdiction otherwise exists, increase or remove the ceiling on an agency's administrative settlement authority, authorize a government official to hear, determine, or settle claims arising from a particular incident, direct straight-out payment of money to a claimant, or provide relief in some other form. The granting of a private act rests solely in the discretion of Congress. However, obtaining passage of a private act to compensate a damaged citizen is a viable course that should be considered.

Illustrative Case

The government eracted a dam on the Willow River where Burkhardt operated a power company. As a result of the dam, the water level rose, and the company lost power capacity. The lost capacity had a significant detrimental impact on Burkhardt's earning capacity, and he sued, alleging that the government's actions had resulted in a taking. Burkhardt won the case in the Court of Claims and was awarded $25,000 in damages. On appeal of the government, the Supreme Court reversed and found that he had no legal remedy for his injury. The Supreme Court said: "Operations of the Government in aid of navigation oft times inflict serious damage or inconvenience or interference with advantages formerly enjoyed by riparian owners, but damage alone gives courts no power to require compensation where there is not an actual taking of property. . . . Such losses may be compensated by legislative authority, not by force of the Constitution alone." Burkhardt went to Congress and had an act passed which directed the secretary of the treasury to pay $31,160 to the Willow River Power Company in full satisfaction of its claim against the United States for compensation for damages resulting from the loss of power capacity caused by the erection of a dam by the United States. The Senate then passed a resolution referring the plaintiff's bill for relief to the Court of Claims for the court to take action. The Court of Claims took jurisdiction over the dispute, noting that it had been well established that Congress not only had authority to create a cause of action where none existed but also had authority to appropriate money to pay the claim.[4]

The theory of congressional reference cases is to compensate parties who have been injured without requiring that the party prove fault. Parties need not even show that the government has been guilty of some wrongdoing.[5] Payments are in the nature of a gratuity, generally based on some moral obligation. It is not necessary to exhaust administrative remedies prior to pursuit of a congressional reference case. Recovery may be had despite failure to seek a remedy from the administrative process.

---

[4]*Burkhardt v. United States,* 84 F. Supp. 553 (Ct. Cl. 1949), *rev. sub nom. United States v. Willow River Power Co.,* 324 U.S. 499 (1945).

[5]*Rumley v. United States,* 169 Ct. Cl. 100 (1965).

Illustrative Case

Adams brought a suit to recover losses caused by delays in the performance of a contract to produce wooden tent pins for the government. He alleged that the delays had occurred because the government inspector required a higher quality of pins than that called for by the contract's specification standards and thus increased the contractor's cost by rejecting a large number of pins. Adams complained to the inspector and the inspector's supervisor but failed to register a protest concerning the arbitrary inspection with the contracting officer. The contract's disputes procedure required protests to be made to the contracting officer. Since Adams hadn't pursued his administrative remedies, he didn't have a claim enforceable in court. His failure to exhaust his administrative remedies did not defeat a claim for damages in a congressional reference case. He needed only to prove an "equitable" claim, not that all the elements of a legal claim were present. Exhaustion of administrative remedies is merely a prerequisite to a legal claim.[6]

TUCKER ACT

The Tucker Act,[7] providing a forum for a number of claims against the government, gives the Court of Claims jurisdiction to render judgments on all claims against the government (except tort claims) based on the Constitution, acts of Congress, executive regulations, and express and implied contracts.[8] District courts have concurrent jurisdiction with the Court of Claims for claims against the government not exceeding $10,000.[9] The most common Tucker Act claims are for an unconstitutional taking and breach of a government contract or a claim for employment benefits. Tort claims which involve damage to property can often be framed to be brought under the Tucker Act so that the many exceptions to the Federal Tort Claims Act are avoided.

Inverse Condemnation

Eminent domain is the power or right of the sovereign to take private property for public use. It is limited only by the requirements that the taking be for a public use and that the owner be awarded just compensation for the taking. Generally, proceedings are initiated by the government when property is to be taken for public use so that the property can be condemned and the owner compensated in advance.

In some situations there is no formal exercise of the eminent-domain power, yet the property is physically taken or is subjected to such rigorous regulations that its value is so diminished as to amount to a taking. When there has in all respects been a taking yet there has been no legal proceeding by the government, the owner may initiate an action pursuant to the Tucker Act against the government claiming entitlement to just compensation. The

---

[6] *Adams v. United States*, 358 F.2d 986 (Ct. Cl. 1966).

[7] 28 U.S.C. § 1491.

[8] 28 U.S.C. § 1346

[9] 28 U.S.C. § 1346 (a)(2).

popular description of the action against the government to recover the value of property which has in fact been taken is inverse condemnation. The suit is, in effect, a condemnation suit in reverse. Even though the government's actions against individuals and businesses are legal, they may give rise to inverse-condemnation rights if the actions amount to a taking of property rights.

It is difficult to determine in what cases a court will award compensation. The Supreme Court admitted that this was a problem when it wrote: "This Court, quite simply, has been unable to develop any set formula for determining when justice and fairness require that economic injuries caused by public action be compensated by the Government, rather than remain disproportionately concentrated on a few persons."[10] Diverse factual situations give rise to a finding that there has been a taking, and seemingly similar situations have produced different results. Some factors have been significant in court decisions.

The decisions are cognizant that the government's exercise of its police power in the name of public good or public welfare often comes in conflict with individuals' rights. That this is a problem requiring a balancing of considerations was recognized by the Supreme Court in an early opinion. The Court stressed that each case must be considered individually and enunciated the general rule that while property might be regulated to a certain extent, if regulation went too far, it would be recognized as a taking.[11]

Governmental actions often damage individuals and businesses. When the damage occurs as the result of a physical invasion by the government, courts will be more likely to find a taking than when the interference arises from a governmental program with a public purpose. However, even when the injury arises out of a program for the public welfare, many courts will reject the inequitable result of placing the burden on one individual and grant compensation.

Illustrative Case

The owner of the old Willard Hotel in Washington was prevented from demolishing the structure and building a new structure. The government further prevented the owner from modifying the exterior of the hotel. Although these restrictions were promulgated under the Pennsylvania Avenue Development Corporation Act of 1972, clearly a program with a public purpose, the Court of Claims found that there was a taking. This was so even though the government had not attempted to prevent the owner from operating the existing structure as a hotel. The court found that the government had effectively prevented him from operating the structure in a profitable manner and therefore held that this was a taking.[12]

All the cases granting compensation recognize that there must be a substantial injury or a "substantial interference with the property so as to

---

[10]*Penn Central v. City of New York,* 438 U.S. 104 (1978).

[11]*Pennsylvania Coal Co. v. Mahon,* 260 U.S. 393 (1922).

[12]*Bennenson v. United States,* 548 F.2d 939 (Ct. Cl. 1977).

destroy or greatly diminish its value."[13] The injury to property for which the government will compensate may involve less than actual condemnation or taking of property. When regulations are so stringent as to have the effect of interfering with an owner's right to use and enjoy property, the government may be obligated to compensate the owner. This includes business whose use and enjoyment of rights have been substantially interfered with by the government or its agencies.

Illustrative Case

Jacob Pete and James Pete owned three large floating cabin barges located on a lake in the Boundary Waters Canoe Area of Minnesota which they operated as hotels. In 1964 Congress passed the Wilderness Act, which established a wilderness area and simultaneously banned structures, commercial enterprises, personal property, motor vehicles, and motorboats in the Boundary Waters Canoe Area. The government compensated the Petes for the taking of the real property which was located in the newly declared wilderness area. However, it contended that it had taken only the real estate and the structures permanently attached to the realty and so refused to compensate plaintiffs for the houseboats. The Court of Claims held that when governmental action was so pervasive as to depreciate greatly the value of property or to interfere substantially with an owner's right to use or enjoy the property, the property had in effect been "taken." When it was shown that the houseboats could not be economically removed from the lake, the Court of Claims found that the cabin barges had been taken and ordered compensation.[14]

The taking may arise from a literal condemnation of the property or from regulations so pervasive and so stringent as to effect a taking. Whatever the means of taking, the loss to the owner must actually be caused by the government's action. If a loss is merely an unintended incident of the government's activity, courts might not award compensation.

To demonstrate that there has been a taking, an individual or a business must first prove that there was some valuable right that had been lost after the government acted. If there was no property interest in something, there could be no argument that anything had been taken. The most common cases occur when there is a taking of property such as buildings or land. The use by the government of an individual's air easement when government aircraft consistently fly low over someone's property generally results in a finding by the courts that there has been a taking.

What constitutes property which can be taken by government action is being given a broader construction by the courts. At one point the courts determined that only realty and tangible personal property such as fixtures could be taken by government action. Now the definition has been extended to include more diverse categories of property. The more difficult cases involve intangible property rights. Courts are more readily finding a taking of intangible property rights in recent cases, and this trend may continue to

---

[13]*Harris v. United States*, 467 F.2d 801 (8th Cir. 1972).

[14]*Pete v. United States*, 531 F.2d 1018 (Ct. Cl. 1976).

create more substantive rights for business to recover damages due to government interference.

Illustrative Case

The Atomic Energy Act of 1946 declared the production of fissionable materials to be a government monopoly. The act thus revoked all existing patents which were useful exclusively in the production of fissionable materials and prohibited the issuance of new patents for that purpose. In addition, it authorized the government to utilize any existing patents in the process of producing fissionable materials without liability for infringement of those patents. The act also established a patent compensation board to award compensation to owners of patents revoked or used pursuant to the act and to developers of processes made unpatentable by the act. The Atomic Energy Act recognized that this was a taking of property and that the government must therefore render just compensation. The court stated that a patent gives a person the right to exclude all others from using an invention and that monopoly is a property right in the patent.[15]

The right to bring a suit against the United States in the Court of Claims for a taking under eminent domain is based upon the existence of an implied contract with the United States. There are also other causes of action which can be filed against the government on the basis of an implied contract with the government.

Implied Contracts

The Tucker Act authorizes the Court of Claims to render judgments on claims against the government based on implied contracts.[16] A distinction has been made in federal case law between contracts implied in fact and those implied in law. The waiver of sovereign immunity applies to contracts implied in fact, not to those implied in law. A contract implied in law is an obligation imposed by the law and cannot be enforced against the United States.[17]

A contract implied in fact is enforceable against the government. This situation occurs when the government's conduct gives rise to an express promise to pay or perform or when its conduct gives rise to such a conclusion. There must be a mutual agreement and promise, but they need not be expressed in words: they may be found by the conduct of the government and the private party. While a contract implied in law is an obligation imposed by the law, a contract implied in fact is a promise implied by law.

Illustrative Case

Cities Service Gas Co. sold gas for many years to the Army at Fort Leavenworth, Kansas, under written contracts. After a dispute over the rates for gas sales, the company terminated the contracts but continued to supply the gas to the Army even though

---

[15] *N.V. Philips' Gloeilampenfabrieken v. AEC,* 316 F.2d 401 (D.C. Cir. 1963).

[16] 28 U.S.C. § 1491.

[17] *J.C. Pittman & Sons, Inc. v. United States,* 317 F.2d 366 (Ct. Cl. 1963).

there were no written contracts. The Army not only agreed to accept delivery of the gas but also demanded that Cities Service continue to make sales and deliveries and issued checks in payment for the gas. Cities Service brought suit to recover on quantum meruit basis for the value of gas supplied to the Army, alleging that the amount paid by the Army wasn't sufficient. The Army contended that the court did not have jurisdiction of the case. However, the Court of Claims held that under the Tucker Act it had jurisdiction of contracts implied in fact. It found a "meeting of the minds" of the parties that Cities Service would sell and deliver the gas to the Army and the Army would purchase and accept delivery of the gas and pay Cities Service for it. The court held that Cities Service's claim was based on a contract implied in fact between Cities Service and the Army. The court held further that the company was entitled to recover on an implied contract the value of all the gas delivered to Fort Leavenworth on a quantum meruit basis.[18]

The bidding process also gives rise to an implied contract which can be asserted against the government. When the government advertises for bids, it is under an obligation to consider honestly and fairly all bids which are submitted pursuant to a request for bids.

Illustrative Case

The Ordnance Tank Automotive Center (OTAC) advertised for bids on 5500 low-voltage circuit testers. Heyer Products submitted a bid in response, together with a sample unit, a letter of explanation, a photograph of the unit, a schematic diagram, and a specification describing the unit. Heyer submitted the low bid, but the government awarded the contract to a higher bidder. Heyer alleged that the government's action was arbitrary and capricious and taken in bad faith. The court held that a bidder did have a right to have a bid honestly considered. If the government breached that implied contract, the bidder could maintain an action for damages for the breach.[19]

In a subsequent case, *Heyer Products, Inc. v. United States,*[20] the court ruled that Heyer's bid was rejected not in bad faith but because the sample submitted by Heyer did not comply with the specifications. However, *Heyer* stated a broad, general rule that every bidder had a right to have his bid considered honestly and that if there was a breach of that obligation by the government, the injured party had a right to come into court and try to prove a cause of action. Not every unsuccessful bidder would be allowed into court. However, when it could be shown that bids had not been invited in good faith but with the intent to disregard willfully and arbitrarily all bids except one previously decided on, then the government had breached its implied contract to evaluate bids fairly and honestly and the unsuccessful bidder was entitled to recover expenses incurred.[21] An unsuccessful bidder can also challenge the award of a bid on the ground that the agency abused its discretion in the award.[22]

[18] *Cities Serv. Gas Co. v. United States,* 500 F.2d 448 (Ct. Cl. 1974).

[19] *Heyer Products Co., Inc. v. United States,* 140 F. Supp. 409 (Ct. Cl. 1956).

[20] 177 F. Supp. (Ct. Cl. 1959).

[21] *Keco Industries, Inc. v. United States,* 428 F.2d 1233 (Ct. Cl. 1970).

[22] *Scanwell Laboratories, Inc. v. Shaffer,* 424 F.2d 859 (D.C. Cir. 1970).

The government procurement process gives rise to other obligations which may be implied against the government. When the government contracts with a private party, other warranties are implied by the contracting. For example, a contracting agency's failure to disclose vital information may establish a predicate for a possible action for breach of an implied contract.[23] When the specifications provided by an agency for use in bidding turn out to be unusable, there has been a breach of an implied warranty that if government specifications are complied with, satisfactory performance will result.[24] Every contract entered into contains some representations which, although not expressly included in the contract, can be implied.

Illustrative Case

Lipsett, Inc., entered into a contract with the Bureau of Yards and Docks of the Department of the Navy to construct aircraft maintenance facilities. The original specifications of the government were defective and caused a delay in the completion of the contract. The court held that when the government ordered a structure to be built and in so doing prepared the specifications, it implicitly warranted that if the specifications were complied with satisfactory performance would result. When defective specifications delay completion of a contract, the contractor is entitled to recover for breach of that implied warranty. Furthermore, the court held that the government's "extremely slow recognition and correction of the defective plans constituted a breach of the implied obligation contained in every contract that neither party will do anything that will hinder or delay the other party in performance of the contract."[25]

The distinction between implied-in-fact and implied-in-law contracts is sometimes nebulous. When an agreement can be inferred from conduct of the parties showing their tacit understanding, the court will take jurisdiction pursuant to the Tucker Act. However, when no agreement can be inferred from the circumstances, the Tucker Act may not be the basis for jurisdiction. That does not mean, however, that an injured individual is without remedy.

Equitable Estoppel

Just as the government's conduct may justify binding the government by an implied contract, so also may that conduct justify estopping the government from denying liability under certain circumstances. Estoppel is a doctrine which is used to adjust the relative rights of parties based on considerations of justice and fairness. It is used when the conduct of one of the parties creates conditions under which it would be unfair to allow it to allege or deny an important fact to the detriment of the other party. Four elements must be present before the doctrine of equitable estoppel will be applied:

- The government must know the true facts.

- The government must act with the intention or expectation that the private party will act thereon.

[23] *T.F. Scholes, Inc. v. United States*, 357 F.2d 963 (Ct. Cl. 1966).

[24] *North American Philips Company v. United States*, 358 F.2d 980 (Ct. Cl. 1966).

[25] *Luria Brothers & Co. v. United States*, 369 F.2d 701 (Ct. Cl. 1966).

- The private party must be ignorant of the true facts.

- The private party must rely on the government's conduct to its detriment.

For example, the government may be bound by an affirmative misrepresentation to an individual despite its being contrary to the law. [26] Conduct far short of actual fraud will suffice to support an estoppel when justice demands it to be applied against the government.

Illustrative Case

In 1934 Coos Bay Lumber Company owned approximately 58,900 acres of timberland in Oregon. Oregon's economy and lumber industry were in a depressed condition, and many timber owners were abandoning cutover lands to eliminate further payment of taxes. Coos Bay Lumber Company entered into a contract with the Forest Service that the government extend the boundaries of the Siskiyou National Forest to include one of its tracts; in return, the lumber company would convey to the government that tract after it had been harvested. In 1958 a public land order retracted the boundary of the national forest and, except for land already conveyed by the lumber company, reestablished the boundary as it had been before the extension. The maps of the forest were changed, and Forest Service personnel began treating the extension as if it were no longer part of the national forest. The government made no claim upon the lumber company or its successors to convey any land under the 1934 contract. Georgia-Pacific acquired title to this tract in 1962, and the government allowed Georgia-Pacific to manage the tract at great expense, adding value to it. In 1967 the government instituted suit to secure declaratory relief and specific performance of the contract. The court entered judgment adverse to the government, holding that estoppel could be raised against the government.[27]

Express Contracts

The Tucker Act also contains the government's consent to be sued on any claims against the government based on express contracts.[28] A contract liability is judicially enforceable against the United States. The United States is liable to the same extent as a private individual under similar circumstances. The government has the same rights and also is subject to the same responsibilities as a private party to a contract.

A limitation on that contract liability enforceable against the government is that it can be created only by an officer of the government who has the power to make a contract and bind the government. An agent of the government without authority to contract for the government may not bind the United States to make it liable. A person dealing with the agent is held to have notice of the limits of the authority of that agent. If an agent of the government exceeds the limits of authority by making a contract for the government, the government is not bound. As long as the contract is authorized, the government is bound by it and the United States submits itself to suit under the Tucker Act.

[26] *Brant v. Hickel,* 427 F.2d 53 (9th Cir. 1970).

[27] *United States v. Georgia-Pacific Corp.,* 421 F.2d 92 (9th Cir. 1970)

[28] 28 U.S.C. § 1491.

Illustrative Case

The National State Bank of Newark and the Bowery Savings Bank purchased mortgages insured by the Federal Housing Administration (FHA) pursuant to the National Housing Act. Both banks brought actions to recover additional mortgage insurance benefits pursuant to their contracts with the FHA. The government filed motions to dismiss, alleging that only the FHA, and not the United States, had consented to be sued in this type of case. The Court of Claims held that the United States was subject to suit on these claims. By using the FHA to carry out public purposes, the United States submitted itself to suit under the Tucker Act unless there was a specific provision to the contrary.[29]

The government is liable on its contracts as a private individual under similar circumstances. When the government enters into contracts, its rights and duties are governed generally by the law applicable to contracts between private parties. The United States is liable in damages for breach of its contracts.

Illustrative Cases

The Chicora Construction Company brought suit against the United States for alleged breach of contract. Chicora had a contract with the Navy for construction of a sewage treatment plant. The government was responsible for building roadways which were necessary before Chicora could complete the contract. The roadways were to be completed by August 1958, but it was actually April 1959 before the roads were usable. The district court held that the government was liable for extra costs or expenses of the contractor resulting from improper or unauthorized delays caused by the government.[30]

The United States contracted with Northern Helex Company to purchase helium to be produced by the company. The agreement was authorized as part of a long-range program designed to conserve helium as a natural resource for future use. The program was designed to be self-liquidating, the borrowed funds to be repaid with interest from helium sales proceeds. However, private helium plants began to operate outside the program and to sell to the "federal market." Consequently there were not enough funds to satisfy the payments due. The government informed Northern Helex that it would be unable to make the payments as they came due. Northern Helex continued to deliver helium to the government in mitigation of damages and in the interest of conservation. The court held that the government's nonpayment was a material breach and that Northern Helex had not waived that breach by continuing to deliver the helium. Northern Helex could bring an action to recover amounts due as a result of a breach of the contract by the United States.[31]

CONTRACT DISPUTES

The Contract Disputes Act of 1978[32] provides another method by which a party contracting with the government may recover compensation for the government's actions. The act was designed to govern the entire disputes process relating to federal government contracts. Replacing the system of

---

[29] *National State Bank of Newark v. United States*, 357 F.2d 704 (Ct. Cl. 1966).

[30] *Chicora Constr. Co. v. United States*, 252 F. Supp. 910 (1965).

[31] *Northern Helex Co. v. United States*, 455 F.2d 546 (Ct. Cl. 1972).

[32] 41 U.S.C. § 601 *et seq.*

separate procedures for each agency, the act installed a uniform scheme which applies to almost all agencies and almost all types of procurement contracts, express or implied. The Contract Disputes Act provides an administrative procedure for solving government contract disputes as an alternative to litigation of claims in the courts.

Should a contractor demand complete judicial due process, direct access to the Court of Claims is still available under the Tucker Act. A contractor may bypass administrative review and proceed to the courts. However, administrative procedures cannot be ignored entirely. The act requires that all claims which relate to a government contract must be submitted to the contracting officer before being taken to a court or a board. The contracting officer is authorized to settle almost all contract disputes. The first step in any dispute with the government over a contract is to request an informal conference, at which point a compromise or settlement might be reached.

If the settlement process fails, the contractor must seek a decision by the contracting officer (CO). The CO's decision must be in writing, stating the reason for the decision and advising the contractor of the rights guaranteed by the act. For claims of $50,000 or less, the CO must issue a decision within 60 days of a written request. For claims over $50,000, the CO must either issue a decision within 60 days or at that time notify the contractor when the decision will be issued. Then the decision must be issued within a reasonable time. The decision by the CO is final and binding unless there is a timely appeal or a suit is filed. If the CO fails to issue a decision in time, the failure is deemed to be a "decision" for purposes of appeal.

The Contract Disputes Act gives a contractor the option of appealing a decision to a board of contract appeals or directly to the Court of Claims. A contractor has 90 days after receipt of a CO's final opinion within which to appeal to a board of contract appeals. The board of contract appeals is authorized to grant any relief that would be available to a litigant asserting a contract claim in the Court of Claims.

There are some differences which are significant in the selection of the forum for an appeal. The most important of these is the length of time for disposition of a case. A case appealed before a board normally takes less time than does one appealed to a court. In addition, accelerated procedures are available for an appeal to the board. Cases involving $50,000 or less are to be decided within 180 days from the time when the contractor elects to utilize the procedure. The accelerated procedure is available only at the election of the contractor. In addition, a small-claims procedure for claims under $10,-000 is available at the election of the contractor when an appeal is made to the board. This procedure provides for simplified rules of procedure with decisions to be made within 120 days from the time when the contractor chooses to utilize the procedure. Decisions reached pursuant to this procedure are final and conclusive and will not be reviewed except in case of fraud. Cases are disposed of much more quickly, and most board decisions may still be appealed to the Court of Claims. So if appeal is made to the board and the decision is adverse, there is still an opportunity for review of the decision.

In lieu of appealing the CO's decision to a board of contract appeals, an adverse decision may be appealed to the Coart of Claims. In addition, board decisions may be appealed to the Court of Claims. An appeal must be initiated by the filing of a petition with the court within 12 months from receipt of the CO's decision. Appeal from a board decision must be made within 120 days of receipt of the decision. Proceedings in the court are governed by the rules of procedure for other breach-of-contract suits. Appeals to the Court of Claims will be treated as are claims made under the Tucker Act.

GOVERNMENT TORT LIABILITY

The Federal Tort Claims Act[33] contains a general waiver provision which provides for the liability of the United States in tort claims "to the same extent as a private individual under like circumstances." It allows monetary recovery against the United States for damages, loss of property, personal injury, or death caused by the wrongful acts of government employees while acting within the scope of their employment. The FTCA was strengthened in 1966 to allow the head of any federal agency to settle claims, the only limitation being that claims in excess of $25,000 must be approved by the attorney general. Allowing the settlement of claims makes the act much easier to use.

A claimant under the FTCA must file an administrative claim in writing with the appropriate federal agency before resorting to the courts. A standard government form is available for use in filing an administrative claim. In addition, federal agencies were given authority to promulgate their own regulations for the processing of claims under the act. Procedures may differ from agency to agency as long as they are not inconsistent with the act itself. A claimant must follow the procedure which has been set out by the appropriate agency. All administrative claims must be filed within 2 years after the claim accrues.

Once a claim has been considered and is denied by an agency, a court action must be initiated within 6 months of the denial. If the agency does not make a determination within 6 months, the claimant may treat that delay as a denial and proceed with an action in court. A court action pursuant to the FTCA must be brought in a federal district court, where it will be tried to the court without a jury. Suit may not be brought for an amount greater than was requested in the administrative claim unless the increase is justified by newly discovered evidence. The administrative claim generally locks in the amount of damages which may be recovered. A claim under the FTCA may be brought only for money damages. No other relief is available to a claimant. The claim must allege damage or loss of property, personal injury, or death.

There are several conditions which a claimant must establish to be able to bring suit under the FTCA. The claimant must establish that the damage was caused by a negligent or wrongful act or omission. The actor must have

---

[33]28 U.S.C. § 1346, 2671–2678, 2680.

been a federal employee who was acting within the scope of employment. In addition, the claimant must establish that the circumstances were such that if the United States were a private party, liability would be imposed.

Illustrative Cases

The United States owned and operated the Marine Hospital in San Francisco. Trubow went with a helper to the hospital to pick up surplus refrigerators which had been purchased from the government and were being stored in the basement until the purchaser picked them up. Trubow and his helper got onto the elevator in the basement. Normally there is a leather or canvas strap that is used to close the elevator from the inside, but the strap was broken. Trubow pulled down with full force upon the metal handles on the outside of the door while standing inside the elevator and caught his hand between the two doors. He brought an action to recover for the injuries sustained. Against an argument that since an employee was not individually liable, the owner could not be held vicariously liable, the court found the government liable. The court held that under the FTCA the United States was liable for an injury resulting from the existence of a dangerous condition in a government building even though the government employee responsible for the condition might not be personally liable.[34]

Mrs. Salim sustained injuries while attempting to descend the icy steps of a United States post office in Leesville, Louisiana. In an action under the Federal Tort Claims Act, the court found that the government was negligent in that it failed to exercise reasonable or ordinary care for the safety of those entering and leaving the post office premises. The court held that the government had the duty to take corrective measures commensurate with the circumstances involved.[35]

Although most cases brought under the FTCA stem from motor vehicle accidents or negligent maintenance of government premises, an increasing number are being brought on the basis of the government's negligence in the provision of services. The United States may be held liable for negligent provision of services upon which the public has come to rely. The theory behind these cases is that if the government undertakes to provide a service, that service must be carried out with due care. In the leading Supreme Court case on the subject, the Court held that if the Coast Guard exercised its discretion to operate a lighthouse, it was obligated to use due care to make certain that the light was kept in good working order. If the Coast Guard failed in its duty, held the Court, and damage was thereby caused, the United States would be liable.[36] Government liability is being extended past liability in ordinary common-law torts to liability when the government undertakes the provision of a service and also in some cases when the government is carrying out a uniquely governmental regulatory activity.

An increasing number of cases under the FTCA stem from the government's involvement in aviation. The government may be liable when an employee is operating an aircraft.[37] In addition, it may be liable when it

---

[34] *United States v. Trubow*, 214 F.2d 192 (9th Cir. 1954).

[35] *Salim v. United States*, 382 F.2d 240 (5th Cir. 1967).

[36] *Indian Towing Co. v. United States*, 350 U.S. 61 (1955).

[37] *United Air Lines, Inc. v. Wiener*, 335 F.2d 379 (9th Cir. 1964).

undertakes to provide a service concerning aviation. For example, liability may be imposed on the United States for negligence in the operation of a control tower.[38]

In addition, in some situations liability may be imposed for negligence in issuing or failing to issue a certificate. Attempts by the government to argue that these activities are regulatory and that liability is therefore excluded have been rebuffed by the defense that if the conduct is regulatory, it is at the operational level and liability may attach. Liability will be imposed when issuance requires the application of clear standards in a given fact situation and there is negligence in the application of those standards.

Illustrative Case

Plaintiff Carl Duncan was a commercial airline pilot employed by National Airlines, Inc. The Federal Aviation Administration (FAA) issued an emergency order revoking plaintiff's airman medical certificate because he had failed to furnish the FAA with certain medical information. Subsequently, plaintiff furnished the medical information to the FAA but was denied recertification. After other proceedings, the National Transportation Safety Board restored plaintiff to flying status. Plaintiff then commenced an action for money damages pursuant to the FTCA for negligence in denying him recertification. The court held that since an applicant was entitled to a certificate if he or she qualified under the regulations, application of that policy was an administrative decision at the operational level which if negligently done would make the government liable.[39]

There are two major exceptions to liability under the FTCA: from liability based on discretionary functions and from liability for certain willful or deliberate torts. The FTCA specifically excepts any claim based upon an act or omission of an employee exercising due care in carrying out statutes and regulations, whether or not they are valid, or based on performing or failing to perform a discretionary function, whether or not that discretion is abused.[40]

The Supreme Court gave the discretionary-function exception a broad construction in its first interpretation of the exception. In *Dalehite v. United States*,[41] it held that the government was not liable for the Texas City disaster which had occurred when a ship loaded with fertilizer-grade ammonium nitrate exploded in the harbor. The manufacture, storage, and transportation of the fertilizer had been controlled by the government as part of an export plan. One of the Court's reasons for exempting the government from liability was that "the decisions held culpable were all responsibly made at a planning rather than operational level and involved considerations more or less important to the practicability of the government's fertilizer

---

[38]*Eastern Airlines v. Union Trust Co.*, 221 F.2d 62 (D.C. Cir. 1955), *aff'd sub nom. United States v. Union Trust Co.*, 350 U.S. 907 (1955); *Ingham v. Eastern Airlines, Inc.*, 373 F.2d 227 (2d Cir.), *cert. denied*, 389 U.S. 844 (1967).

[39]*Duncan v. United States*, 355 F Supp. 1167 (D.D.C. 1973).

[40]28 U.S.C. § 2680(a).

[41]346 U.S. 15 (1953).

program."[42] Although many other aspects of the *Dalehite* case have been modified and ignored by successive cases, the planning-operational distinction remains the most important criterion in determining whether the discretionary-function exemption will be applied to deny recovery. The *Dalehite* case gave the government broad immunity from liability by including within the planning level "determinations made by executives or administrators in establishing plans, specifications or schedules of operation, and the acts of subordinates in carrying out the operations of government." The Court held that where there was room for policy judgment and decision, there was discretion. However, as the Court found the government immune from liability, Congress passed legislation to compensate the victims.

Although the *Dalehite* case is still the leading case on the discretionary-function exception, it has been seriously undermined. Many courts will construe the exception much more narrowly by requiring that the government show more than that some choice was part of the decision-making process: that it show that the discretion involved the evaluation of factors such as the financial, political, economic, and social effects of a given plan or policy. This kind of construction places a definite limitation on the discretionary-function exception. If a court will follow that construction, it won't exempt decisions relating to the day-to-day operations of government even though they may involve discretion. The exception will be applied primarily when the decision involves a policy judgment made in the upper echelon of government. It is important that, in framing a request for relief, the action of the government be classified as being at an operational level.

Illustrative Cases

Eunice Swanson brought an action against the United States under the FTCA seeking damages for the wrongful death of her husband, Franklin R. Swanson, Jr. Swanson, a technical representative of Lockheed Corp., was killed in the crash of an Air Force Lockheed Constellation which occurred when the plane was being flown to check the modification of the elevator mechanism of the tail assembly. The government contended that the case fell within the discretionary-function exception to the FTCA. The court held that the exemption might apply if the action was based on the government's decision to develop a modification of the elevator assembly of the airplane. However, when the action was based on the government's negligence in the manner in which the modification was designed or installed, the discretionary-function exception would not apply. The court stated that even though necessary to the execution of a planning-level decision the alleged negligence was at the operational level.[43]

Mrs. Griffin brought an action against the government for injuries sustained as a result of the administration to her of live-virus poliomyelitis vaccine. The vaccine had been released to the public by the Division of Biological Standards (DBS), a division of the Department of Health, Education, and Welfare (HEW). The approval of the vaccine by the DBS was found to be negligent. The court held that this approval by the DBS did not fall within the discretionary-function exception to the FTCA: "Where decisions have not involved policy judgments as to the public interest, the courts have not held

---

[42]346 U.S., at 42 (1953).

[43]*Swanson v. United States,* 229 F. Supp. 217 (N.D. Cal. 1964).

the decisions to be immune from judicial review." To determine the applicability of the exception the court analyzed "not merely whether judgment was exercised, but also whether the nature of the judgment called for policy considerations." It held the government liable even though this was a highly discretionary action.[44]

The promulgation of a regulation falls within the discretionary-function exception. The formulation of a regulation requires consideration of many policy factors, and the action will be protected most of the time. However, when an official has not acted in conformity with delegated authority, there is no immunity. If a regulation is promulgated in excess of the authority delegated, there may be a possibility of actions stemming from that regulation. In addition, not all regulatory activities are protected. For example, the mere fact that Occupational Safety and Health Administration (OSHA) inspectors are engaged in regulatory activities may not exempt the United States from liability.[45] While the formulation of the policy contained in the regulations might be a protected action, the application of the policy in those regulations to individual cases may not be protected. Sometimes a slight difference in the wording of the cause of action will place it outside the reach of the discretionary-function exception and into the realm of operational activities. An agency must exercise due care in following its regulations. That is an administrative, not a discretionary, function.

Another major exception to the FTCA is for "any claim arising out of assault, battery, false imprisonment, false arrest, malicious prosecution, abuse of process, libel, slander, misrepresentation, deceit, or interference with contract rights."[46] The act does not subject the government to liability for the listed willful or deliberate torts. However, a good many intentional torts do not come within the exception. The list does not include some important unintentional torts, such as trespass, conversion, and unlawful invasion of the right of privacy.

Illustrative Case

Fred B. Black, Jr., was a Washington lobbyist affiliated with Robert G. Baker, secretary to the majority of the Senate. The Federal Bureau of Investigation (FBI) installed a microphone through the common wall of a room adjoining Black's suite at the Sheraton-Carlton Hotel in Washington, D.C., and listened to Black's conversations and activities. Black was also beset by a number of difficulties. The Internal Revenue Service (IRS) had been investigating him for income tax evasion, had completed its investigation, and had recommended that the Justice Department undertake a criminal prosecution. Black had also become entangled in a Senate investigation of Bobby Baker. Black was convicted of income tax evasion in 1965. By this time Black was unable to obtain employment in Washington. When the Supreme Court learned of the eavesdropping, it vacated and remanded for a new trial. Upon remand, the district court found that the government's evidence had not been derived from the eavesdropping. On retrial, however, Black was acquitted. Black then filed this action seeking monetary recovery for injuries caused by the illegal eavesdropping operation. He

[44] *Griffin v. United States,* 500 F.2d 1059 (3d Cir. 1974).

[45] *Blessing v. United States,* 447 F. Supp. 1160 (E.D. Pa. 1978).

[46] 28 U.S.C. § 2680(h).

invoked theories of trespass, invasion of privacy by intrusion, invasion of privacy by publication, and violation of constitutional rights. The court held that the claim was not barred by the doctrine of sovereign immunity on the theory that because plaintiff sought to recover for injury to his reputation, he was really alleging libel and slander, which are excepted from the liability of the FTCA. The court determined that plaintiff was not simply suing for damage to his reputation and loss of earning ability but was suing for unlawful invasion of his privacy and for physical trespass.[47]

The intentional-tort exemption was limited by an amendment to the FTCA in 1974 which fixed liability on the government for claims for assault, battery, false imprisonment, false arrest, abuse of process, and malicious prosecution arising out of investigation or law enforcement. This amendment may allow recovery of damages by individuals and businesses relating to administrative, investigative, or law enforcement officers. There have been very few cases arising out of this statute, which could be a vehicle for fixing liability on the government under abuse of process or malicious prosecution for unjustified civil actions and administrative enforcement.

The FTCA provides for payment of some claims, but at the same time it retains aspects of sovereign immunity by excepting certain other claims. Although the act has some serious shortcomings, there are other means of obtaining compensation from the government on a tort claim.

TORT LIABILITY OF FEDERAL OFFICIALS

The general rule of sovereign immunity did not at common law extend to officials of the government. Government officials were supposed to be answerable for their actions just as any citizen was. Therefore, a government official could be sued individually for acts performed in the exercise of an official function. A tort action against an individual official could be used to obtain judicial review of an administrative action. The officer was at the same time liable for damages.

The common-law rule of officer liability has been continuously modified. Most actions by government officials which can be classified as "judicial" will be protected. The immunity for judicial acts is also being extended to immunity for discretionary acts. What constitutes an exercise of discretionary power is not clearly defined. An argument could be made that immunity should be limited to those discretionary actions which have the characteristics of a judicial action. In any event, an officer who performs only a ministerial function will not be immune from liability. If an action can be classified as ministerial, it will not be protected.

The courts have not extended the principle of official immunity to police officers sued for torts committed in the performance of their official duties. Most commonly, actions have been allowed against a police officer individually for false arrest, false imprisonment, and excessive force. The Supreme Court extended the liability of federal agents to liability for violation of Fourth Amendment rights.

---

[47] *Black v. Sheraton Corp. of America,* 564 F.2d 531 (D.C. Cir. 1977).

Illustrative Case

Federal officers without a warrant made an early-morning intrusion into Bivens's house. They searched his home, handcuffed him in front of his family, took him to the police station, and booked, fingerprinted, photographed, and questioned him; then when he was brought before a United States commissioner, the complaint was dismissed. The Supreme Court held that the plaintiff could bring an action for damages against the officers for violation of his Fourth Amendment rights. On remand the court of appeals held that damage suits could be brought against police officers for violations of constitutional rights, not limiting grounds to deprivation of Fourth Amendment rights.[48]

In a reaction to the outrageous action of the government agents in the *Bivens* case, Congress amended the FTCA in 1974 to provide specifically for government liability for claims arising out of assault, battery, false imprisonment, false arrest, abuse of process, or malicious prosecution with regard to acts and omissions of investigative or law enforcement officers. Unjustified actions by government agencies against individuals or businesses may amount to abuse of process or malicious prosecution, which under the 1974 FTCA amendment could give a right of action for damages directly against the government in the Court of Claims.

The Supreme Court has extended the *Bivens* rule to violations of constitutional rights by school board officials.[49] If the tortious acts of a government official can be described as a constitutional violation, the door is open for the courts to place liability on the official. For example, illegal detention can be recast as a constitutional deprivation of liberty, abusive treatment of prisoners as infliction of punishment without due process, and seizure of property to satisfy a pretended tax lien as a taking of property without due process. Any claim which can be framed in terms of violation of constitutional rights would seem to have a greater chance of success.

In many of those cases in which the doctrine of official immunity does prevent recovery against an official, the injured citizen is not left without a remedy. Governmental liability has been substituted as a method for recovery of damages to an individual. Governmental liability may also be provided in addition to, rather than in substitution for, an action against an official.

Illustrative Case

Marie Green brought an action on behalf of the estate of her deceased son, alleging that while a prisoner in a federal prison he suffered personal injuries from which he died because prison officials failed to give him proper medical treatment. The Supreme Court held that a *Bivens* remedy was available to respondent even though she could also bring a suit under the FTCA against the United States. The Court stated that the FTCA provision allowing an action against the government for intentional torts committed by law enforcement officials contemplated that victims of these kinds of intentional torts should have an action under the FTCA as well as a *Bivens* remedy against the individual officers.[50]

[48]*Bivens v. Six Unknown Named Agents,* 403 U.S. 388 (1971)
[49]*Wood v. Strickland,* 420 U.S. 308 (1975).
[50]*Carlson v. Green,* 446 U.S. 14 (1980).

12 FIGHTING CITY HALL

McNEILL STOKES
Stokes & Shapiro
Attorneys at Law

State and local governments affect the everyday lives and activities of citizens and businesses. Units of local government—cities, towns, counties, townships, parishes, and villages—can operate facilities and institutions, build and maintain recreational areas, provide for streets and public ways, license businesses, furnish police and fire protection, and perform many other services necessary to modern society. Because of their capacity to touch directly so many lives, they also have the capacity to cause many injuries. In the exercise of their powers and in the performance of their duties local governments injure people and businesses in many ways. They may cause physical injury to an individual or to property, overtax or tax unequally, breach contracts, wrongly refuse to issue a license, create a nuisance, arbitrarily zone or rezone an area, or cause injuries in other ways. Contrary to common belief, local and state governments are highly suable for the injuries they cause. More important than that fact is the fact that they have money to pay any judgment.

State and local units are also subject to certain restrictions which create rights in private parties. Local units have no inherent authority; all their powers are derived from the state. Therefore, if a local unit hasn't expressly been granted a particular power, the chances are that it hasn't that power. Many actions of a local unit may be challenged because they are not authorized. In addition, state and local units must comply with the constitutional restrictions placed on government in general.

Illustrative Case

The owner of a commercial warehouse refused to permit a city fire inspector to enter and inspect his locked warehouse without a warrant. The inspection was being conducted as part of a routine, periodic citywide canvass to obtain compliance with the city fire code. After he refused to allow the inspector to inspect the warehouse, the owner was arrested for violating a provision of the fire code which provided for the inspection of buildings. The owner contended that if the fire code was interpreted to authorize warrantless inspections, it would violate his rights under the Fourth and Fourteenth Amendments.

In a companion case, the Supreme Court held that the Fourth Amendment bars prosecution of a person who has refused to permit a code enforcement inspection of a
personal residence without a warrant. The court held that in this context the owner of
a commercial building also had a right to be free from administrative searches conducted without a suitable warrant procedure.[1]

INVASIONS OF PERSONAL RIGHTS

At one point in history the rule of sovereign immunity protected governmental units from suits against them. As a sovereign entity, a state could be
sued only if it consented to the suit. The immunity was extended to local
governments as creatures of the state. A local government, as an organ of the
state, is obligated to serve local citizens and to supply them with some services and conveniences. But local governments have another role. At times
they act as corporate bodies doing those things which private corporations
might do. Their different roles gave rise to different liabilities; when acting
in a governmental capacity they enjoyed the immunity of a governmental
unit, but when acting in a private or proprietary capacity they were liable
for all the things for which a private corporation would be liable. Because of
this dual role, whether or not a local unit could be sued depended on whether
the action of the unit was characterized as governmental or proprietary. In
some states the distinction still is made that a unit may be sued for actions
in its proprietary capacity but not for those carried out in its governmental
capacity. There is no clear distinction between the two. In states which rely
on the distinction an attempt should be made to frame a claim as one arising
from an action done by the unit in its proprietary capacity.

Regardless of whether or not an act is a governmental function, even in
states which adhere to the distinction there are actions for which a municipality is nevertheless held liable. For example, a municipality is generally
held liable for the creation of a nuisance. Courts hold that the power to carry
out whatever governmental function is involved doesn't authorize a city to
create a nuisance. This is so even when the city is not negligent.

Illustrative Case

The owner of certain property in Brookfield installed drains from the cellar and exterior of the premises leading into a common drain which was then connected with a
storm sewer installed in Horseshoe Drive, which he also then owned. Later he conveyed several parcels of land including Horseshoe Drive to the town of Brookfield. At
some point, Brookfield removed the drain which the property owner had installed without notifying him. As a result, the property owner's premises were severely damaged
by water which could not flow into the storm sewer and so accumulated on his premises. The court held that even if the town had no duty to maintain the drain and even
if it had a legal right to sever the drain without notice to the owner of the property, it
could still be liable if the manner in which it did so was unreasonable and created a
nuisance which resulted in damage to someone's land. The court emphasized that it

[1]See v. City of Seattle, 387 U.S. 541 (1967); *Camara v. Municipal Court of City and County of San Francisco,*
387 U.S. 523 (1967).

was a well-established principle that a municipality might be liable for injury resulting from a nuisance created and maintained by it.²

Even in states which adhere strictly to the doctrine of sovereign immunity, there are generally statutes which provide for liability for damages in certain instances. For example, almost all municipalities have statutes providing liability for damages caused by defects in streets and sidewalks when the municipality knew or should have known of the defect. The obligation to use due care in the maintenance of streets, sidewalks, and public ways includes the maintenance of traffic signals and signs when the city chooses to furnish them. Although a city is not obligated to provide lights, signs, and signals, once it chooses to do so, it will be liable for negligence in the maintenance or operation of them.

Illustrative Case

The plaintiff incurred injuries when he drove his car past the dead end of a street and crashed into a tree. Evidence was presented to show that the intersection was improperly illuminated. The plaintiff brought suit against the city of Chicago Heights for personal injuries. The court held that even though the city was under no obligation to provide signs, barriers, or reflectors, once it undertook to provide lights, it was liable for injuries which resulted from deficient or inadequate ones. A municipal corporation, like an individual or a private corporation, was required to exercise its powers with such precautions as should not subject others to injuries.³

One problem which a citizen injured by a defect in a street or a sidewalk may encounter is that the city must have had prior notice of the defect before liability will attach. As a practical matter this is always so because if a city isn't aware of a defect, there is no negligence in a failure to correct it. However, some statutes require that a municipality receive written notice of a defect prior to an accident; otherwise liability will not attach. In such municipalities, even if the city was actually aware of the defect, a suit may be barred if there has been no written notice.

In the majority of states, the doctrine of governmental immunity no longer applies to cities. Courts or legislatures have abolished the governmental-proprietary distinction and fix liability generally for the acts of cities. In many of those states which haven't abolished the doctrine of governmental immunity, courts have held that the purchase of liability insurance waives the immunity of a city at least to the extent of coverage. If an individual is injured on city property by a city's actions or failure to act, it is better to assume that there is a right to sue than to assume that the city won't be liable because it is a governmental unit.

A city is responsible for the provision of many services to its citizens and may be liable for failure to provide a service or for negligence in the provision of that service. It is a general rule that a city is not liable for failure to provide

²*Cyr v. Town of Brookfield*, 216 A.2d 198 (Conn. 1965).

³*Baran v. City of Chicago Heights*, 251 N.E.2d 227 (Ill. 1969).

police service because a duty is owed to the community as a whole: there is no duty to a particular individual. There are many ways around the general rule. If a city narrows its obligation into a special duty to an individual, a breach of that duty will subject the city to liability. For example, when a domestic relations court issued to a woman an order of protection which authorized the police to take her husband into custody if he threatened her, a special duty to that woman was created. The duty was extended to her child, and suit against the city was allowed when the child was severely injured by the husband after repeated requests by the mother for protection were ignored by the police.

If a city undertakes to provide police service and does it negligently, liability might also attach. Once a city undertakes to provide a service, it must carry it out with due care.

Illustrative Case

A suspect in Deputy Watter's custody in a courthouse managed to seize a gun and took the deputy hostage. They drove to an airport where the plaintiff, Johnson, was in charge. A scuffle ensued in the airport, and the suspect shot the plaintiff. Johnson brought a personal injury action against the county and its deputy sheriff. The court held that the policeman could be held liable for negligence committed in the performance of his duties. The court also held that it was clear under Illinois law that a municipality was liable for negligent injuries proximately caused by its officers.[4]

INTERFERENCE WITH CONSTITUTIONAL RIGHTS

Another means of placing liability on a municipal unit is through a 1983 suit; 42 U.S.C. § 1983 is a one-sentence statute which has been on the books since 1871 but which has recently been expanded into an effective means of recovery from a local government. The law could be applied to almost any action taken by a local government and could be interpreted very broadly.[4a] The act provides:

Every person who, under color of statute, ordinance, regulation, custom or usage, of any state or territory, subjects or causes to be subjected, any citizen of the United States or other person within the jurisdiction thereof to the deprivation of any rights, privileges, or immunities, secured by the Constitution and laws shall be liable to the party injured in an action at law, suit in equity or other proceeding for redress.

The types of actions which can be brought under Section 1983 are almost limitless. Whenever a person is deprived of any constitutional right by a local government or governmental agency, recovery might be had under 1983. Actions have been maintained under 1983 for illegal arrest and detention, failure to provide medical attention during incarcerations, use of unreasonable and malicious force, defamation, unlawful searches and seizures, withholding of vested pension benefits from a former county employee, a city-

---

[4]*Johnson v. Gallatin County, Ill.,* 418 F.2d 96 (7th Cir. 1969).

[4a]The Supreme Court held in *Owen v. City of Independence, Mo.,* 100 S. Ct. 1398 (1980) that a municipality has no immunity from liability under Section 1983 and may not assert good faith as a defense.

mandated unpaid maternity leave commencing 4 months after the beginning of pregnancy and extending 4 months after birth, and systematic discrimination in tax assessments.

Illustrative Case

Taxpayers sued county and taxing authorities seeking compensatory and punitive damages under 42 U.S.C. § 1983 for injuries caused by tax assessment discrimination. The taxpayers alleged that the taxing authorities had systematically, knowingly, intentionally, fraudulently, and invidiously discriminated against them by assessing their property at levels not permitted by law. The court determined that an action for tax assessment discrimination could be brought under 42 U.S.C. § 1983 and that the county could be held liable for systematic tax assessment discrimination by the county assessor and the county board of appeals.[5]

A claim under 1983 can be based on the negligent conduct of a government official as long as the constitutional provision said to be violated does not specifically require a greater degree of culpability. A failure to act can also provide the basis for a claim under 1983. For example, when law enforcement personnel fail to enforce the laws and thereby deny equal protection of the laws to people or businesses that are legitimately exercising their fundamental rights, they may be held liable.

An action under 1983 can also be brought when a local unit fails to afford an individual or a business due process. There are many examples of actions by governmental units which cannot be taken without due-process protection. When a local government unit undertakes to provide a service even though it is not obligated to do so, a property right which cannot be divested without due process of law may vest in the recipient of that service. For example, once a local government unit undertakes to provide gas or electric service to its citizens, it cannot merely unilaterally cut off that service without due process.

Illustrative Case

The Crafts moved into a residence which had previously been used as a duplex. Accordingly it had two separate gas and electric meters. They were told by the seller that the second set of meters was inoperative. However, they began receiving two bills. The Crafts then hired a plumbing and electrical contractor to combine the meters into one. The contractor did not do the job properly, but the Crafts were not aware of that fact. They continued to receive two bills, and their service was terminated five times for nonpayment. The Crafts sought in good faith to determine the cause of double billing but didn't receive any real help from the Memphis Light, Gas and Water Division. The Crafts and other customers of Memphis Light, Gas and Water brought a class action under 1983, seeking declaratory and injunctive relief against the utility and damages for termination of utility service without due process of law. The Supreme Court held that because Tennessee decisional law provided that a utility might not terminate service "at will" but only "for cause," the Crafts asserted an interest in property which was protected by the due-process clause. The Court held that the utility had deprived the Crafts of an interest in property without due process of law. [6]

---

[5] *North American Cold Storage Co. v. County of Cook,* 468 F. Supp. 424 (N.D. III. 1979).

The list of suits which can be brought pursuant to Section 1983 is virtually endless, and the potentiality for such suits is constantly being expanded. It appears that 1983 will play an increasingly important role in controlling the actions of local government units. An important aspect of a 1983 suit is that counsel fees will be awarded to a party who is successful against the local unit or its officials.

ZONING

A city may take other actions which may vest a property right in an individual or a business. For example, when a person makes substantial expenditures in reliance on a zoning ordinance, that person may acquire a vested property right which is protected by the Constitution. When the property right becomes vested and the owner attempts to use that property in accordance with the zoning ordinance, the zoning authority may not be able legally to divest that right by the adoption of another ordinance which prohibits that use.

Illustrative Case

The city of Atlanta rezoned a tract of land from a residential classification to an apartment classification. At the time of the rezoning there was correspondence with the owner regarding some conditions to the zoning, but the conditions were not made a part of the ordinance. The property was subsequently sold to Westinghouse. Westinghouse obtained a building permit which authorized the construction of apartments on the tract. Before completion Westinghouse had to suspend construction because of economic conditions, and the building permit expired. Westinghouse had expended over $1 million in connection with the development of the tract. When Westinghouse subsequently applied for another building permit to finish the apartments, the city refused. The city determined that the ordinance which had rezoned the property from residential to apartment use was invalid because the proposed conditions had not been incorporated in the ordinance. The city subsequently passed an ordinance downzoning the property from apartment use to residential use. Westinghouse then filed an action against the city of Atlanta. The court held that the original ordinance had rezoned the property without conditions. The fact that the city intended to apply conditions did not invalidate the zoning. Furthermore, the court held that the law in Georgia was clear that a property owner acquired a vested right to the continuation of a zoning classification when the owner incurred expenses in acquiring property and developing it in reliance upon the zoning classification. [7]

One of a municipality's most important regulatory powers is zoning. Through the zoning power a city can mandate the way in which land can be used in a particular area, the kind of activities allowed in a particular zone, the kind of structure and where it must be placed on a lot, the size of a building, and the area of a lot which must be free of construction. In exer-

[6] *Memphis Light, Gas & Water Div. v. Craft,* 436 U.S. 1 (1978).
[7] *City of Atlanta v. Westinghouse Corp.,* 241 Ga. 560 (1978).

cising this power, the city also determines who will occupy the land and, by means of lot sizes, the minimum size of a residential structure, etc. Zoning thus becomes an even more important power. Because businesses often own a great deal of property, an exercise of the zoning power can intimately affect a business.

The zoning power is an aspect of the police power of government. The police power establishes a very broad authority to promote the health, safety, morals, and general welfare of the public. However, the power is not limitless. The means used must be reasonable, and zoning ordinances will be overturned if they are not. Each zoning case will be considered individually.

There are usually two ways to influence a zoning decision. Most zoning decisions are ultimately made by an elected local board. This fact opens up the decisions to all the pressures of the political system. Applying political pressure through a show of public backing is one means of influencing zoning decisions. In some cities there are provisions for public input in zoning decisions. If a structure is already available, it makes sense to obtain support there. If there is no organized group, a pressure group can be created. The zoning board can be requested to inform interested individuals and businesses of any activity with respect to a zoning decision. Freedom of information acts, if available, may be used to examine the files. A strong pressure group with a solid basis in fact can exert a great deal of influence on a local zoning board.

Larger cities have, in addition to an elected board, a professional planning staff which makes recommendations on zoning decisions. The staff consists of permanent professional people who will probably not be influenced by group political pressure. However, they can be influenced, as can anyone, by friendly relations and strong, solid arguments. It is important to sell the planning staff on the benefits of a particular decision. It never hurts to have an ally on the planning staff if you intend to influence a zoning decision.

Zoning ordinances are subject to exceptions or variances. If a particular zoning law works an unnecessary hardship on an individual or a business, a variance may be granted. Generally, variances are granted only when property in a particular zone cannot reasonably be used in the way mandated for that zone. There are specific requirements which the property must meet for a variance to be granted, and there is not much discretion in whether a variance will be granted or denied. For this reason court review of a grant or denial of a variance is readily available. However, in most jurisdictions review must be pursued very quickly; otherwise the challenge will be lost.

INVERSE CONDEMNATION

If a variance is not available yet a zoning ordinance renders property almost worthless, an alternative challenge is available. Zoning restrictions can be challenged as being so confiscatory that they actually amount to a taking. A zoning ordinance must substantially diminish the value of land to be regarded as a taking.

Illustrative Case

> After 5 acres of unimproved land had been acquired by the present owners, the city adopted a zoning ordinance that placed that land in a zone which restricted them to between one and five single-family dwellings on the tract. The owners brought suit against the city, alleging that the city had taken their property without just compensation. The Supreme Court held that the application of a general zoning law to particular property could effect a taking if the ordinance didn't substantially advance legitimate governmental goals or denied the owner an economically viable use of his or her land. The Court held in this case that although the ordinance limited development, it neither prevented the best use of the land nor extinguished a fundamental attribute of ownership. Therefore, the zoning ordinance did not on its face effect a taking of the owners' property without just compensation.[8]

When a city government's actions do render property almost worthless, the courts will require that the city compensate the owner for the property. This taking can come about as a direct result of the city's actions, for example, by regulating the property so that it cannot be used for what it was previously used for, or as an indirect result of the city's actions. (See Chapter 11, subsection "Inverse Condemnation.")

Illustrative Case

> Pursuant to an area redevelopment plan, the Bridgeport Redevelopment Agency advised the owners of particular property that their property would be taken by eminent domain unless the owners accepted its offer for their property. The owners rejected the offer, and the city of Bridgeport approved the acquisition of the property by eminent domain, but the agency refused to acquire the property. As a result of the uncertainty of the neighborhood during redevelopment activities, the owners lost their tenants and were unable to relet their property. The owners brought suit against the city and its redevelopment agency for refusing to acquire their property by eminent domain after they had lost their tenants as a result of the redevelopment activity. The court held that although it was settled law that a municipal corporation was not liable for negligence in performance of a governmental function, willful and wanton negligence would subject the municipality to liability. Since the owners did not allege mere negligence, the doctrine of sovereign immunity was held to be inapplicable. As an alternative theory, the court held that the complaint stated a good claim for relief when it alleged that the city and its agency had created a nuisance by their actions, for a municipality's liability for nuisance could not be avoided by sovereign immunity. Notwithstanding the other legal theories, a claim for relief could be premised on the claim that the city's actions constituted a taking of property without just compensation.[9]

EMINENT DOMAIN

The government can actually condemn private property, compensate the owner for it, and appropriate that property for a public use. That power to take private property for a public purpose is the power of eminent domain. A governmental unit can be enjoined from acquiring land in a condemnation setting if the condemner is exceeding its powers, or the condemnation is for

---

[8] *Agins v. City of Tiburon,* 447 U.S. 255 (1980).

[9] *Haczela v. City of Bridgeport,* 299 F. Supp. 709 (D. Conn. 1969).

an improper purpose, or the condemner hasn't complied with statutory requirements. An injunction then is available to prevent the governmental unit from taking property through an unlawful exercise of eminent domain. Zoning cannot be used as a substitute for eminent domain by so depressing property values that when the property is ultimately taken, the amount of damages will be low.

If the taking of the property cannot be prevented, the important thing is to receive adequate compensation. The owner of the property must be formally notified of the condemnation and be paid for the value of the property. At one time this proviso didn't adequately compensate the owner because payment was only for the bare value of the land and building, not for any value to the owner. Steps are being taken to ease the standard condemnation formula. Some states now provide for relocation benefits and moving costs. Congress has placed conditions on municipalities that receive federal moneys for projects so that persons whose property is condemned because of a federally supported project receive relocation benefits and moving expenses. Homeowners can also receive many of the incidental costs of a forced move. They can receive the value of the land and building, the difference between what is awarded to them and the cost of a new home, the difference between the interest rate on the old mortgage and the rate on a new mortgage, closing costs on the purchase of a new home, and moving expenses. Businesses may now receive more adequate compensation than was previously provided. A business may now be entitled to the actual cost of relocation. That cost may include disassembling the facility and equipment, moving it to a new location, and putting it back together again. If there is federal involvement in the project which is causing the condemnation, the federal agency involved will send to any affected individuals information explaining what they are entitled to.

Condemnation is another area in which it may pay to fight the government in order to receive the highest value for property. The government will attempt to obtain the property for as little as possible. Property owners who settle with government negotiators usually get much less than the estimated value of their property. However, when individuals are prepared and vigorously represented by counsel, with professional appraisers, they may receive more than the government's estimated value of their property. Since condemnation lawyers generally take such cases on a contingency basis, it need not cost property owners anything to challenge the government's award. The courts commonly award property owners more than the government's estimated value upon the condemnation of property.

LICENSES AND PERMITS

The power to grant licenses and permits is the power to regulate and tax professions, occupations, trades, and businesses. The purpose of a license is to confer a right which does not exist without it. Licenses are especially important to businesses and occupations. A license to do business may be required of any business. The activities of a business may be restricted by license. In fact, some businesses may be altogether prohibited. A licensing authority may control the actual existence and profitability of a business.

A state has the power to regulate activities and occupations through the issuance of licenses and permits. Although a city has no inherent power to license or issue permits, the powers and duties as to licenses and fees are usually delegated by ordinance to a board or an agency. The board must act within the bounds of the authority delegated to it. For example, when a county has no authority to impose occupational taxes and licenses for businesses and professions in unincorporated areas of the county, an ordinance purporting to do so is invalid. Not only must the local unit act within the authority granted to it, but that grant of authority must include specific standards to govern the exercise of administrative discretion. If discretion is granted to an administrative body to license and impose fees without sufficient governing standards, that delegation may be struck down.

Requirements for licenses and permits vary from city to city. The occupations and activities which require licenses vary from area to area. However, at this point almost all trades or businesses require some kind of license or permit. Generally, licenses and permits are granted merely upon application and payment of a fee. Some grants require an inspection of buildings or facilities or an investigation of the person applying for the license. A municipality may classify persons, activities, and things separately for licensing reasons, but the regulations must apply equally and uniformly to all members of a particular class. If a classification applies unequally, it will be invalidated. Imposing an occupation tax on a gas plant but not on an electric plant, prohibiting illuminating signs except for theaters, discriminating between dealers in solid and liquid fuels, and imposing a business license tax on a particular business in addition to the taxes imposed on businesses generally are examples of classifications deemed discriminatory or unequal.

Not only must the classifications be uniform and apply equally to individuals and activities, the licenses must be issued fairly and reasonably. Licensing authorities cannot arbitrarily or unreasonably refuse a license or a permit. A license cannot be denied except for a valid reason relating to the fitness of that particular person to conduct the licensed activity. In addition, once a license has been granted, the licensee obtains a vested property right that cannot be suspended or revoked without just cause and without authority of law. A license cannot be suspended or revoked without due process of law, notice, and a hearing into the matter. In some cities review before a license review board must be obtained before an action can be brought in court. Since the time for court review is limited, review proceedings should be pursued quickly.

TAXATION

Municipal taxes are distinguished from the imposition of fees, special assessments, water or sewer charges, or a taking under the power of eminent domain. Municipal taxes are those charges imposed by a municipality for the support of the government and public needs. The power to tax is inherent in the state and is merely delegated to the municipality. The power to tax is vitally important. Chief Justice Marshall said, "The power to tax is the power to destroy." The power must be granted expressly; it will not be implied unless it is a necessary implication. For example, even the imposition on a municipality of the duty to erect a hospital does not include by implication the power to levy a tax to pay for the building. When examining a tax imposed by a municipality, the first question always is "By what authority is the tax levied?" If the city has no authority to levy a tax, the tax will be invalid.

Illustrative Case

The city of Bellingham, Washington, adopted an ordinance which required, among other things, that all employees within the city secure a yearly license and imposed a tax on all persons receiving compensation for services performed within the city. A resident and wage earner in the city brought an action to enjoin enforcement of the ordinance. The court held that the city had no power to control the right to work for wages and therefore had no power to levy an excise tax based upon such right.[10]

If a tax has been validly authorized, it is then subject to constitutional restrictions. An ordinance must operate uniformly and equally. Although classifications may be created for taxing purposes, the classifications must have a reasonable basis.

Illustrative Case

WHYY, Inc., was a nonprofit corporation incorporated in Pennsylvania. It operated a noncommercial television station which broadcast cultural, educational, and recreational programs. The broadcasting facility for one of its television channels was located in New Jersey. The station registered and qualified to transact business in New Jersey. WHYY requested an exemption, as a nonprofit organization, from state real and personal property taxes. The request was denied. On appeal the superior court held that the statute in question exempted only nonprofit corporations which were incorporated in New Jersey. WHYY argued that the statute denied it equal protection of the law by discriminating against it solely on the basis of its foreign incorporation. The Supreme Court held that while a state might impose conditions on the qualification of a corporation to do business within the state, once it had qualified, the foreign corporation was entitled to equal protection with resident corporations. The Court concluded that WHYY had not been accorded equal treatment. [11]

When taxes have been lawfully ordered, an assessment or list of taxables must be drawn up before a tax can become a charge on a person or property. The assessment presents another basis for challenge of a taxing result. Local laws are so different regarding the method of assessing property for taxation that no general rules concerning the appropriateness of a particular procedure can be made. In making the assessment the method provided for a particular city or county must be substantially followed. Exact conformity with

[10] *Cary v. City of Bellingham*, 250 P.2d 114 (Wash. 1952).
[11] *WHYY, Inc. v. Borough of Glassboro*, 393 U.S. 117 (1968).

the directions may not be necessary, but substantial conformity will be required. The requirements usually set out when the assessment must be made, who should make the assessment, and how the property should be valued for the assessment. There is also generally a day or a number of days following the completion of the assessments during which a protest may be made. Unless a protest is filed on the day set aside for it, the right to protest an assessment is lost. The owners of large real estate holdings almost without exception protest the assessment of their property while small property owners seldom do. It is important to note that a protest of an assessment usually results in a reduction of that assessment.

Two challenges generally can be made to any assessment. The property owner may protest that the property has been overvalued or that valuations are not uniform or equal. The first challenge, that the property is not worth the value at which it has been assessed, can rarely be made. Assessments are usually done at less than the true value of the property, so property is very rarely overvalued. The second challenge, that the property has been assessed unequally in comparison with other properties, can more easily be made. In some tax districts there is no uniformity of valuation. Valuations are not made annually, so that an old building will generally have a lower valuation placed on it than a new building. If other similar property is assessed at a lower percentage of its value than your property, you may request a reduction in the assessment. It doesn't matter that the assessment is still less than the value of the property; the challenge is that the valuations are not uniform.

It is important to check the tax assessment rolls to compare an assessment with the assessments of other similar properties. If there is an inequality in the assessments, a protest must be filed on the specific day set for grievances. A claim should be substantiated through the facts obtained from the assessment rolls. There is generally an assessment appeals board to which an appeal can be made if the assessor's determination is not favorable. Court review may also be available. Pursuing a protest often results in a reduction of the assessment.

SPECIAL ASSESSMENTS

While taxes are laid for purposes of general revenue without regard to direct benefits, a special assessment is a local charge imposed on property because of a direct benefit which that property receives. A special assessment is a charge actually imposed on the property to pay for a local improvement made by the municipality. Because the property being assessed has received some direct benefit from the improvement, the theory is that payment ought to be made accordingly.

A municipality has no inherent power to impose a special assessment; that power must be expressly granted by the state or arise by necessary implication. If there is no grant of the power to the municipality, the assessment can be challenged as being beyond the authority of the municipality. If a special assessment is authorized, the apportionment must be made according to a specific rule. The apportionment must be made equally and uniformly among the properties benefited by the improvement. Some ordinances require that the assessment be apportioned according to the proportionate benefit, while others require that another method be used. Whatever method is used, the property being assessed must receive some special benefits, and the assessment must not exceed those benefits received.

Illustrative Case

The city of Owatonna levied a paving assessment against property owned by the Chicago, Rock Island & Pacific Railroad. Rock Island contested the assessment, which was for the conversion of the dirt road which ran contiguous to the railroad property into a paved street. The court held that the amount of the city's assessment against the railroad was greatly in excess of the benefit to the railroad and that the residential property which abutted the street and had ready access to the street benefited more and was assessed less than the railroad's property. Accordingly, the court held that reassessment was required.[12]

CONTRACTS

State and local governments are among the biggest users of goods and services. In providing services to the public, local units necessarily contract with many businesses for supplies, materials, services, and construction. Local units are a continuous source of business. There are many advantages to dealing with a local unit. However, in choosing to deal with a local unit, business people must take extra care. Rules and regulations govern every aspect of a contract, and they must be complied with.

A city is limited in what contracts it can enter into. If a contract is beyond the power of a city to make, there may be no recovery against the city. This is so even if the city has received benefits from the contract. A person dealing with a city is presumed to know the nature and extent of the city's authority to contract. So the most important principle to remember in dealing with a city is that unless the city has the authority to make a particular contract, no payments will be made pursuant to that contract.

On the other hand, if a city has the power to make a contract but the contract suffers from some defect, the city will generally be held liable for damages or for the benefits retained. The city cannot avoid liability on the ground of the invalidity of an agreement if it had the power to make that agreement. There is at times a fine line between a contract which is not authorized and one which suffers from some other defect. It is important to establish in some way that the contract itself was authorized.

Illustrative Case

On November 23, 1971, the city of Lawrence, Massachusetts, entered into a contract with a contractor for the construction of a hospital. The next day the city learned that on November 15 of that year a statute had taken effect which prohibited the commencement of major renovation on a health care facility unless a certificate of need

---

[12] *Owatonna v. Chicago, Rock Island & Pacific R.R. Co.*, 450 F.2d 87 (8th Cir. 1971).

was obtained from the department of public health. The city informed the contractor and applied for a certificate of need. No work was actually performed on the contract, although the contractor signed some subcontracts and moved some equipment to the site. The city wasn't able to obtain a certificate of need, so the parties agreed to terminate the contract, although the contractor reserved his right to seek damages. Since the contract had included an arbitration clause for all claims arising out of the contract or its breach, the contractor requested arbitration. The city defended that since the contract was illegal and unenforceable, the arbitration clause was also. The arbitrators rejected the city's argument and awarded delay damages and lost profits to the contractor. The Massachusetts Supreme Court also found for the contractor. The court held that the fact that performance of the contract without a certificate was illegal did not make the contract itself illegal. Since the contract was valid, the arbitration clause was binding on the parties. Thus the court affirmed the arbitrator's award to the contractor for delay damages and lost profits.[13]

When a contract is valid and within the power of a city to make, the rules of law governing the performance and liability for the breach of private contracts generally are applicable to municipal contracts. However, there are some specific rules and regulations which apply to contracts with a city. For example, there is generally a short period of time during which claims arising out of a contract with a city can be made. If a notice of claim is not presented within the time specified, the claim is lost.

In addition, although the credit of most cities is good, they are almost invariably late with payments. It is often advisable to factor a payment delay into any price given to a city. Even a judgment awarded by a court may be paid slowly. Municipal property is not subject to levy or attachment and so cannot be reached in that way. However, often a court order directed to an individual city official can obtain fast results. An action directly against a city treasurer to compel payment will probably result in fast payment. Although there are pitfalls in dealing with local governments, they remain one of the largest sources of business. If care is taken to comply with the rules and regulations governing dealings with the government, those dealings can be profitable. The advantages to dealing with the government generally far outweigh the disadvantages.

However, to assert a right against a local unit the limitations placed on the exercise of that right must be avoided. Local governments are notorious for placing strict, detailed limitations on the right to sue.

PROCEDURAL LIMITATIONS ON A SUIT

To sue a municipality in almost any state, a written notice of claim must be served on the municipality within a short time after the claim has arisen. Under some statutes almost all claims for damages, whether for personal injury, property damage, or breach of contract, must be presented to the municipality in the manner specified and within the time designated to the board or person designated. The directives in the statute are generally a precondition to payment of the claim or maintenance of a lawsuit on the claim.

[13]*City of Lawrence v. Francis G. Falzarano,* 402 N.E.2d 1017 (Mass. 1980).

Usually it is a good idea to comply completely with the directives of the statute because failure to do so may bar payment or suit on the claim. Notice-of-claim statutes set out specifically what must be included in the notice. At a minimum the statute generally requires the name and address of the claimant, the date, the place and nature of the claim or event giving rise to the claim, the way in which the claim arose, and the injuries or damages. A statement that the notice includes other injuries from the event which are as yet unascertained should always be included. The notice may be required to be notarized, and a copy should be kept. Many local government units provide notice-of-claim forms for use in complying with the statute. However, they often request more information than is required by the statute. It is best to give the minimum amount of information required by statute and to strike out the surplusage on the form.

The notice of claim must then be filed with the proper person or department. You should make certain when serving notice that the person served is the one who is supposed to be served. The notice should be served in person, and the person who receives the notice should stamp a receipt for it on your copy. You should serve the notice of claim within the time designated by the statute.

Although it is best to comply completely with the statutory requirements, if for some reason the deadline is missed, you should not give up. It is possible that the requirements of the notice-of-claim statute will not be sustained upon a challenge. Courts are loosening up on technical compliance with statutes, especially if the result seems unjust.

Illustrative Case

A 19-year-old passenger in an automobile sustained injuries when the car struck a rut or chuckhole in a city street, causing the driver to lose control of the car and strike a tree. The passenger was physically and mentally incapacitated as a result of the accident and did not nominate a guardian to file notice until more than 60 days after the accident. The guardian filed a notice of claim with the city, and the city moved to dismiss for failure to serve written notice on the city within 60 days as required by statute. The court held that that requirement was unconstitutional as applied to a minor claimant who was rendered physically and mentally incapacitated as a result of the accident. The court added that even if it were to assume that the policy considerations for the rule were once valid, they had lost their validity and ceased to exist owing to changed circumstances. Whereas the purpose had been to provide notice of a claim to municipal authorities, most units and agencies now had police departments, full-time attorneys, and investigators to investigate accidents promptly. In addition, most governmental units were covered by liability insurance so that the reasons behind the requirement were no longer valid.[14]

Courts have found other ways to get around the harsh results caused by a failure to comply with the technical requirements of a statute. For example, some courts have held, even in states which require notice of claims in both torts and contracts, that when property is damaged as a result of a

[14] *Grubaugh v. City of St. Johns,* 180 N.W.2d 778 (Mich. 1970).

public improvement project of the city, a claim is not necessary because the property owner really is only recovering what would have been received if the city had used its power of condemnation and compensated the owner for the property before rather than after it had been damaged. Although there has been a loosening up of technical requirements, every attempt should be made to comply totally and to avoid the notice-of-claim trap.

Once the notice has been properly served, there is usually a specific time within which an individual or a business must file suit. Municipalities often have specific statutes of limitations; the general statutes for private suits don't usually apply. The statutes of limitations for suit against a municipality are generally shorter than the common limitations. In addition, there is usually a time limit before which you cannot file suit. If suit is filed before the time, it will be dismissed and must be filed again. It is best to file suit as soon as possible after that time. Then there is plenty of time to negotiate a settlement before the statute of limitations runs.

13 POLITICAL ACTION COMMITTEES*

JUSTIN DART
Chairman of the Board, Dart Industries Inc.,
and Chairman of the Executive Committee
of Dart & Kraft, Inc.

How do we elect a responsible Congress? One of the most effective methods is providing funds to political action committees (PACs). An all-important part of any successful political endeavor is money. Congress has provided the most efficient vehicle that we have ever had available to us for political fund-raising purposes. It is extremely important because in any corporation the amount of money raised by an organized program (called a PAC) will be approximately 10 times the money that would go for political purposes without an organized program. In addition, the out-of-pocket expenses paid by the corporation mean that 100 percent of the contributions go to the candidate. An individual can give only $1000 to a federal candidate. A PAC can give $5000.

Illustrative Example

A very important businessman said to me in his office before a recent election, "I have been asked to raise $500,000 for a senator in my state. This is almost an impossible task." "Quite to the contrary," I said. "Let me give you an example—I'll send you tomorrow morning $5000 from our PAC. If 200 corporations in the United States also sent you $5000 from their PACs, you'd have a million dollars (not half a million dollars), and you'd have it without any exertion at all." He said "Oh." There were thirty-four senators up for election in 1980, fourteen of them in small states which obviously required less funding.

Now let's look at what the PACs could do on a hypothetical basis. A thousand PACs at $50,000 per PAC (our PAC raised $125,000 last year) would collect $50 million. A thousand PACs at $20,000 per PAC would collect another $20 million. Two thousand PACs at $5000 per PAC would collect $10 million, and 10,000 small PACs at $1000 per PAC would collect $10 million, for a total of $110 million. I feel confident that this sum, along with other normal contributions, will provide an adequate balance between the

*The assistance of the University of Southern California Center for the Study of Private Enterprise is greatly appreciated.

power of labor and the power of the forces working for free enterprise. PACs really work. They work if the chief executive officer takes the lead. The CEO must take the lead. If the CEO doesn't, PACs won't work.

Money is a vital and essential ingredient of politics. In the case of unions, money comes from the Political Contributions Committee of the AFL-CIO Committee on Political Education (COPE) and similar organizations. It is, therefore, of paramount importance that corporations and individuals provide funding for fiscally responsible candidates (Democrats, Republicans, or independents) to preserve a proper balance of representation in government.

Whom does a PAC support? The only criterion, and the final criterion, is responsibility. A PAC must support inflation fighters, waste fighters, people who are trying to bring the cost of government in line and the tax burden on the average citizen into reasonable proportion. The money must be spent on challengers, not incumbents who are irresponsible. If we don't do it that way, the PAC will be self-defeating. How do you know where the money should go? The National Association of Manufacturers, the Chamber of Commerce of the United States, state chambers of commerce, and many other organizations keep careful track of the responsibility and voting records of members of Congress. These data can be used along with your own analysis of the candidates. It is counterproductive to raise money for legislators who are irresponsible and who are perpetuating our problems. Most money should go to federal offices, for if things go well in Washington, they will go well in the fifty states.

As I have said, the CEO must take the lead. When the CEO requests money for a PAC, the person asked is going to say, "Well, boss, how much do you give?" The CEO should tell him or her. In my case I give $5000, which is the limit that an individual can give to a PAC. My wife also gives $5000, and many of our directors give very generously. The person then will say, "What's my fair share?" In our company we have suggested a guideline of giving, without which people have no idea of what to give. Our guideline is very modest. For instance, at an annual salary of $25,000 we suggest $100, which is $50 out of pocket after tax. At $50,000 we suggest $325, which is $275 after tax; and at $100,000 or more $1000.

Another way to win elections is through employee economic education programs. The economic illiteracy in the United States—not just on the part of employees but, perhaps, of the majority of Americans—is a serious problem. We try to bring economic facts to our employees in a very simple way. We tell them about what makes our economic system function, and we teach them about profits—why profits are a good thing. Employees are inclined to think that companies make aftertax profits of 25 to 35 percent, whereas they really make 4, 5, or 6 percent, depending upon the industry. Additionally, they want to know where the profits go and how they are used in their interest as well as in the shareholders' interest. We teach them about the deadliness of inflation and why it is a real enemy of them and their families. Employee education is easy, and it doesn't cost much to administer. We use posters on bulletin boards, payroll stuffers, house organs, face-to-face meetings, and the like, all of which cost a minimal amount of money. However, this effort can't be a 2-, 3-, or 6-week process; it must continue month after month and year after year. You might ask, "How many people can you influence? Is the effort really worthwhile?" Let me remind you that President Carter was elected by a margin of 1 percent of the voters in 1976. I feel completely confident that we can influence more than 10 or 15 percent of our employees not with rhetoric but with facts, incontrovertible facts. And that's what the employees will believe if the material is presented in a way that has credibility and is not just propaganda.

With a PAC to raise funds to elect and support the election of responsible members of the House and Senate, regardless of party, and with an employee economic education program, we can turn the country around, further the free enterprise system, and increase productivity at the same time. CEOs must have the will, the determination, and the dedication to carry out such a project if we are to change the face of Congress to one of greater fiscal responsibility.

FORMATION OF A PAC

Following the Supreme Court's 1972 decision permitting union PACs to make contributions to federal candidates if those contributions have been paid voluntarily by members, the Federal Election Commission (FEC) issued an advisory opinion permitting corporations to establish PACs. Meanwhile, Congress passed the Federal Election Campaign Act of 1971, which specifically allows the creation of political action committees by unions, trade groups, and corporations. Through these PACs labor and corporate groups can solicit funds from members to be used to contribute to federal election campaigns and parties.

In 1978 labor PACs contributed over $10 million to the federal elective process. Corporate PACs have lagged behind labor groups in their contributions: in 1978 business PACs raised something over $9 million. Business PACs must be instituted and supported to provide a balance in the democratic process.

A business PAC must have as its purpose the improvement of the environment in which a business operates so that the business will succeed. Any other purpose would generally be inconsistent with the needs of the firm's employees and shareholders. Business PACs must support the election of people who will provide a government in which the private enterprise system can prosper. Candidates who believe in private enterprise, fiscal responsibility, and economic and personal freedom must be supported for election to public office. Corporate PACs must be employed to create a balance between labor power and corporate power.

The Federal Election Campaign Act of 1971, as amended in 1974 and 1976, provides the legal basis for the involvement of PACs in federal election campaigns. The Federal Election Commission was created to administer the act. Since each state has different regulations governing contributions to state candidates, it is much simpler to use a PAC for federal elections only. Then the PAC need comply with only one set of rules and regulations.

All PACs are subject to various reporting requirements. PACs must register and file reports including:

- *Quarterly reports.* Reports must be filed in each quarter in which a particular PAC's contributions or expenditures exceed $1000. They must include lists of all contributions, debts, and expenditures of the PAC.

- *Preelection and postelection reports.* These reports disclose contributions and disbursements on behalf of federal candidates as of the fifteenth day preceding an election and the twentieth day after an election.

- *Monthly reports.* The FEC may permit PACs to file monthly reports instead of quarterly, preelection, and postelection reports in an election year.

The law imposes other requirements on a PAC. Each PAC must have a treasurer. In addition, most PACs will have a chairperson and a vice chairperson to assume the duties of the chairperson in the former's absence. The chairperson may be assigned other duties, but this is not required by the FEC.

The treasurer is responsible for maintaining the financial records of the PAC. He or she must keep detailed accounts of all transactions of the PAC, including the names of persons making contributions, the amounts of the contributions, the names of persons to whom expenditures are made, and the amounts of those payments. The treasurer is also responsible for making certain that all the transactions of the PAC are legal. Generally, the treasurer is assisted by an assistant treasurer who will be ready to assume the duties of the treasurer if needed.

A typical PAC is generally run like any other organization. It is composed of its officers. A majority of the officers constitutes a quorum and can transact any legitimate business of the PAC. A majority vote of the officers determines what transactions a PAC will undertake, including the candidates to whom contributions will be made and the amount of those contributions. A PAC may delegate authority to its treasurer to determine which candidates or political committees will be supported.

Although a corporation cannot contribute funds to a PAC, it may exercise control over the PAC. The PAC must be kept separate from the corporation in most respects. However, the corporation may pay all the establishment, administration, and solicitation costs of the PAC from general corporate funds. There is no limit on the amount of expenses incurred by the corporation for operation of the PAC, and this is one of the selling points in the solicitation of contributions. The entire amount of any contribution is paid to the candidates, for the corporation defrays all the costs incurred by the PAC. These costs include, but are not limited to, rental of office space, insurance, utilities, supplies, salaries, professional (legal, accounting) fees, and expenses incurred by solicitation and fund-raising activities.

SOLICITATION BY A PAC

Federal law governs the solicitation of funds for a PAC. In the first place a PAC must clearly state the political nature of the fund and the purpose of the solicitation. It should also give an individual an idea of the type of candidate supported by the PAC and the reason why a particular candidate is supported. It is also important for a PAC to urge employees to take a personal interest in the political and economic problems of the country. It is essential that employees feel that contributions are necessary for the survival of the present economic system.

Contributors must be United States citizens or have been admitted for permanent residence in the United States. A management PAC[1] may solicit only its stockholders and their families, executive or administrative personnel of the corporation and its subsidiaries, and their families. It appears from recent decisions that this permitted group includes the executive and administrative personnel of a corporation's franchises. FEC regulations stipulate the employees who are considered "executive or administrative personnel." These include employees paid a salary, rather than on an hourly basis, who have policymaking, supervisory, professional, or managerial responsibilities. Excluded from this group are members of a labor union and employees who have supervisory responsibility over hourly employees.

A PAC may solicit individuals in its eligible class as often as it wishes. However, it must be clear to those solicited that the contribution is voluntary and that they won't be advantaged or disadvantaged by a decision to make or not to make a contribution. Contributions may not be solicited by threats of job discrimination or financial reprisal or be made a condition of employment with the corporation. As long as the corporation follows these guidelines, however, the administrators of the PAC may solicit as aggressively as they choose.

Many methods can be used to solicit contributions. One approach is included here for illustration. First, an announcement explaining what a PAC is may be sent to all members of the eligible class. At this point, the administrators should include information about their particular PAC, including the reasons for its establishment, its purposes, and the reasons why it is essential for each employee to make a contribution. The administrators may include bylaws of the organization, although federal law does not require that a PAC have bylaws. It is recommended that a PAC present to potential contributors a guideline of suggested giving. Such a guideline would merely give participants an idea of the range of appropriate contributions. It should be stressed that any amounts mentioned are merely suggestions; no minimums or maximums are prescribed. This announcement can also state how much the solicitor and the other officers of the PAC or the sponsoring company have given. It is essential that a potential participant know that the officers have paid more than lip service to the organiza-

---

[1] In distinction from a PAC that solicits contributions from all employees. This type of PAC is not discussed here, and the reader is referred to the FEC rules and regulations pertaining to it.

tion. This information is a demonstration that the officers really do consider participation in a PAC important enough to the survival of the economic system to warrant a contribution of their own money.

Active leadership and commitment by the chairperson and the president of the company are essential. Correspondence with participants should include a statement of the amounts given by the chairperson and the president; and, of course, these amounts must at least be in accord with the suggested guidelines. A typical set of guidelines follows.

Compensation	Contribution	Compensation	Contribution
$25,000	$100	$ 70,000	$ 500
30,000	150	80,000	700
35,000	200	90,000	800
40,000	250	100,000	1000
50,000	325	Above 100,000	1 percent
60,000	400		

Amounts contributed by individuals in excess of $200 are filed with the FEC and are published as a matter of public record. Amounts of $200 and less may be reported and, if so, will be part of the record.

It is essential that all persons solicited are convinced that they will not be advantaged or disadvantaged by their participation or nonparticipation. Having made this clear to participants at all levels, PAC administrators have a right to sell the benefits that a PAC can provide in the elective process. People want to participate in an intelligent way, but generally they don't know how to do so. A PAC provides a vehicle for them to participate.

Following the announcement of the formation of a PAC, the administrators can send out a more specific letter to executive and administrative personnel. This letter should advise participants of the laws and the FEC regulations governing contributions to a PAC. It generally contains a more specific request for a contribution. The letter should again stress the importance to the individual of supporting the PAC. Enclosed with it should be a card requesting specific information from the contributor which must be filed with the FEC.

As with any fund-raising activity, a follow-up is essential. Additional letters can be sent to those who have not made a contribution, reiterating the importance of making one. Follow-ups can also be conducted in person or by telephone. Supervisors can be requested to sell the PAC to their own people. While it must be stressed that no one will be disadvantaged by choosing not to contribute, the administrators may push the PAC as hard as they can.

Tax advantages accompany the making of a political contribution. The first $50 of a contribution is a tax credit on an individual return or $100 on a joint return. Individual donors are permitted to make a maximum annual contribution of $5000 to a PAC. A corporation and its affiliates may set up more than one PAC, but if the committees are affiliated, they share the same contribution limit. That is, an individual donor cannot make $5000 contributions to several affiliated PACs.

Illustrative Dos

- It must be firmly stated that giving or not giving to the PAC advantages or disadvantages nobody. And the administrators must mean it.

- The chief executive and other leading officers must enthusiastically endorse the PAC.

- A scale of suggested giving is a must.

- The corporate leaders should give something more than the scale calls for.

- After a strong sell, there must be a follow-up (obviously without coercion).

- Giving to candidates must be carefully analyzed, and only candidates who meet the test of fiscal responsibility and support of the free enterprise system should be recipients of funds.

- Responsible challengers must be supported even though they don't have the best chance of winning. Otherwise they will have *no* chance.

Illustrative Don'ts

- Don't make your PAC a Republican or a Democratic instrument. It should be nonpartisan. The criteria should be the fiscal responsibility of the candidate and the candidate's full support of free enterprise. The candidate could be an independent, a Democrat, or a Republican (*R* stands for responsibility, not Republican).

- Don't give money to incumbents who are not responsible.

- Don't use PAC money to contribute to state elections. If everything goes well in Washington, the states will survive.

CONTRIBUTIONS BY A PAC

Not only does the law place limits on the amount that an individual donor may contribute, it also places restrictions on how much a PAC may contribute to an individual candidate. A PAC has a limit of $1000 per election for a particular candidate until it has qualified as a multicandidate committee. This is the same limitation as that placed on individual contributions.

To qualify as a multicandidate committee, a PAC must have been registered with the FEC for at least 6 months, have had more than fifty contributors, and have supported five or more federal candidates. Once a PAC has qualified as a multicandidate committee, it is no longer subject to the $1000 limitation. The PAC may now contribute $5000 to a candidate or that candidate's authorized committee for each primary and general election. It may contribute an additional $5000 to any other committees which are not authorized by any candidate. In addition, a PAC may give up to $15,000 annually to national party committees. In other words, a PAC can give $15,000 each to three kinds of committees: a party's national committee and its Senate and House campaign committees. There actually is then no limit on total annual contributions by a PAC. Contributions of goods or services must be assigned a fair market value and are to be included for purposes of figuring contribution limits.

The officers of the PAC determine to whom contributions will be made.

It is up to the particular PAC whether individual contributors can designate candidates to whom they wish their contributions to be made. It is generally a good idea to allow contributors to designate favored candidates but to advise them that contributions will be given to these candidates only if they meet the criteria or philosophy established by the PAC. In any event, the PAC will have described the type of candidate it supports prior to the solicitation of any potential donor. Business PACs must support the election of candidates who meet the test of fiscal responsibility and support of the free enterprise system. The PAC should not support a particular party but must be nonpartisan. The criterion must be who will best improve the environment within which the business must operate. This stipulation applies to both incumbents and challengers. The business PAC must be used to protect the corporate and personal welfare of the participants. Corporate PACs must be established and supported to strike a balance in the democratic process between the powers of labor and the powers of business.

A business PAC must state its purpose to those solicited. The purpose should be improvement of the environment in which a business operates so that the business will succeed. Any other purpose will generally be inconsistent with the needs of the firm's employees and shareholders.

Business PACs must support the election of people who will provide a government in which the private enterprise system can prosper, or business will fail. Candidates who believe in private enterprise, fiscal responsibility, and economic and personal freedom must be supported for election to public office. Some shortsighted business PACs support incumbents who have assignments to committees with influence over the activity in which the particular business is engaged. In the long run this parochial approach is self-destructive. One line of activity cannot prosper alone; it can succeed only as part of the entire economic system. Legislators with a record generally harmful to our economic system must be replaced by those with a positive philosophy. Business PACs should use their funds to aid the election of those challengers and not help to continue in office those whose views are contrary to our general well-being.

As an illustrative example of how to establish and operate a PAC, the University of Southern California Center for the Study of Private Enterprise has a carefully prepared manual of illustrative examples and forms. It serves as a guide to the formation and operation of a PAC. For complete details on management of a PAC, consult *Code of Federal Regulations,* Title 11. The following descriptive material sets forth one manner of implementing these regulations and of helping assure success.

Illustrative Example

Good Industries Inc. established GOODPAC in 1977 and registered it with the FEC as a nonpartisan federal PAC. Although federal regulation does not require PAC bylaws, Good prescribed a manner of operation which formed the basis of its operation, and this was made available to all interested employees.

An announcement was sent out to all executive and administrative personnel introducing the GOODPAC and explaining the necessity of establishing a PAC. It is important that a company do an effective job of demonstrating to the persons solicited why political and economic problems are something in which they should take a very personal interest. For example, it may be pointed out (as the Good announcement does) that in the United Kingdom taxes on dividends go up to 98 percent and taxes on earned income go up to 83 percent. Regardless of the approach, it is important to have employees feel that they are not merely making a donation but are taking out an insurance policy for the future based on the survival of our economic system. To facilitate the fund-raising process for both contributors and solicitors, general guidelines are provided by Good Industries. The Good scale of giving is low. It does not go much below an annual compensation level of $25,000. At $25,000, it is suggested that a $100 contribution be made. Since there is a $50 tax credit on a joint return, the net cost to the giver is $50. Suggested contributions scale up gradually to $325 at $50,000 and to 1 percent for $100,000 or more. It is required that those solicited be advised that they will be neither advantaged nor disadvantaged by their decision to give or not to give or by the amount of their contribution. Guidelines are merely suggestions. This means that a PAC should stress its merits.

Very important to any fund-raising campaign are the amounts that the solicitor and other key supporters give. In the case of GOODPAC, the chairman gave the maximum amount allowed ($5000), and the vice chairman and president gave $4000 each. These sums were noted in their solicitation of others.

Following the announcement sent out by the chief executive officer of Good Industries Inc., the treasurer of the GOODPAC reached executive and administrative personnel with a letter explaining some of the laws and regulations regarding donations to a PAC. Accompanying the letter was a card requesting specific information (required by the FEC) from all donors.

The chief executive at Good Industries makes the following points regarding the PAC program:

If all the *Fortune* 500 companies raised through their PACs an equivalent percentage of net earnings, this would add up to approximately $50 million. This certainly should be less than half of the potential to be raised from other secondary companies, transportation, financial institutions, merchandisers, etc.

Labor reports that somewhere between $10 and $12 million was given to candidates in the 1976 election. How much more labor gave we don't know (probably a lot), but we have the power to raise very substantial moneys and power enough to offset a lot of labor's efforts. GOODPAC has already given funds to several Democrats who, it was felt, have the same responsible goals that Good has; so the campaign is truly nonpartisan. As reported, organized labor gave $10,208,000 to Democratic candidates in 1976, while Republicans received $380,000.

We must quit fighting rearguard actions. We have to spend enough money to get the right people to run, and we have to spend enough money to get them elected.

We have the PAC instrument set up by the Congress of the United States. We would be out of our minds not to use it.

We have learned that when you ask people for money, they want to know what you are doing personally and what you expect from them. We tell them what we are doing personally, and the guidelines provide the other side of the coin.

In any fund-raising activity, for instance, United Way, a persuasive selling job is of paramount importance, and follow-up is essential to a successful campaign. We emphasize that nothing is at stake except the survival of the free enterprise system.

Nothing is at stake except a government so big that it demands confiscatory taxes and the destruction of incentives.

The result, of course, is declining productivity and rampaging inflation, which is the greatest enemy of every American.

Additional material from the GOODPAC is provided in the following pages as an example of the types of correspondence, publications, and follow-up that may be sent to prospective donors. There are many different approaches, but the important thing is to become involved. PACs help business in general and individuals in particular to become active participants in the federal political process. Our future welfare, corporate and personal, depends on helping to provide the kind of government that will keep economic and personal freedom flourishing.

BYLAWS OF THE GOOD INDUSTRIES INC. POLITICAL ACTION COMMITTEE

ARTICLE I: NAME AND LOCATION

The name of the committee is GOODPAC, a voluntary not-for-profit unincorporated body established in Los Angeles, California, with the principal office located at P.O. Box 0000, Terminal Annex, Cucamonga, California 00000.

ARTICLE II: PURPOSES

The purpose of GOODPAC is to encourage protection and development of the democratic system of government in the United States, the private enterprise system, and the basic freedom of the American people and to promote good citizenship of executive or administrative personnel of Good Industries Inc. (Good) and its affiliated companies, through personal and financial participation in the federal elective process. To achieve these purposes, GOODPAC is empowered to solicit and accept voluntary contributions from the above individuals to further the nomination and election of candidates for federal office who believe in and support the need to protect, preserve, and further the free enterprise system in general and the principles set forth herein. All contributions and expenditures shall be in conformity with applicable laws and regulations.

ARTICLE III: ORGANIZATION

Section 1. GOODPAC shall be completely independent of and not affiliated with any political organization and shall be composed of its officers, who shall be individuals. The officers of GOODPAC shall be those individuals as specifically set forth below. In the exercise of their responsibilities under these bylaws, officers of GOODPAC shall act solely in their capacity as such, and their decisions and determinations shall be independent of any other relationship or duty they may have with Good. Good shall defray all costs and expenses incurred in the establishment and administration of and in the solicitation of contributions to GOODPAC, to the extent and in the manner in which such costs and expenses may be defrayed by Good under applicable federal law. All financial records of GOODPAC shall be kept separate and apart from those of the corporation.

Section 2. The officers of GOODPAC shall be a chairperson, a vice chairperson, a treasurer, and an assistant treasurer. The initial officers and their mailing addresses are:

Chairperson:
James O. Martinez
GOODPAC
P.O. Box 0000, Terminal Annex
Cucamonga, California 00000

Vice chairperson:
Richard K. Jones
GOODPAC
P.O. Box 0000, Terminal Annex
Cucamonga, California 00000

Treasurer:
Donald P. Lyons
GOODPAC
P.O. Box 0000, Terminal Annex
Cucamonga, California 00000

Assistant treasurer:
Steven Chew
GOODPAC
P.O. Box 0000, Terminal Annex
Cucamonga, California 00000

Section 3. The chairperson shall be the chief executive officer of GOODPAC and shall preside at all meetings.

Section 4. The vice chairperson shall, in the temporary or permanent absence or incapacity of the chairperson of GOODPAC, automatically assume all powers and duties of the chairperson and in any event in the aforesaid circumstances shall be deemed the chairperson for all purposes of the Federal Election Campaign Act of 1971, as amended, or any successor provision of law. The vice chairperson shall perform such other duties as are assigned by these bylaws or by the chairperson.

Section 5. The treasurer shall be the financial officer of GOODPAC and also shall be responsible for all contributions made to or by GOODPAC and shall maintain all financial records. The treasurer shall also take minutes of all meetings, give oral or written notice of all meetings, and prepare, sign, file, and maintain copies of all reports required by applicable federal law or regulations and by GOODPAC. The treasurer also shall make recommendations to the officers for action and shall keep detailed accounts of:

a. The full name and mailing address (occupation and the principal place of business, if any) of every person making a contribution to GOODPAC and the date and amount thereof

b. The full name and mailing address (occupation and the principal place of business, if any) of every person to whom any expenditure is made and the date and amount thereof

c. Appropriate records, stating particulars, for all expenditures made by GOODPAC

d. Any other records deemed necessary or required by, and in a manner consistent with, federal law or regulations

In addition, the treasurer shall utilize any reputable and federally chartered bank having safety deposit boxes and insured accounts as repositories for the funds of GOODPAC.

Section 6. The assistant treasurer shall, in the temporary or permanent absence or incapacity of the treasurer of GOODPAC, automatically assume all powers and duties of the treasurer and in any event in the aforesaid circumstances shall be deemed the treasurer for all purposes of the Federal Election Campaign Act of 1971, as amended, or any successor provision of law.

Section 7. The officers of GOODPAC shall determine by a simple majority vote the candidates and/or political committees to which contributions shall be made and shall direct the treasurer to make such contributions. The officers may delegate to the treasurer responsibility for selecting candidates and/or political committees to receive contributions within the guidelines set forth by the officers.

Section 8. There shall be an annual meeting of GOODPAC at a time and place designated by the chairperson. In addition, a meeting of GOODPAC may be called by the chairperson, vice chairperson, or treasurer whenever such officer deems it necessary. A majority of the officers of GOODPAC shall constitute a quorum thereof for the transaction of business. GOODPAC shall act by a simple majority of its officers present. Any officer may participate in any meeting of officers by telephone or other communications device and shall be deemed present for all purposes of these bylaws if he or she can be heard or understood by all officers physically present at any such meeting.

ARTICLE IV: CONTRIBUTIONS

Section 1. To the extent permitted by law, contributions may be solicited from time to time from executive or administrative personnel of divisions and subsidiaries of Good in accordance with federal law or regulations. No contributions to GOODPAC may be solicited or secured by job discrimination or financial reprisal, or by threat of job discrimination or financial reprisal, or as a condition of employment by Good.

Section 2. All contributions made to GOODPAC shall be maintained by the treasurer as separate, segregated funds, and no contributions made to GOODPAC shall be accepted when designated by the contributor for a named candidate or party.

Section 3. No officer of GOODPAC shall share personally in any funds or assets of GOODPAC upon dissolution or at any other time.

ARTICLE V: AMENDMENTS

These bylaws may be amended from time to time by action of a simple majority of the officers of GOODPAC.

ARTICLE VI: DISSOLUTION

Although the duration of GOODPAC is intended to be perpetual, GOODPAC may be dissolved at any time by action of a simple majority of its officers. In the event of such dissolution, the balance remaining, after paying any remaining costs and expenses of GOODPAC, shall be promptly distributed to candidates for federal elective public office, political committees supporting such candidates, or national, state, and local committees of national political parties in a manner consistent with applicable federal law and for the purposes set forth in Article II hereof.

GOODPAC bylaws.

LIMITS ON CAMPAIGN CONTRIBUTIONS

Contribution from	To candidate or his or her authorized committee	**To national party committees[a] (per calendar year)[b]	**To any other committee (per calendar year)[b]	Total contributions (per calendar year)[c]
Individual	$1000 per election[d]	$20,000	$5000	$25,000
Multicandidate committee[e]	$5000 per election	$15,000	$5000	No limit
Party committee	$1000 or $5000[f] per election	No limit	$5000	No limit
Republican or Democratic senatorial campaign committee[g] or the national party committee, or a combination of both	$17,500 to Senate candidate per calendar year[b] in which candidate seeks election	Not applicable	Not applicable	Not applicable
Any other committee or group[h]	$1000 per election	$20,000	$5000	No limit

[a]For purposes of this limit, national party committees include a party's national committee and the Republican and Democratic Senate and House campaign committees established by the party's national committee, provided they are not authorized by any candidate.

[b]For 1976 elections only and solely in the case of contribution limits established in the 1976 amendments (indicated by double asterisk), the calendar year extends from May 11 (date of enactment of the act) through December 31, 1976.

[c]Calendar year extends from January 1 through December 31. Individual contributions made or earmarked to influence a specific election of a clearly identified candidate are counted as if made during the year in which the election is held.

[d]Each of the following elections is considered a separate election: primary election, general election, runoff election, special election, and party caucus or convention which has authority to select the nominee.

[e]A multicandidate committee is any committee with more than fifty contributors which has been registered for at least 6 months and, with the exception of state party committees, has made contributions to five or more federal candidates.

[f]Limit depends on whether or not party committee is a multicandidate committee.

[g]Republican and Democratic senatorial campaign committees are subject to all other limits applicable to a multicandidate committee.

[h]Group includes an organization, partnership, or group of persons.

FEC limits on campaign contributions. (Based on Federal Election Commission, *Code of Federal Regulations*, Title 11.)

ARTHUR GOOD,
TOM THOMPSON, AND
DON VICTOR
INVITE YOU TO CONTRIBUTE TO
GOOD INDUSTRIES'
POLITICAL ACTION COMMITTEE
(GOODPAC)

The United Kingdom has proved a tragic example of what happens
when a nation stresses redistribution of wealth rather than the
creation of wealth. Every effort has been made to destroy almost
every kind of incentive. Success has been remarkable.

During the celebration of the twenty-fifth anniversary of Queen
Elizabeth's coronation, Eric Sevareid commented:

> English sickness keeps Britain stagnant and stationary. Here,
> organized labor is a juggernaut. It gets what it wants for its
> members. The middle classes are slowly dragged down. They
> don't organize. They don't fight back. They grow rather
> bitter. But they also grow apathetic. They seem to constitute
> the first example of a revolution of declining expectations.
> Today England is the example of what not to do.

More than 60 cents out of every dollar generated by every man,
woman, and child in Britain goes to government. Income taxes
take up to 95 percent of income. In the United States we've gone
from the government taking 20 percent of our income to almost 40
percent in the last 10 years. This trend of increasing federal
bureaucracy must be stopped.

We are at a crossroad. Either we continue to follow Britain's
tragic pattern, or we organize to protect the free market and the
free enterprise system.

GOODPAC is a political action committee organized under federal
law and is registered with the Federal Election Commission. It
is an unincorporated political committee for independent
support of candidates to federal office who, regardless of
political party affiliation, believe in the need to protect,
preserve, and further freedom and the free enterprise system.

GOODPAC will solicit voluntary contributions and use these
funds in accordance with election campaign laws and the judgment
of the committee. As you know, no corporate contribution can be
used directly or indirectly for candidates for federal offices.

GOOD Industries Inc. provides staff, facilities, and administrative assistance from corporate sources. Thus, all of your contribution will be used solely in support of candidates for federal offices.

So far there are 530 other corporations which have established PAC programs. The following is a suggested guideline for contributions to GOODPAC. It is only a guideline, and you should therefore feel free to give more or less. Your contribution will neither favor nor disadvantage you in your company in any way.

For purposes of this schedule, participants in the bonus plan should add their bonuses to their salaries.

Salary	Contribution
$ 25,000 and below	$100
30,000	150
35,000	200
40,000	250
50,000	325
60,000	400
70,000	500
80,000	700
100,000	1000

Qualified political contributions are deductible from income for federal income tax purposes to a maximum of $200 on a joint return; on separate returns the maximum is $100.

You may do more if you feel strongly about salvaging our free enterprise system.

When I am asking somebody else to give money to any cause, it has always been a cardinal principle with me to state what I am doing. Because no one individual can give more than $5000 to a political action committee, that is the amount that I'm giving to GOODPAC. In addition to this, I will give another $5000 to $10,000 directly to candidates.

Tom Thompson and Don Victor are putting in $4000 each.

Please think of this as an investment in the future of your country and that of your children rather than as a contribution.

Thanks for your cooperation.   ARTHUR GOOD

Good announcement from chief executive officer to all executive and administrative employees.

GOOD
INDUSTRIES, INC.

August 10, 1977

Dear Fellow Employee:

Now that you have read the announcement of the formation of our
GOODPAC and hopefully have decided to join those of us who feel
that our way of life is worth a contribution, there are a few
operational items with which you should be acquainted. First, we
must comply with the law and regulations of the Federal Election
Commission (FEC). Second, we plan to be completely open in the
conduct of our affairs.

Contributors must be United States citizens or have been
admitted for permanent residence in the United States. GOODPAC
will not accept contributions earmarked for a particular
candidate. However, it will accept recommendations from
contributors for candidates to support. Candidates recommended
will be evaluated against other candidates, and the decision
will be made by the committee. Candidates must be compatible
with GOODPAC principles as stated in the attachment. A majority
vote of the four GOODPAC officers, Tom Thompson, Don Victor,
Donald Lyons, and myself, will determine which campaigns
GOODPAC will help.

The federal laws under which GOODPAC will function give many
specific duties to the treasurer. The treasurer is in charge of
the fund and is responsible for reporting to the FEC
contributions received and expenses and campaign
disbursements. He is required to report to the FEC the names of
all who contribute in excess of $100 during a calendar year, and
this becomes public information.

Your personal check must be accompanied by the enclosed card.
The data requested on the card are required by the FEC. You
should place the card in the envelope provided, making sure that
the address appears in the window.

Please contact me with your questions. I will be delighted to
communicate with you. My telephone is (222) 000-0000.

Sincerely,

ARTHUR GOOD

Good letter to all executive and administrative employees.

GOODPAC PRINCIPLES

Good Industries Inc. has established a nonpartisan political action committee to help foster an environment in which both individual freedom and American business can flourish. As a consumer products company, we depend on a free marketplace in which Good Industries can respond to the consuming public rather than the economic planners. More and more, our ability to meet demands of the people is being hampered by restrictions on free enterprise. Restriction of business results in loss of individual freedom for the American people.

Our American system has given us the highest standards of living. However, one of the freest, richest societies ever known may be in peril. In recent history one can see examples of what happens when a nation stresses redistribution rather than the creation of wealth. Enterprise falters, and people begin losing, not gaining.

It is incumbent on all citizens to become active in government to ensure that it is responsive to the wants of the majority and does not become an end in itself or a tool of utopians. As employees of a company owned by and serving people, we have an individual responsibility to engage actively in the political process for the purpose of preserving freedom and the free enterprise system, with which personal freedom is intertwined.

GOODPAC is a political action committee organized under federal law and is registered with the Federal Election Commission. It is an unincorporated political committee for independent support of candidates to federal office who, regardless of political party affiliation, believe in the need to protect, preserve, and further freedom and the free enterprise system. GOODPAC will solicit voluntary contributions from legally allowable sources and use these funds in accordance with election campaign laws and the judgment of the committee.

In supporting GOODPAC, you will be joining others associated with Good Industries who accept the challenge to defend their way of life through legal processes. GOODPAC will be an active voice in representing the interests of you, your company, and the system within which we do business and live. It is your committee for political action and will be as effective as you make it.

Statement of GOODPAC principles.

REMITTANCE ADVICE This is my voluntary contribution. I understand no one will be favored or disadvantaged by reason of contribution amount or their decision not to contribute. Guidelines are merely suggestions.

IMPORTANT: Government Requires —

This is my voluntary contribution to GOODPAC	(PERSONAL CHECK ONLY) $
Full Name	Social Security Number

Residence	Street	City	State	Zip

Association with Good ☐ Employee   ☐ Other
Principal Place of Business   Name   Address - STREET   CITY   STATE   ZIP

Occupation

	Self-Employed	☐ Yes	☐ No
(This Form is to be mailed with check to address on reverse) *READ REVERSE SIDE BEFORE SIGNING	Signature		Date

403-8/78

PLEASE MAIL IN ATTACHED ENVELOPE —
BE SURE ADDRESS SHOWS THROUGH WINDOW.

GOODPAC
UNITED STATES BANK
Box 0000
CUCAMONGA, CA. 00000

Attention: A.J. BROWN

INFORMATION FOR CONTRIBUTORS
TO GOODPAC

I understand the funds received will be used for political contributions as directed by GOODPAC. The purpose of GOODPAC is to effect the nomination and election of federal candidates favorable to economic and personal freedom.

We report the data on the reverse of the card with respect to all individuals who contribute regardless of amount. A copy of the reports filed by any Political Action committee with the Federal Elections Commission are available for purchase (FEC address: 1325 K Street, N.W. Washington D.C. 20463)

(403-8/78)

Two sides of card accompanying letter to employees, requesting information required by FEC.

14 TAMING THE AGENCIES

CONGRESSMAN ELLIOTT H. LEVITAS

U.S. House of Representatives

In the preceding chapters you have gained a better understanding of how to deal directly with our nation's regulatory system. In effect you have taken a regulatory survival course intended to help you cope with the regulatory system you face on a day-to-day basis. Your reading has probably confirmed something you already suspected: regulators are omnipresent and omnipotent.

While you may feel more capable of dealing with the regulators now, you may be wondering how such a system came to exist in the first place. You may also have asked whether we as a nation have collectively decided to accept the present regulatory system, for better or for worse, and simply live with it. These would certainly be valid questions at this point.

This chapter will outline briefly how we came to create the regulatory system that you now face. More important, I hope to assure you that not everyone views the existing system as the best we can do. There is a broad-based effort to reform the system, one that I believe will ultimately be successful.

Reforming our regulatory system has been a major goal of mine since coming to Congress. I had asked myself the same questions that have come to your mind, and I concluded that positive reform is in everyone's best interest. Moreover, I am convinced more than ever that such reform is imperative to the continued vitality and well-being of our nation. It is this reform that is the major subject of this chapter.

Some reform proposals deal with actions that Congress should take to improve the quality of its oversight of agency activities. Both the legislative veto and sunset proposals would give the Congress, an outside institution, greater sway over the regulatory system. Other reform proposals would affect the internal operations of the agencies and provide for greater coordination of those operations between agencies. Internal procedural improvements include the use of economic-impact analysis of regulatory proposals, greater responsibilities to agency heads for improved regulatory development, flexibility in the application of regulations, improvements in the participation of the public in the development of regulations, and review of existing rules.

Improvements in interagency coordination include publication of a regulatory calendar to permit a comprehensive review of regulatory proposals and the monitoring by an outside agency of compliance with regulatory process improvements. While President Carter implemented some of these reforms when he signed Executive Order 12044 in March 1979, congressional action is necessary to ensure that the reforms apply to the independent regulatory agencies as well as to those of the executive branch and to make the reforms permanent. If the reforms continue to be mandated only by executive order and not by legislation, they may not bind Presidents with different concerns. Thus it is important that Congress make all these reforms the subject of legislation, either through a comprehensive bill or with the passage of several specific laws. Although I will discuss the reforms separately, it is highly likely that they will be combined into one or two pieces of legislation when Congress acts.

EVOLUTION OF THE REGULATORY SYSTEM

Let us start with an explanation of how and why this system evolved to its mammoth size. It did not spring full-blown into being. The process was much more gradual, building upon itself and the initial success of government regulatory activities.

Regulatory laws and agencies, like other types of law, are normally created in response to a problem or a perceived need. Regulations and the agencies that write and enforce them commonly are used to address problems of health, safety, exploitation, and unfair competition. They are intended to provide protection when other institutions fail to do so.

For the first century of the nation's existence, there was no real ongoing federal regulatory activity. However, as the country expanded and industrialized in the years following the Civil War, our society became increasingly complex. Transportation of goods and the sale of products in one state that had been manufactured in another posed continuing problems for all involved. Requests for help from the federal government prompted the creation of the Interstate Commerce Commission in 1887. The commission was charged with protecting the public interest by regulating public carriers engaged in interstate commerce. This included the certification of carriers and the establishment of reasonable rates.

For the time being there was no great rush to create other federal regulatory agencies. In 1914 the Federal Trade Commission was established to encourage and maintain the nation's competitive enterprise system and to discourage monopolies or unfair restraints on trade. In 1931 the Food and Drug Administration came to life to protect the public against impure or otherwise unsafe foods and drug products. These agencies did their work, but there was still no urgent pressure to utilize the regulatory approach in other areas.

The real stimulus for boosting federal regulatory activity came in the form of our worst economic disaster, the great depression. This catastrophe was so pervasive that it touched every person in the nation. People who had worked all their lives were suddenly without jobs. Savings were wiped out. Homes and property were lost. Intervention by government was viewed as essential, and the federal government was the only level of government capable of handling such an all-encompassing disaster.

Franklin D. Roosevelt came into the presidency in 1933 with the promise to create a federal government that could meet the problems of the nation. The New Deal called for a major expansion of the federal government, and the regulatory wing played a prime part in that growth. The Securities and Exchange Commission, Federal Deposit Insurance Corporation, National Labor Relations Board, and many others were created in the process. Their success was a key to the nation's eventual emergence from its economic woes. That success also spawned the belief that all types of problems could be solved by a willing federal government using special regulatory agencies to combat specific problems. This faith on the part of the public and willingness to respond on the part of elected federal officials led to a new round of federal regulatory innovations during the 1960s and early 1970s.

The problems of this next generation of Americans were more easily classed as social than as economic, but the federal response was the same: more regulation. The Equal Employment Opportunity Commission, the Occupational Safety and Health Administration, the Environmental Protection Agency, the Consumer Product Safety Commission, and many others were created throughout this period. As had occurred during the depression, each agency was created to address a strongly perceived need and with the view that the particular problem should be the focus of attention of the federal government. The New Deal had created the impression that the federal government could and would act to cure the nation's ills.

The direct success of regulatory activities created an impression in the minds of our people and elected officials that regulation was always an effective way to solve problems. For example, in 1933 bank failures were running at a rate of 40 percent. Since the imposition of federal regulation this figure has been reduced to less than 1 percent, and no depositor has ever lost a penny in a federally insured bank. Since federal standards for infant cribs were imposed, crib deaths by strangulation have been reduced by one-half and injuries have been cut by 45 percent.

The record of success of some federal regulatory activities argued strongly for expansion into other areas. This attitude led directly to the complex regulatory system we have today. There are now at least 95 federal regulatory agencies issuing over 10,000 regulations per year. The process has truly created a fourth branch of government.

CONCERNS ABOUT THE REGULATORY SYSTEM

The pressure to create new regulatory agencies is being replaced by concerns about the comprehensive system that has been put in place. Our national enthusiasm for specific regulatory protection has been tempered by the realities of the total system. We are coming to realize that our sincere efforts to solve problems have ballooned into a massive, often incomprehensible regulatory structure that creates its own set of brand-new problems.

This large and powerful regulatory system has institutionalized a whole new way of life for our citizens and businesses. Increasingly, regulations are becoming another problem to be dealt with in one's daily routine. Even a partially objective look at the system we have created reveals that regulation collectively increases costs, imposes delay, stifles competition, overlaps and often conflicts with other regulations, and concentrates too much power in the hands of unelected government officials or employees.

The sheer costs of regulation are now awesome. Estimates differ, but Dr. Murray Weidenbaum (now chairman of the Council of Economic Advisers), in a study conducted for the Joint Economic Committee of Congress, estimated that the total cost to the nation for complying with federal regulation in 1979 was $102.7 billion. By any measure, that is a sobering figure.

Delays occur more commonly now as businesses are required to complete and submit necessary forms or to receive approval to offer a new product or service. This delay adds to costs and increases the frustration of doing business. It can also mean another major hurdle in efforts to develop innovative technology. Regulatory agencies are commonly reluctant to approve new technology, at least in a prompt fashion. This can be a frustrating disincentive for large businesses, but it can be a disaster for small businesses that may not have the funds to survive while the regulators make up their minds.

Small businesses generally have a much more difficult time in coping with the cumulative impact of regulatory requirements than do their larger competitors. Big business and big labor can afford to hire the staffs it often takes to deal with regulators. The heads of small businesses frequently do not have that financial capability. Frequently they must do this work themselves, taking time away from the normal responsibilities that go with running a business operation. In this way federal regulation often serves to protect established business activities from potential competition.

Regulations also have an increasing tendency to be counterproductive or confusing or to create contradictory overlapping. The Congress passed the Employee Retirement Income Security Act (ERISA) in 1974 with the goal of eliminating many of the problems that existed in individual pension programs around the nation. Unfortunately the regulations developed under the act required so much additional cost that more than 13,000 businesses simply terminated their plans. The costs of additional regulation are passed on by businesses in higher consumer costs. Other companies choose not to establish plans, and their employees thus have less security.

With such a massive uncoordinated system, conflicts occur. For example, one agency has required that meat-packing plants wash their floors several times daily to remove meat particles that might decay or create an unsanitary situation. Another agency has told those same plants to keep their floors dry at all times to protect workers' safety.

Costs and confusion are significant problems, but I believe our present regulatory system presents a far more serious threat: the potential for the abuse of power. Regulators have been vested with an awesome power both to write and to enforce regulations. Under the Constitution these powers are separated between two branches of government, the Congress and the President. Yet in the interest of effective regulation that fundamental principle of separation of powers has been violated. These two important powers of government are vested in one entity which is not directly answerable to the public. Unelected government officials now write rules which have the full force and effect of law. This practice violates another fundamental principle of our form of government: that elected officials should make our laws. Any agency, any official, and any enactment of and by government which is not accountable and seen to be such is to that degree a step toward despotism. A large measure of power has been entrusted to unelected, almost unknown government officials. It is too much to hope for to tell them effectively to protect us without abusing their authority.

Used properly, the power to write and enforce rules can be an effective tool for the general good. Used improperly or without ample forethought, that power can become oppressive. In the rush to solve problems through regulation we created this powerful fourth branch of government. We did not at the same time establish the necessary checks and balances to keep its power in bounds. Now we must take steps to establish those checks and balances.

Fortunately, we have entered a period with a satisfactory climate for instituting these checks and balances on the regulatory system. People are looking for some commonsense reforms. For the first time there is a national willingness to raise questions about the extent of regulatory power. While the goals and concerns that led to establishing the regulatory agencies remain, we are now willing to recognize and correct the problems that accompany regulation. We can trust our good sense and reason to make reforms which will improve the system without destroying it.

These reforms can and must take a number of forms. We already have a wide range of proposals which are designed to get at various aspects of regulatory problems. True reform will not mean viewing these as conflicting solutions from which we must choose one. Rather, we must enact a combination of solutions if we want to address the full problem. The only simple solutions in terms of action will be cases in which we choose to eliminate regulation completely. While this is not a likely or advisable solution in most cases, it can work well in some areas.

For example, legislation was passed during the Ninety-fifth Congress to institute a phased deregulation of the airline industry. For the first time Congress took steps to return an entire industry to a basically free market economy. At the end of the phaseout, the agency which currently regulates the industry, the Civil Aeronautics Board, will be abolished. This is a monumental action and one that was accomplished only after protracted debate, but it was accomplished nevertheless. A whole industry is being deregulated; a federal agency is going out of business. Only a few years ago that step would not have been seriously proposed, much less taken.

So there is real hope for regulatory reform. Certainly, not all of it will take the form of total deregulation, but there are many other proposals which can work effectively to solve the problems of regulation, problems both with specific agencies and with the cumulative impact of regulatory requirements. Congressional control over agency rule making, sunset provisions, economic-impact analyses, and interagency review of regulatory activities are all positive solutions to problems created by the regulatory system. These are practical solutions, short of total deregulation, which have been proposed and are now being considered by the Congress.

The underlying concerns upon which all the reform proposals are based are a recognition of the vast power concentrated in regulatory agencies and a better understanding of the cumulative impact of the regulatory system. I think we have an obligation to diffuse the power of the regulators as a means of guarding against abuse of that power. We can approach the cumulative-impact problem by requiring regulators to take a broader perspective as they develop regulatory proposals. We can be more selective and considerate in our use of regulatory authority and still produce regulations that effectively meet our needs. To do this will require that the agencies adopt improved internal procedures for developing regulations while Congress and the President adopt new procedures for overseeing and supervising the activities of these agencies.

There are a wide variety of suggestions for reforming the regulatory system, but basically they can be broken into three categories: (1) reform of internal agency procedures, (2) establishment of more effective coordination and exchange of information between agencies, and (3) creation of greater review and control by Congress. Congress ought to take a stronger role in the control of the regulatory activity, and proposals for congressional involvement should be the first priority.

LEGISLATIVE VETO

The legislative veto is the key to returning the balance of power over regulatory matters to elected officials, and I have sponsored and advocated this program during my years in Congress. Simply stated, the legislative veto is designed to restore to Congress a part of its legislative authority in the rule-making process. Here it is important to understand that rules and regulations are actually written under a delegation of legislative authority. Regulatory agencies do not have the inherent authority to write regulations. Because regulations become a part of the law, they are written by the agencies using legislative authority delegated by the Congress. When Congress writes a new law, it delegates to the agency which will be responsible for that law the authority to write rules to implement it; this is a delegation of legislative authority. As a practical matter, authority is delegated because the regulatory agencies possess the expertise necessary to develop and write the regulations needed to implement general legislation passed by Congress. However, this expertise should not be used as an excuse for an agency to employ its rule-writing authority in a manner contrary to Congress's intentions when it enacted the enabling legislation. At all times, the agency should seek to write regulations in keeping with the objective that Congress sought to reach when it passed the original enabling legislation.

Unfortunately, regulators all too often have demonstrated a belief that their special knowledge gives them license to write the law in a way which they feel is best, regardless of the views of Congress. The agencies have often forgotten that they are arms of the government and not the government itself. The basic attitude demonstrated by such an approach is chilling: it assumes that unelected officials will use power more wisely than elected officials. This is contrary to the very premise of our form of government. It demonstrates the type of arrogance in government that our forefathers feared. Such an attitude is the reason why we initially placed government power in the hands of elected officials, people who are answerable to their fellow citizens at the ballot box.

We now are realizing that in our regulatory system we have strayed too far from our principles of government. When adjusting to a more complex society which called for greater involvement by the federal government, Congress vested too much unchecked authority in the hands of the bureaucracy. The broad grant of legislative authority to the agencies has precipitated much of the regulatory excess we have today. The regulators have simply abused their authority. They have demonstrated an attitude of independence which should have been anticipated and yet was not. We must now correct that mistake.

The legislative veto is a useful means of making that correction. Basically it is a means of conditioning the grant of legislative authority that Congress previously has given to the rule makers. That condition would require that the agencies, once they developed their rules but before putting them into effect, submit those rules to Congress for a period of review. During this period, one or both houses of Congress could pass a resolution disapproving the rule or rules in question. Aside from this change, the agencies' authority would remain the same.

The net effect of the veto would be a shift of ultimate authority over rule making from the agencies to the Congress. The agencies would be left with authority to propose rules based on their special expertise and to enforce the rules once they were reviewed by Congress. The change would come in the type of rules the agencies would write. The agencies would no longer be unencumbered writers and enforcers of regulations, free from any effective check on their authority. The legislative veto would give Congress that check. It would place Congress squarely between an agency's responsibility for the writing of regulations and its enforcement of them. This clearly would mean that every regulatory proposal would have to be written with Congress and its veto in mind. That simple change would significantly affect the content of any proposed regulation or rule.

The legislative veto is not a new concept. It has been used by Congress many times but has not been applied uniformly to federal regulatory agencies. Until recently, it has generally been associated with activities other than the development of rules. When the concept of a congressional veto was proposed for application to rule making, it soon became viewed as a major regulatory reform device. The veto is simple and to the point. It answers the ultimate question: "Who makes the laws in the country, the elected Congress or the unelected bureaucrats?"

Once the question of ultimate authority has been settled in favor of the Congress, many of the objectionable regulation-writing practices will be eliminated without frequent need to resort to the veto. When Congress establishes its veto power, the regulation writers will be much more conscious of congressional views about the content of regulations. The agencies will consider congressional intent. They will gain a new appreciation for congressional comments about the content of proposed rules. In short, there will be far greater interaction between the agencies and the Congress about the rules the regulators write.

This has consistently been the experience in states in which a procedure for a legislative veto has been enacted. Uniformly, state legislatures have found that the authority to veto regulations has made state agencies much more considerate of the legislatures' views about the scope and content of regulations. An agency tries to find out what a legislature's views are before it writes its rules. In some cases a number of rules had to be vetoed until the agencies got the message that legislatures took the matter seriously, but in all cases the results were the same: legislative intent became the order of the day. In states in which the procedure has become established, legislative vetoes are rarely necessary. I expect that congressional experience will be much the same.

The bill I introduced to give Congress a legislative veto over agency regulations has been cosponsored by more than 230 members, or more than a majority of members of the House. In addition, various forms of the veto have been added to more than sixty-five public laws since I came to Congress in 1975. A legislative veto was a part of the legislation creating the Department of Education and was added to all rules developed by the Federal Trade Commission, ending a 3-year battle to give Congress veto authority over FTC regulations.

The veto is gaining widespread acceptance and becoming a valuable tool for those intent upon reforming the regulatory system. I firmly believe that a uniform congressional veto procedure is a key element in the reform. If Congress has a veto over rules, the effectiveness of other reform proposals will be enhanced. The veto will mean that the agencies must comply with any other reforms which are implemented. If they do not, Congress can veto their regulations. It's that simple.

SUNSET

Under this proposal, Congress would be required to review and reauthorize federal programs and agencies every few years. If the program was not reauthorized, the "sun would set" and the program would literally be terminated.

Several states are now implementing the sunset concept, and several pieces of legislation are pending in Congress to provide for a federal sunset procedure. The sunset approach has two potentially beneficial aspects, one relating to the Congress and the other to the agency or program.

From the standpoint of Congress, sunset should make us do a better job of fulfilling our responsibilities in the area of agency oversight in two ways. First, the sunset concept puts oversight on a systematic basis by establishing a regular schedule of review of programs and agencies. With the implementation of an orderly procedure, oversight will no longer be the haphazard, hit-or-miss process it is today. The Congress, over a fixed period of time, will be required to take a look at what every agency is doing rather than selecting targets and thereby avoiding many of the agencies and their activities. Second, by forcing Congress to conduct its oversight in the shadow of agency or program termination, the quality of that oversight is likely to improve. Regardless of its decision as to an agency's fate under sunset, Congress will be forced to justify to the voters its actions on sunset reviews, and the best justification will come from the revelations of thorough oversight hearings. Therefore, it is in Congress's own best interest to do a good job in every review.

From the standpoint of individual agencies or programs, the threat of sunset will encourage a strong effort to avoid termination. Agencies will become much more conscious of meeting their responsibilities in a fashion that Congress and the country expect. The instinct to survive will operate, and the agencies will know that their own actions hold the key to their fate in Congress. The fact that Congress undertakes a systematic review of programs and agencies will put these activities on notice that a time of review will definitely come. The agencies will conduct themselves accordingly to avoid the ultimate prospect of sunset. In this fashion, accountability will be restored as Congress demands answers about actions which have or have not been taken by each agency and program.

Under the major sunset proposals now before Congress, agencies and programs scheduled for review would be required to submit a complete report of activities to Congress no later than 6 months before scheduled completion of congressional review. At the same time, a copy of the report would be submitted to the Office of Management and Budget (OMB). This provision would allow OMB to submit to Congress an assessment of each report along with its own comments about the program in question. In this situation, OMB would act as the President's representative in the review and thereby give the President an important voice in the sunset process. This particular provision would help to reinforce the President's overall role as the chief administrator of the federal government, a role frequently ignored by the executive branch agencies and their supporters in Congress and outside government. The President has both a right and an obligation to provide leadership in the performance of the executive agencies. The President's authority to provide this leadership has been called into question, and the sunset review process would afford the President one opportunity to reassert authority. Other reform proposals would provide additional opportunities for the President to help tame the agencies.

In the actual review process conducted by Congress, an agency would be evaluated under several criteria. For example, Congress would look at the cost effectiveness of the activity and, along these lines, at some alternatives for achieving program goals. Congress would also consider the age and origin of the program and any changes in those factors. The program's effectiveness in meeting its responsibilities and goals would be the primary subject of the oversight review.

One final feature that is incorporated in many pieces of sunset legislation involves the coordination of sunset reviews of related programs. One of the key problems with the existing regulatory system is the cumulative burden it imposes. The actions of individual regulatory agencies are often applauded and encouraged with little thought for how those actions might interrelate with the activities of other agencies. We must attack this problem of the cumulative regulatory burden if we are to succeed in our efforts to reform the overall system.

The sunset concept presents an opportunity for assessing the combined impact of several agencies by providing for a coordinated review of the related activities of these agencies. This gives us a chance to analyze the activities of interrelated programs and, it is hoped, to correct any duplication or conflict. The failure to provide for a coordinated review would mean that these programs could easily be reviewed in different years. If that were the case, we would not only miss the chance to get a grasp of the larger picture of cumulative impact but also lose an important criterion for evaluating each program. If an agency or activity is reviewed only on its own merits, it is much more likely to be reauthorized than if its activities are viewed in light of other programs operating in the same area.

Sunset review is one of our best chances for meaningful reform of our regulatory system. It will place the responsibility on Congress to improve significantly its oversight procedures. It will make the agencies more accountable for, and therefore, more attentive to, their regulatory activities. And it will provide the President with a greater opportunity to exert leadership in program evaluation and improvement. In short, sunset can be a very effective tool in our effort to improve the regulatory system and tame the agencies.

ECONOMIC-IMPACT ANALYSIS OF PROPOSED RULES

Another reform for which I have introduced implementing legislation would require agencies to compare potential costs and benefits of the rules they propose. With the increasing cost of regulation, this procedure makes good sense. There is clearly a need to establish the economic impact of government regulations before they go into effect. Such information is valuable not only to the regulators but also to the Congress and the general public.

The legislation would require a detailed analysis that would address the cost impact of the regulation on consumers, businesses, markets, and federal, state, and local governments. It would deal with the estimated cost to the government and affected parties of implementing, monitoring, and enforcing a rule, the effect of the rule on employment, and the fiscal effect of any predicted increase in unemployment if the analysis so indicates, and the effect of the rule on the productivity of wage earners, businesses, and government. It would also require the agency to consider alternatives to the rule and to publish those alternatives along with a finding as to why they were not proposed.

The evaluation process, though improved, would still not allow for a complete quantification of costs and benefits (most frequently the latter). Quantifying the benefits of regulations can be an impossible task. How can one place a true value on seeing a sunset, or breathing air that is free of pollutants, or preserving a human life? These factors are certainly difficult if not impossible to quantify in terms of monetary value. Nonetheless, they are benefits that can readily be identified and taken into consideration as regulations are developed and reviewed. The fact that they are not quantifiable makes them no less important or worthy of consideration.

Obviously, the most significant aspect of this review is the requirement that the agencies look at the cost impact of regulatory alternatives. The blending of costs with alternatives will force the agencies down from their perch of aloofness and make them conscious of the positive and negative impacts of their regulatory proposals. This is a crucial step in sensitizing regulators to the real world and their role in it.

EXPANDED RESPONSIBILITIES FOR REGULATORY AGENCY HEADS

This proposal follows upon the requirement that agencies make more detailed analyses of the economic impact of their regulations. Specifically, an agency head would be responsible to ensure that the agency complied with all aspects of a regulatory analysis. In addition, the agency would be held responsible for ensuring that each regulation was necessary, was clearly written, and had reasonable means of enforcement and that the public had ample opportunity to participate in developing the rule.

By designating the agency head's specific responsibilities in the regulatory development process, the possibility of greater accountability would be enhanced. In addition, internal agency management should be improved as the responsibilities of the agency head are clearly defined. It may seem almost incredible that these responsibilities are not defined at present, but they are not.

REGULATORY FLEXIBILITY

Another concept that is gaining attention is regulatory flexibility. Under this approach, regulatory agencies are required to seek alternative regulatory proposals having less impact on individuals and small businesses or governments that would be affected by a proposed rule. The agency could choose to exempt any of these groups from compliance entirely or to alter compliance requirements or their time periods. If the agency chose to include such groups after it completed the required analysis, it would have to explain why it did so.

In 1980 the Regulatory Flexibility Act was signed into law. The act requires federal agencies to consider the impact of their rule making on small businesses and local governments. All agencies are required to publish semiannually an agenda of proposed regulations which would have a significant impact on small businesses. Any agency proposing a rule must prepare a regulatory flexibility analysis which explains the legal basis and the purpose for the rule, projects reporting and record-keeping burdens on small businesses, and proposes less burdensome alternatives to the proposed rule. After a rule has been adopted, the agency is required to issue a statement explaining why it was adopted over available alternatives. In addition, the agencies are to begin a systematic review of all existing rules which affect small businesses, annually announcing the rules that they expect to review in the coming year.

This approach has the obvious attraction of differentiating between businesses and activities having a major impact, and therefore most in need of regulatory supervision, and those having little impact and most likely to suffer adversely from the regulatory burden. It brings to the regulatory system an understanding that regulations impact different groups and businesses in drastically different ways. It also demonstrates a sensitivity to special situations that has been lacking in our regulatory system.

IMPROVEMENTS IN PUBLIC PARTICIPATION

One of the best ways to improve the quality of the regulatory product is to improve the level of public participation in the development of regulatory proposals. To become sensitive to the need for and problems with regulation, agency officials should solicit the views of people and organizations on all sides of a regulatory issue. Like Congress, the regulatory agencies are not reservoirs of infinite wisdom. Like Congress, the regulators should seek the views of those impacted by their activities. This can be a truly enlightening experience. It can certainly bring a new perspective to what might have seriously been considered a problem with only one regulatory solution.

More fundamentally, the effort to improve public participation in the regulatory field is basic to our form of government. By tradition, our government has operated under the watchwords "of the people, by the people, and for the people." While these words were applied initially to a government founded in a simpler time, they still have application today and not only for elected officials. The growth of government by regulation allows many important decisions to be made by unelected officials. While these officials are not directly answerable to the electorate, the government they help run is still intended to be operated "by the people," and the decisions they make are intended to work "for the people." It makes sense, therefore, that "the people" have a direct voice in decisions which regulate their lives.

A number of proposals for increasing the public's opportunity to participate in the rule-making process are now being considered. Two of the most frequently discussed proposals are the publication of a regulatory calendar and the expansion of public participation opportunities, including direct notification of public groups that would like to participate in the process of developing specific types of regulation.

One of the most fundamental problems for any group, business, or consumer interested in participating in the rule-making process is the lack of information about pending regulatory proposals. Many groups that want to express their views about rule-making ideas do not do so because they are not aware that any matter of interest to them is the subject of consideration by a regulatory agency. Simple ignorance about ongoing regulatory action frequently prevents groups from becoming involved in rule making.

The publication of a regulatory agenda is intended to open up the regulatory process and provide advance notice of regulatory proposals to interested groups. Under this proposal, regulatory agencies would be required to publish a list of the regulatory proposals they intend to make during a fixed time period (generally 12 months). This would allow interested groups to prepare their comments about proposed regulations in an orderly fashion. There should be an improvement in the quality of their comments and, therefore, in the quality of the information available to the regulatory agency.

The agenda would provide useful specific information about each rule. It would list the rule's legal basis, its objectives, deadlines for action pertaining to the rule, and the name, address, and telephone number of an agency official designated to handle inquiries and provide information about the rule. Some proposals also would require the agenda to include cost estimates for each proposed rule. Most agenda proposals would require the agency to list existing policies, rules, and procedures which were expected to undergo review.

As often occurs with regulatory reform proposals, the concept of a regulatory agenda has more than one purpose. Not only would the proposal expand significant opportunities for public comment, it should also improve the understanding of regulatory activities between the agencies. The proponents of regulatory agendas would like to have the information combined into a comprehensive regulatory calendar containing agendas from all the agencies. This compilation would allow all the agencies to know what each one was doing. It would point up potential conflicts and overlapping as well as possibilities for cooperation. The calendar could thus serve as an agency management tool as well as a public information device.

Other frequently mentioned proposals to increase public participation in the regulatory process center on directly notifying interested groups that would be affected by a particular rule-making proposal and expanding their opportunities to contribute comments and questions. The direct notification of groups, either by mail or through advertising in interest-group publications, reinforces the publication of a regulatory agenda as a means of notifying the public about pending regulatory actions which might be of interest.

The intent is to improve the regulatory process by opening it up to comments from all sides of the interested public. The reform is reinforced by proposals to conduct more numerous regional public hearings away from Washington and to modify or eliminate entirely procedural rules which tend to discourage the participation of the public. Again, the reforms are intended to increase the exposure and sensitivity of regulators to the public and its many concerns. The result should be a better regulatory product.

REVIEW OF EXISTING REGULATIONS

Another proposed reform of internal agency procedures involves the review of existing rules. As many people have pointed out, existing regulations frequently become obsolete or obstructive as conditions change. Fast-paced changes in the economy, technology, business practices, consumer activities, etc., often make specific regulations out of date. This process is frequently compounded by the introduction of new regulations promulgated either by a particular agency or by another agency responsible for similar matters.

Most proposals for review of existing regulations would require that these rules be reviewed in a periodic manner similar to the agency review schedule that Congress must set under the sunset concept. Then, as a rule came up for review, a period of public comment would be set. Afterward, the agency would provide an assessment of the rule including the benefits provided by the rule, the costs of compliance, and the potential for the rule's goals to be accomplished in a different way. The agency would then recommend whether the rule should continue unchanged, be amended, or be eliminated.

A separate set of proposed reforms involves the vitally important area of coordination between the regulatory agencies. In the relatively rapid development of our regulatory system, a large number of the regulatory agencies which have been established have fairly narrow purposes. Each of these agencies has been given responsibility to regulate in its own specific area, and each has generally done so in a vigorous manner. A resulting problem is that the agencies have had little interest in or concern for the cumulative impact of regulations. Their specific interests are only in the areas that they are responsible for regulating. They have demonstrated little inclination to compare the impact of their own rules with those developed by other agencies or even with regulations previously developed by the agency in question. The system has shown a glaring lack of any requirement that these cumulative impacts be considered.

Only recently have more than a few voices been raised to question the cumulative impact of regulation. We have begun to take a comprehensive look at what has been imposed and have found that the regulators have had little concern about the interaction of regulations. Clearly this situation must be corrected as one step toward reforming the regulatory system. The individual regulatory agencies have demonstrated a lack of interest in the problem, but even if they demonstrated sincere concern, these special-purpose agencies frankly would not be equipped to evaluate the broadest implications of regulatory overlapping. The answer must lie in a review outside the

specific agencies. Several proposals along these lines would involve the establishment or authorization of a special-purpose group to review regulatory
actions, the designation of a multifunction agency such as the OMB to coordinate regulatory activities, or some combination of the two.

As one example of a step in the right direction, the Paperwork Reduction
Act attempts to coordinate the reporting and record-keeping requirements
of the various agencies and to concentrate control over all agency reporting
and record-keeping regulations in the OMB. The act consolidates within the
OMB authority over the overall direction of federal information policies. The
OMB has the responsibility for developing and establishing uniform information management policies, reviewing proposed regulations, and coordinating agency information activities. It creates the Federal Information
Locator System (FILS), which is designed to reveal duplication, identify
information being collected by the federal government, promote greater
sharing of information by agencies, and assist the OMB in its clearance process. The Paperwork Reduction Act is expected to minimize the federal
paperwork burden on private parties, minimize the cost to the federal government of information collection, and maximize the usefulness of the information that is collected.

U.S. REGULATORY COUNCIL

The concept of a regulatory agenda for every regulatory agency and incorporation of these agendas into a single regulatory calendar is intended in
part to provide a working guide for evaluation of the overall regulatory system. As such the calendar can serve as a tool for any activity that is intended
to coordinate or evaluate regulatory proposals on an intraagency basis. At
present, such a calendar is developed under the guidance of the U.S. Regulatory Council, a group composed of representatives of thirty-six executive
departments and agencies. The council now plays mainly an information-
gathering role, and through its regulatory calendar it helps each regulatory
agency to know what the others are doing. It could obviously take on a large
role if we were so inclined. The importance for now is that we have taken a
step toward establishing a framework for the coordination of the entire regulatory system. That is a significant beginning.

EMPOWERING AN AGENCY TO ENFORCE REFORMS

Beyond basic coordination of the regulatory system, proposals are being considered to empower a central agency to ensure that individual regulatory
agencies comply with any required internal improvements in their rule-making activities. It has been pointed out that without an effective enforcement
mechanism the regulatory agencies may ignore completely or apply selec-
tively internal reforms. Obviously, this would effectively negate those
reforms, and the regulators could continue unimpeded in their normal fashion. In effect, there would be no guarantee that comprehensive reforms
would occur.

To avoid this situation, I have suggested that an agency be empowered to

monitor and enforce the reforms imposed on the regulators. I have specifically suggested that the OMB could be strengthened to serve this purpose.
But regardless of whether the OMB or another existing agency is directed to
ensure compliance or a new agency is established for the purpose, there must
be a supervisory authority. Otherwise our reforms will likely fall far short of
our expectations.

PRESIDENTIAL AUTHORITY

Many would argue that regulatory reform is not necessary because the President already has the requisite authority to exert his will on the regulatory
process if he chooses to use it. However, this authority has been questioned
by many groups, including the regulators themselves. Most of this chapter
has discussed reform proposals which have a strong chance of being implemented. By this point you may be inclined to believe that the real battle of
regulatory reform has been won. It has not. The regulators are not taking the
push for reform easily, nor is the wide spectrum of interest groups they serve.
The regulators may suffer from internal confusion and conflict, but they are
united in their unwillingness to yield any of the vast powers they have accumulated. They jealously guard these powers, in some cases to the point of
arrogance. The question of presidential authority in the rule-making activities of the executive branch agencies is a good case in point.

Most people believe that the President, as the head of the executive
branch, has the right to involve himself in the rule-making activities of his
agencies. That seems reasonable since the President actually serves as the
manager of his branch of the government. Yet many of the regulators have
objected to presidential efforts to manage their activities. Some have suggested that he has no right to participate in rule-making proceedings except
during periods of public comment. They would effectively relegate their boss
to the role of a private citizen in regulatory matters. In at least three
instances, the President has been challenged in efforts to influence regulatory proposals after the period of public comment had ended. While these
challenges may eventually prove groundless, the fact they have occurred
gives a clear indication of the extent of independent-mindedness that our
regulators have assumed. Along with decisions to ignore clear congressional
mandates, this treatment of the President serves to demonstrate that we
have a long way to go before the regulators rediscover their place in the
exercise of governmental power.

Several suggestions have been made for resolving the question of the President's authority in rule-making matters. The President's authority is clear
under the Constitution. From a practical standpoint, however, it would probably be useful to identify specific times when the President should become
involved in the rule-making process. At the very least, the President should
consider regulatory proposals in light of the administration's basic policy
positions on matters that might be affected. Such a review, exercised by the
President or his designee, would help to provide a needed measure of uni-

formity in public policy. This type of review would reinforce reforms in congressional and agency procedures designed to reduce conflict and confusion in the regulatory process. Greater participation and guidance by the nation's chief executive officer would effect a valuable improvement in the regulatory process. It would also help to restore clarity to our government's lines of authority. The present vagueness provided an opening for the regulators to expand their authority to the point of arguing that the President has no special right to participate. Over time, the exercise of regulatory power free from effective outside restraint has led the regulators to assume that no restraints can be imposed. The President as well as Congress has a responsibility to see that attitude reversed.

NEED FOR PROMPT ACTION

The goal of taming the federal regulatory agencies is a vital one. It is also one which will require a number of reforms touching all aspects of the regulatory system. Congress, the President, the agencies, and the public will all have to change their existing roles if the system is to be improved. For the Congress and the President, change must come in the form of expanding their roles to exert much greater guidance and review in the process. These two constitutional branches of government must make it clear to the agencies once and for all just where ultimate authority in the regulatory process lies. From the standpoint of the public, parties interested in specific regulatory matters have a responsibility to participate in the regulatory process at the appropriate times. Their comments should be substantive and their questions constructive. The agencies themselves must accept a changing role in the regulatory process. Their powers will be altered while their responsibilities expand. They will be required to pay far greater attention to the impact of regulations and the procedures that should be followed in their development.

I have tried to provide an overview of the numerous proposals for regulatory reform that are circulating today. Many of these specific ideas have been combined in broad pieces of legislation designed to foster comprehensive reform of the regulatory process. I believe this is the most effective approach. As I hope I have made clear, simple or piecemeal solutions will not provide the type of reform we need to reverse the course that has led the regulators to assume that no restraints can be imposed.

The most important point is that major efforts are under way to reform drastically our regulatory system. Common complaints about the system have been considered and generally found to have validity. The reform process has begun. It is a cooperative effort centering on the Congress and the President, each prompted by the public's demand for improvements. The Carter administration introduced reform legislation based upon the President's Executive Order 12044. The Reagan administration almost immediately took steps to provide regulatory relief. President Reagan issued Executive Order 11291, setting up the Presidential Task Force on Regulatory

Relief and imposing a cost-benefit analysis on the promulgation of new regulations and imposing the standard on existing regulations. Members of Congress have offered their own ideas in the form of legislation, some providing for comprehensive change and others addressing specific problems. Almost completely, however, there is agreement that a comprehensive set of reforms must be adopted. We are now well along in the process of deciding just what should be included in that comprehensive legislative package. We are going to institute much-needed accountability in the regulatory system and impose meaningful restraints on the authority of the regulators. These reforms are long overdue. They are vital for our continued well-being as a nation. They will be accomplished because they are needed. The public demands them.

TABLE OF CASES

265

SUBJECT INDEX